SMALL GARDENS

A Creative Approach to Garden Design

SMALL GARDENS

A Creative Approach to Garden Design

WARD LOCK

This paperback edition first published
in Great Britain in 1993
by Ward Lock Limited, Villiers House,
41/47 Strand, London WC2N 5JE

A Cassell Imprint

The material in this volume is taken from titles previously
published in the Ward Lock Gardening by Design series:
Town Gardens; Container Gardening; Window Boxes; Herbs.

Text filmset in Bembo
by TJB Photosetting Ltd., Grantham, Lincs.
Printed and bound in Singapore
by Kyodo Printing Ltd

Cataloguing in Publication Data for this title is
available from the British Library

ISBN 0 7063 7153 4

CONTENTS

GENERAL INTRODUCTION

There have always been small gardens. Even in the less densely populated past, cottagers often had limited space, even though they lived in the country, but filled it to capacity with flowers, fruits and vegetables. Understandably many town dwellers had only pocket-handkerchief-sized backyards, especially those who lived in terraced houses.

Today there are even more small gardens due to the trend for high-density housing – indeed, pocket-handkerchief plots are the norm with most new houses.

However, tiny plots have their advantages. For a start, many busy working people actually prefer small gardens as they are easier to maintain than larger patches when time is limited.

Secondly, they are more economical to lay out and plant, an important consideration these days as construction materials and plants are not cheap.

Possibly the main disadvantage is insufficient space for all the features one would like to include. But having said that, it is surprising how many features can be incorporated into a small plot: a tiny patio, pool, rock or scree garden, raised beds for various plants, to name some of the most popular.

By choosing mainly small and restrained kinds, a great many plants can be incorporated into a pocket-handkerchief plot. The occasional larger plant can be used to create variation in height – even a small ornamental tree. Of course, one should make the most of vertical space by growing climbing plants.

Even more plants can be grown if containers are used: tubs, pots, urns and other ornamental containers on the patio; window boxes and hanging baskets on the house. There is a vast range of plants suited to container growing, a fact not realized by many gardeners, who think that spring and summer bedding and bulbs are the only subjects that will tolerate the limited volume of soil.

If you are among those people who think that little can be done with a small garden, then you are in for a pleasant surprise as you scan these pages: they will reveal a wealth of inspired ideas.

Small Gardens is mainly an ideas book and is very strong on design. It is aimed at the home-lover who sees the garden as an extension of the house and thinks in terms of the garden as an outside room which needs as much attention to design as a room inside the home.

The book opens with stimulating ideas for town gardens – which is natural enough, for the majority of people live in towns and invariably the gardens are small. It considers the requirements of the whole family – not just the gardener!

A considerable selection of plants is recommended, from climbers and small trees to annuals, bulbs and water plants. The 'hard landscaping' side is considered – like hard surfaces, as well as special features such as pools.

Because gardening in containers is so important to small-garden owners, this subject follows next and is considered in great detail. It embraces not only the kinds of containers available, from ornamental to utility, but also a wide range of plants, ornamental and culinary, to grow in them, plus cultural requirements.

Still on the subject of containers, window boxes have a large section to themselves. Hanging baskets are included here, too, for never before have elevated containers been so popular as they are today. Both types of container can be used to provide colour and interest around the house all the year round.

These sections between them recommend a wide range of plants, but herbs have a section all to themselves as they are so popular today, particularly with small-garden owners. Most are small-growing and therefore ideally suited to limited space. They can be used to create attractive features in their own right, or mixed with other plants.

Small Gardens is rounded off with a substantial Appendix of Plant Lists covering the whole book, enabling you to select plants quickly with particular characteristics or for special purposes.

TOWN GARDENS

INTRODUCTION

It is easy to dismiss a small town garden, thinking that it does not get much light so nothing will grow there. But this is far from the truth and this part of the book will show what can be achieved with a little imagination and well thought out planting schemes.

How does one define the size of a town garden? Traditionally it can be as small as 3.7 by 1.8 m (12 ft by 6 ft), probably walled on all sides and possibly completely paved. But any small garden could fit into this category, even if it is only a passage way, and the same advice applies when planning and planting.

Planning the garden to suit your requirements is the key to a successful small town garden so it is worth spending some time deciding what you actually want from your garden – what you want to hide and what you want to see from your windows, whether it is a garden to potter in or sit and look at, and what special features would add interest.

After designing a garden, plants need to be chosen. As will be seen in Chapter 2, there are plants suited to every situation, from sun to shade. An especially good range of shade-loving plants is included, for often town gardens have more than their fair share of shade.

Climbers and wall shrubs are particularly recommended for small gardens, to make the most of vertical space. There may be room for a small tree to act as a focal point in the garden. Shrubs, herbaceous plants, bulbs and annuals, though, will be the main subjects of planting schemes.

Paving is important in a small garden as it probably will not have any lawn. Carefully chosen, this can be a most attractive feature of a small town garden. Plenty of design ideas are given and numerous materials to consider.

If a garden is large enough to allow part of it to be screened to provide a private sitting area, then this is strongly recommended. There is a choice of solid walling or fencing, or more open screens such as trellis or patterned concrete-block walling.

Ideas for special features to add the finishing touches to a garden are given. We take a look at statuary, especially for creating focal points in a garden; garden furniture; pools, which really help to bring a garden to life; and even small greenhouses which, if well designed, can be attractive features in their own right, especially hexagonal models.

Whatever type of garden you have designed it will need some sort of maintenance to keep it looking good, so this subject rounds off the section.

1

AIMS OF SMALL-GARDEN DESIGN

The aims of designing a garden for a small space vary according to different needs. But the basic requirement must be to have something pleasant to look out on all year round. The garden should complement the house and the design should take into account the type of brickwork or facing, colour of paintwork and any special features such as a balcony or French windows. As well as thinking about the view from the ground floor also consider what it will look like when seen from the upper windows.

Most people want an area for sitting in and this will usually be in the sunniest part of the garden, not necessarily nearest to the house. Attractive garden furniture can be made into a feature and with only a small garden to look after you should have plenty of time to sit down and relax!

Barbecues are very popular and these can be built as a permanent feature rather than having a portable one that has to be stored somewhere. There will also be things that need to be hidden such as dustbins, garden tools and possibly a compost heap if you are very enthusiastic. Whether or not you have children or pets will influence the design and also how much time you will be spending in the garden. If there is a disabled person in the house their needs should be considered at the earliest planning stage.

Many people will want to go for low maintenance and this is easily achieved with a mixture of hard surfacing, shrubs and ground cover with the odd plant pot or ornament strategically placed. Once the plants have established themselves they will cover the soil and stop the weeds from growing. All that will need doing is a little feeding occasionally and some pruning to keep the shrubs in shape.

You don't even need many plants to achieve a pleasing effect. Just a few climbers and two or three planted pockets of soil among the paving or some containers can often suffice. Choose plants with attractive foliage and which have different shapes.

If you like gardening you will probably want a mixture of evergreens, herbaceous plants and annuals. Because of limited groundspace you need to 'think vertically' and one of the first jobs is to decide what climbers you want to grow. If the garden is overlooked it is important to get things growing quickly to supply privacy as soon as possible. It is also important to think about the aspect of the garden. Most small gardens and backyards are in the shade for the greater part of the day so any sunshine that filters through should be given a clear unimpeded run.

This Cheltenham garden belongs to Mr & Mrs W A Batchelor and is designed along simple lines to create a low-maintenance garden with something of interest to look at all year round.

A well-filled garden with dense planting can make the area seem larger than it really is. Here a path in this delightful corner of Lys de Bray's garden lures the visitor on further.

Whether you want a neat and tidy garden or a jumbled one, never be tempted to plant too much at the start. Although it will give an instant effect the plants will soon overcrowd each other and, as you only have a small space, you will not be able to move them to another part of the garden. A good idea is to plant the shrubs at a reasonable distance apart, bearing in mind the eventual spread, and fill in the gaps with annuals. The better the soil the quicker the plants will grow so if the ground is poor it will pay to buy in some good quality top soil or dig in plenty of compost, peat and fertilizer or manure before planting.

Hidden corners are always exciting and they can be created quite easily. The thing to avoid is lots of small, divided areas making it look too 'twee'. A natural effect can be achieved by curving a path round a large bush or having an archway near the bottom of the garden so that you can't quite see what is on the other side of it.

A focal point is a good idea to lead the eye to a certain part of the garden. A statue viewed through an archway or a fountain bubbling up through the undergrowth will catch the attention. Sometimes it is not easy to make things look natural and casual especially when the plants are young. But as they become established you will have more idea of the finished effect and any glaring mistakes can be remedied.

With an enclosed garden you will not have to pay as much attention to the surrounding area as you would with a more open aspect. Existing trees will probably be the main external features to influence the overall design and these should be taken into consideration when planning the garden.

A colour scheme is important so that flowers don't clash and there is not a jumble of too many different colours. The whole garden could run on the same theme, for example green and silver foliage plants with pink, blue and white flowers. Yellows and white look good together and create a cheerful effect. It is the strong colours that are the most difficult to accommodate and they should be used with care to avoid a garish colour scheme. A lot of the modern hybrids are bred for their bright colours and double flowers and they often look too brash.

PRACTICALITIES

How you go about planning your garden depends on whether it is brand new or an existing one. It is often easier to start from scratch with your own ideas rather than trying to incorporate existing features into a new scheme. A lot of the old terraced houses, which are so popular now for renovation, have walled backyards which give a good basis on which to start. Many of these types of backyard look very dingy and depressing and it is often difficult to see how they can be transformed. But it is possible for even the most unpromising site to be made into a haven of peace and tranquillity in a short time—a far cry from the old-style backyards that were bare except for a mangle and an outdoor privy. These were not seen as potential gardens, they were used merely as a place of work, and it shows how our attitudes to leisure and lifestyle have changed.

With a new house you will probably want to erect walls or fencing and clear away builder's rubble before buying in some good quality top soil.

One of the major problems with the construction of small back gardens is likely to be getting the materials into it. Often the only access is through the house, or possibly over the wall, so this is a point to consider when buying large stone statues or tall trees!

CHILDREN AND PETS

If you have children you may feel that you want a lawn, however small, for them to play on. This is fine as long as you are prepared to keep it cut and have somewhere to store a mower: a small hand mower is probably all that is needed. If you are going to have a lawn make sure that it is a good one. The area should be completely flat and can either be laid with good quality turf or sown with a fairly tough seed mixture.

If there really is not enough space for a lawn you could have a sandpit for the children so they have something soft to play on.

When choosing plants go for tough shrubs, but not prickly or poisonous ones, and avoid delicate plants that can easily be snapped off. Children will need space to play in the garden so it should not be overcrowded with plants.

Children usually have bikes or toy cars on which they want to race around the garden, so any paving slabs or bricks should be completely flat to avoid hazardous bumps. Water features should be avoided as even a few inches of water can be dangerous with children about. Wait until they have grown up and turn the sandpit into a pool. Swings and slides take up a lot of space but if there is an old tree you could make a rope swing on one of the branches, making sure that it is quite strong enough first.

An informal garden is best suited to children, then it does not matter if toys are scattered about the place and they will not feel restricted as they would do in a formal garden. Also, it is no good having winding paths if you have children—they will just take the shortest route across the garden. The best way to encourage them to respect plants is to give them a small plot of their own in which to grow things.

If you have a dog, raised beds would be sensible, so long as there is plenty of paved area for it to run around in. Cats cannot be so easily restricted but you could try planting their favourite nepeta (catmint) in one corner of the garden, to encourage them to keep off the other plants.

Fig. 1. A neat and unobtrusive way to store coal or wood, incorporating a compartment for the dustbin. For best effect, use material that fits in with the surroundings.

OUT OF SIGHT

If you have a town house you may not have room at the front of the house for storing a dustbin so this will have to be accommodated somewhere within the garden. A purpose-built brick construction (Fig. 1) with a wooden door on the front can be made to fit in, if the brick is the same as the house or garden walls.

Alternatively a fence can be erected to screen off one part of the garden and this can hide all the things you don't want to see, such as the compost heap, dustbins, coal or wood stores and maybe even a washing line if you have room. Plants can be put in to cover up the bricks or fencing.

A small shed might be necessary if you have no garage or basement for storing garden tools, garden furniture etc. With sufficient plant screening a shed will fit quite happily into the scene provided it is kept in good order with wood preservative.

You may also want to hide an unsightly view, possibly a neighbour's unkempt yard or an ugly building. Quick-growing evergreen plants will be needed, but don't fall into the trap of planting Leyland cypress; they will certainly grow fast but they will get out of

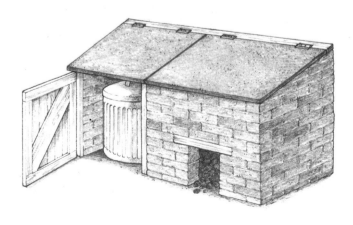

A shaded place in Lys de Bray's garden to sit and relax in. The canopy of trees and shrubs blocks out any external features and creates an air of seclusion.

This shaded arbour also includes a small pool which adds to the feeling of tranquillity. The stone bench merges in with the rest of the scenery and is an attractive permanent feature (courtesy Lys de Bray).

Fig. 2. Tranquil and uncluttered—a Japanese garden maintains the correct balance between plants and hard surfacing.

hand in a small area and completely dominate the scene. There are other evergreen shrubs that can be used—*Garrya elliptica* is one of the best and it has the advantage of being suitable for growing in the shade.

OUTDOOR LIVING

The trend now is to integrate the garden and the living area so that the transition from one to the other is less noticeable. One good way of achieving this is to have a clear roof covering a patio area with French windows leading out from the house. The same floor covering, or similar colour, could be used in the house and patio, quarry tiles for example. Potted plants in both sections will amplify the garden theme. The advantage of having a covered area is that you can enjoy sitting in the garden even on wet days when the weather is warm and it is ideal for evening dinner parties.

Even though your garden may be in the middle of a town it is still possible to create a wild effect and bring a bit of the countryside to a built-up area. Wild gardens should be allowed to grow at random and you will find that all sorts of plants will appear from seed carried by birds or blown in the wind. You don't need to worry about what are weeds and what are not; just keep anything that looks attractive.

This type of garden will attract all sorts of birds, butterflies and insects and perhaps even hedgehogs. If you provide water you may get frogs too, if there is a way in to the garden.

Another type of garden that is becoming increasingly popular is the Japanese garden (Fig. 2). Tranquillity is the theme here and the effect is provided by uncluttered planting surrounded by stones and gravel and some sort of water feature. Running water has a most soothing effect in any sort of garden and is easier to keep fresh than still water. If you have a pond you will need to create the right balance with oxygenating plants to prevent the water becoming green and slimy.

Watering is going to be necessary in the garden especially if there are a lot of plants in pots and hanging baskets. Plants next to walls also dry out quickly. An outside tap is extremely useful, preferably with a reel-type hosepipe that can easily be stored. Another method, which can be fitted when the garden is under construction, is to have an underground hose system with countersunk nozzles that push up when the hose is turned on.

One word of warning—when constructing the patio or hard surfacing bear in mind that water should drain away from the house. If you have all hard surfacing and raised beds it may be necessary to have drainage holes somewhere in the garden.

Lys de Bray's garden in Wimborne, Dorset incorporates a paved area which she has filled with a mixture of plants in terracotta pots, to give an informal effect.

2

CHOICE OF PLANTS

Just because an area is often heavily shaded does not mean that the choice of plants is very small. There is a wide range of plants that will grow quite happily in the shade, in fact there are so many it is difficult to choose just a few to fit in to a small garden. A backyard has the added advantage of being sheltered, so slightly tender plants can be grown that would not survive in a more open situation. There are no hard and fast rules about what plants will grow in a certain spot but the following categories can be used as guidelines.

CLIMBERS AND WALL SHRUBS

Climbers are the plants to start with. If you choose these first the other plants can be selected to fit in with them. Some will climb quite happily up a wall or fence without any help but others will need some support.

Shade

Ivies will provide a good cover once established and they only need support in the early stages. *Hedera colchica* 'Dentata' is a large-leaved ivy with dark green leaves and 'Variegata' has cream markings. *Hedera canariensis* 'Gloire de Marengo' is another popular large-leaved variety; it is not so hardy as *H.c.* 'Dentata' but should grow quite happily in the shelter of a backyard. The smaller leaved ivy, *Hedera helix,* is also attractive and good varieties include 'Glacier' with silver-grey variegated leaves; 'Goldheart', green with a gold centre and 'Buttercup' with golden young foliage. Bear in mind that the colour will not be so good if the plants are grown in heavy shade. *Garrya elliptica* is a vigorous evergreen shrub that grows well against a wall and makes an ideal screening plant. It has thick, leathery leaves and long drooping grey-green catkins on male plants. The catkins on female plants are smaller and less attractive.

If you want to cover an eyesore quickly you will not do better than *Polygonum baldschuanicum*, the Russian vine. It is essential it is grown on its own rather than in a border because it will rapidly smother other plants.

Semi-shade

Hydrangea petiolaris is an excellent choice. It is self-clinging and the flat white flower heads produce a lovely display in early summer. For colourful foliage there is parthenocissus (Virginia creeper) and the best variety is *Parthenocissus henryana* (Chinese Virginia creeper) which is not so vigorous as the others and clings to a wall without support.

For winter colour *Jasminum nudiflorum* will brighten up dark days with its bright yellow flowers and chaenomeles (flowering quince) will provide flowers in spring followed by yellow-green fruits which can be used for making jelly. There are many different forms of *Chaenomeles speciosa* with flower colours ranging from deep crimson to white. *Chaenomeles japonica* is a smaller variety with orange-red flowers.

The pyracantha is tough and easy to grow, if you don't mind the prickles. As well as the common red-berried variety there is *Pyracantha atalantioides* 'Aurea' with bright yellow fruits that have the advantage of not being popular with the birds. Honeysuckle will grow well in partial shade and the evergreen or semi-evergreen *Lonicera japonica* is a useful cover-up plant. 'Aureoreticulata' has lovely bright green leaves with golden 'netting' and white fragrant flowers. 'Halliana' has white flowers changing to yellow.

The deciduous *Lonicera periclymenum* flowers in late summer with yellow blooms flushed purple. 'Serotina' is the late Dutch honeysuckle, flowering through to the autumn.

A lot of roses need to be grown in full sun but there are also many climbers which will stand partial shade and still produce plenty of blooms. They flower over a long period if dead-headed regularly and make good covering plants for trellis and pergolas.

'Danse du Feu' is a modern climber with double orange flowers which last well into the autumn and 'Golden Showers' is a double yellow with masses of scented blooms. 'Zéphirine Drouhin', an old favourite with its thorn-free stems and pink, semi-double flowers, provides a welcome second flush in autumn. Particularly good for a shady spot is the old-fashioned 'Mme Grégoire Staechelin' with sweetly perfumed

double pink flowers—the only disadvantage is that they are not so long lasting as the other varieties. 'Mme Alfred Carrière' (pinky white) is another lovely old variety that's ideal for a north-facing wall.

Sun

The choice of climbers and wall shrubs increases if you have a sunny wall to grow them on. Both ceanothus and wisteria have attractive blue flowers and both will need to be trained as they are not self-clinging. Ceanothus produces its flowers from summer to early autumn and 'Gloire de Versailles' is one of the best varieties. If you buy a wisteria make sure it is a grafted one because plants grown from seed will often take years to flower. *Wisteria sinensis* is the most widely grown and it has large mauve-blue flowers in late spring.

Actinidia is a deciduous climber and one variety, *Actinidia chinensis,* is the Chinese gooseberry or Kiwi fruit that is so popular now. It is often thought of as a greenhouse plant but it will grow quite happily outside and will thrive on a sheltered, sunny or partly-shaded wall. To produce fruits both male and female plants are needed so buy sexed plants from a reputable grower. The other variety, *Actinidia kolomikta,* has most attractive heart-shaped leaves with pink and white tips and it has small white flowers in early summer.

Of course I can't forget the clematis. These contain such a wide range of flowers—large and small, mauve, white, yellow and pink, with various markings. There is even an evergreen form, *Clematis armandii,* with white flowers, although it is not very widely available. Of the large flowered hybrids 'Nelly Moser' (pink with crimson stripes) and 'Jackmanii Superba' (dark purple) are probably the best known. 'Lasurstern' (lavender blue), 'Ernest Markham' (red) and 'The President' (purple with paler stripes) are also a good choice.

Clematis montana is a particularly vigorous small-flowered variety and is very easy to grow. It has white flowers but *C. montana rubens* with pink flowers is also widely available. *Clematis tangutica* is a pretty yellow and the flowers are followed by attractive silky seed heads. Although clematis like the sun their roots should be in the shade, so plant low-growing shrubs or perennials around the base.

A much wider selection of roses can be grown in a sunny position and you can choose between the modern and the old-fashioned climbers and ramblers. The modern ones flower over a longer period and tend to be more disease resistant. They include the well-known 'Ena Harkness' with scented red flowers; 'Iceberg', a pure white; 'Queen Elizabeth', pink; and 'Pink Perpetue', a fairly vigorous variety with a good perfume.

I find that the old-fashioned roses have more appeal and am particularly fond of 'Albertine' a vigorous rambler with masses of double pink scented blooms. 'Albéric Barbier' is also attractive with yellow buds opening to white and 'Mermaid' is a good candidate for a south or a north wall. It's a vigorous, almost evergreen climber with large bright yellow blooms.

In a very sheltered spot *Eccremocarpus scaber* (the Chilean glory flower) will scramble up walls and trellis. It is evergreen and has tubular orange flowers from summer to early autumn.

Another tender climber is *Passiflora caerulea*, the passion flower. It will survive in a very sheltered place and is ideal for growing under a canopy or conservatory. The fascinating white and purple flowers are produced in late summer and are sometimes followed by oval, yellow fruits.

SMALL TREES

The choice of tree for a small garden must be very carefully thought out. It is going to be a dominant feature and will shade other plants. Also, if it becomes too big it will be very difficult to dispose of. If in doubt it would be better not to plant a tree at all and just stick to shrubs.

There may be an existing tree which you will probably want to leave. A good tree surgeon will remove any dangerous branches and thin it out a bit to let in more light.

Flowering cherries, crabs and crataegus all produce medium-sized trees from about 4.5 m (15 ft). Choose one with an attractive shape that will look good in winter, such as *Prunus subhirtella autumnalis* or *Malus* 'John Downie'. Steer clear of the stiff upright growth as in the 'Kanzan' cherry or, even worse, 'Amanogawa'.

The acers (maples) are excellent small trees to grow in limited space and most of them will grow on acid or alkaline soil. Some produce large trees but there are also smaller ones with a wide variety of shapes and leaf colours. *Acer griseum* is a slow growing tree reaching about 4.5 m (15 ft). The green leaves turn red in autumn and it has flaking orange-brown bark which provides winter interest.

Acer palmatum also grows about 4.5 m (15 ft) high and forms a rounded head. *Acer palmatum* 'Dissectum' has light green leaves, finely divided, and 'Atropurpureum' has bronze-coloured leaves. They all produce beautiful autumn colour.

The magnolia is a small tree that will benefit from the shelter of an enclosed garden. *Magnolia soulangiana* is one of the most reliable. It grows about 3–4.5 m (10–15 ft) high and the lovely white tulip-shaped flowers with a pink tinge open in spring before the leaves. 'Lennei' has rose-purple blooms with a white inside.

If you don't have enough room for this one you could grow *Magnolia stellata* which only reaches 2.5–3 m (8–10 ft) and is slow growing. The white flowers are star-shaped and fragrant.

Lilacs and laburnums both make small trees. If you want a laburnum choose the variety 'Vossii' which has long, drooping flowers and does not produce much

Two stone urns planted with geraniums and *Begonia semperflorens* accentuate the change in level provided by the steps. Bulbs could be planted in autumn, when the geraniums and begonias are removed, to give spring colour (courtesy Lys de Bray).

A blossom-strewn path turns a hidden corner, with the two large clay pots containing fuchsias standing guard on either side (courtesy Lys de Bray).

seed. *Rhus typhina,* the stag's horn sumach, is also popular in small gardens although the suckers can be a nuisance.

For leaf colour you could choose *Gleditsia* 'Sunburst', a small tree with golden leaves and a round head. Then there is *Eucalyptus gunnii,* which will grow into a large tree but can be cut back to the ground each spring, after the first year, to produce new growth.

If you want to try something a little more unusual why not grow *Arbutus unedo,* the strawberry tree. It grows about 4.5–6 m (15–20 ft) high and has dark green glossy leaves and small pink, bell-shaped flowers in autumn. The orange strawberry-like fruits appear at the same time, from the previous year's flowers. 'Rubra' is the best form being more compact.

Cercis siliquastrum (Judas tree) is a small spreading tree with heart-shaped leaves and pink pea-like flowers in spring followed by green seed pods. It likes a sunny sheltered spot.

Amelanchier canadensis is a lovely tree that grows well on moist soil. It does tend to produce suckers, though, and may need pruning to keep it in shape. Masses of white star-shaped flowers open in spring followed by edible black berries. The brilliant leaf colours provide an added bonus in autumn.

If you like weeping trees there is *Betula pendula* 'Youngii' which is a smaller tree than the silver birch. I find *Pyrus salicifolia* 'Pendula' (willow-leaved pear) a better shape as it looks more natural.

Figs can be grown successfully on a south-facing wall although they need quite a lot of attention in the form of training, pruning and thinning if they are to produce fruit.

SHRUBS

In a small garden it is important to have attractively shaped shrubs and to avoid planting them too close together, thus spoiling the form. You could choose all evergreen plants but you will probably want to have a balance between evergreen and deciduous and with the right choice it is possible to have something of interest to look at all year round.

Shade

If you have acid soil you can grow camellias which thrive in sheltered, shaded conditions. One of the most popular varieties is 'Donation' with pink, semi-double flowers. 'Anticipation' is hardier with large crimson flowers and it is one of the best camellias for a small garden. Another acid lover is the skimmia, an evergreen that produces white flowers in late spring followed by bright red berries that last all winter.

Holly bushes will grow in the shade and variegated ones such as 'Silver Queen' and 'Golden King' will brighten up a dark corner. For berries to be produced you will need a male and female variety and strange though it may seem 'Silver Queen' is male and 'Golden King' is female!

Cotoneasters provide a good show of red berries in autumn and there are spreading plants such as *Cotoneaster horizontalis* (useful for covering manholes), upright ones such as *Cotoneaster franchetii* that will fan against a wall and large ones like *Cotoneaster cornubia* that will grow up to 6 m (20 ft) high. Some are evergreen and others are deciduous.

Hydrangeas like a sheltered position where the buds will not be damaged by late frosts. The lace-cap hydrangeas are particularly attractive with their large, flat flower heads. 'Blue Wave' and 'Mariesii' are both good varieties and their flower colour will depend on what type of soil they are grown on; blue on acid soil and pink on alkaline.

Yellow flowered shrubs suitable for the shade are *Hypericum* 'Hidcote'—not to be confused with the ground-cover hypericum—and *Potentilla fruticosa.* There are also pink and red potentillas but I still prefer the original yellow.

If you have an acid soil you can grow rhododendrons and azaleas. There are some splendid dwarf rhododendrons, growing about 1 m (3 ft) high, and the yellow flowered 'Cowslip' does particularly well in the shade.

The Japanese azaleas do better than the deciduous ones in shade and there are some lovely subtle colours such as 'White Lady' and 'Hinomayo' (pink) as well as the stronger oranges, scarlets and bright pinks. If you do not have an acid soil they can always be grown in tubs containing ericaceous compost, which can be bought at garden centres.

Bamboos are popular and look especially good in a modern design or Japanese-type garden. It is best to grow one of the smaller varieties such as *Arundinaria murielae* or *Arundinaria viridistriata* which are not so invasive as the larger ones.

Semi-shade

For all soil types there is the evergreen elaeagnus and the variety *Elaeagnus pungens* 'Maculata' creates a splash of colour with its green and gold leaves. For more sombre tones the larger grey-leaved *Elaeagnus × ebbingei* is particularly attractive. *Euonymus fortunei* can be grown against a wall or free-standing. 'Emerald 'n Gold' is a variegated form although the colour may not be as good in heavy shade.

Fatsia japonica is often thought of as a tender plant but it is hardy in many areas and is well suited to walled gardens in sun or shade. It can be planted in the garden but also looks good when grown in a pot. It has large glossy leaves and small white flowers in early autumn.

It really is worth growing a philadelphus if you have got room. The lovely white flowers look especially good in evening light in summer and they fill the air with their orange-blossom scent. 'Manteau d'Hermine' only grows 1 m (3¼ ft) high and 'Belle Etoile' reaches 1.5 m (5 ft) and has white flowers with a purple blotch.

Also grown for its scented flowers is the daphne and *Daphne mezereon* provides welcome colour early in the year with its clusters of pink flowers followed by red berries. It is a deciduous shrub but *Daphne odora* is evergreen, again flowering early, with pinkish-purple blooms. 'Aureomarginata' has cream-edged leaves.

The pink flowered weigela is another attractive shrub and there is a variegated form called *Weigela florida variegata*.

Hamamelis (witch hazel) flowers in winter on bare stems, like the daphne. It prefers a slightly acid soil and a sheltered position to do well. *Hamamelis mollis pallida* produces the best flowers, bright yellow and fragrant.

For early summer flowers there is *Deutzia* 'Mont Rose', a deciduous shrub with rose-pink flowers and arching stems. Then later in the summer come the buddleias with their blue, purple or white flower spikes that attract butterflies—giving them the common name of butterfly bush. Hybrids of *Buddleia davidii* include 'Black Knight' (deep purple), 'Royal Red' and 'White Bouquet'.

Griselinia and pittosporum are both grown for their foliage. The griselinia is a slightly tender shrub that may need protection until it becomes established. It can grow up to 7.5 m (25 ft) high but can be kept smaller by pruning. *Pittosporum crassifolium* is one of the hardiest varieties and it has leathery green leaves with white undersides. The deep purple flowers appear in the spring followed by seed capsules.

Hardy fuchsias will make quite large shrubs in many areas and even if they are cut back by frost they will often survive. 'Riccartonii' is one of the hardiest, growing to about 1.5 m (5 ft) and it has crimson and mauve flowers. 'Lady Thumb' and 'Tom Thumb' are both good small varieties.

If you want something a bit more exotic you could grow desfontainea, an evergreen shrub which needs the shelter of a wall. It has dark green holly-like leaves and produces tubular scarlet flowers with yellow tips in early summer.

Bricks provide the edging for the lawn, making it easier to mow the grass, and they also make a step down to the lower level of paving surrounded by dense planting (courtesy Mr & Mrs D B Nicholson).

Another view of Mr and Mrs Ninnis' garden shows a seating area with crazy paving. The small well-kept lawn sets off the foliage plants.

Then there is *Eriobotrya japonica* (loquat) which is growing in popularity. It is also an evergreen with leathery leaves and will bear fragrant white flowers in winter, providing it has plenty of warmth in summer. If you are lucky it will produce yellow pear-shaped fruit.

There are several good roses for semi-shaded conditions and one of these is 'Nozomi', excellent as a ground cover plant or for trailing over a low wall with small, pinky-white flowers.

Among the old-fashioned Bourbon roses there is 'Mme Isaac Pereire' with beautifully fragrant deep pink blooms and 'Kathleen Harrop', a soft pink colour. Some of the *Rosa rugosa* hybrids are well worth growing and they produce lovely large hips after the flowers. They are more suited to a wild garden than a formal one and they include 'Frau Dagmar Hartopp (Hastrup)' with pink flowers and 'Blanc Double de Coubert' a lovely semi-double white. 'Max Graf' can be used as ground cover and it has scented single pink flowers with white centres. *Rosa moyesii* is a species rose that will grow free-standing or against a wall. It has dark red, single flowers followed by glossy hips. The variety 'Geranium' is probably a better bet for small gardens as it is not so rampant.

Sun

In a sunny position you can grow the grey-leaved shrubs such as lavender, santolina and senecio. They all produce a low mound and contrast well with pinks and pale blues.

Cistus (rock roses) need plenty of sun and do best in a sheltered place. They flower between late spring and early summer and have saucer-shaped flowers in pink, white and yellows. *Cistus corbariensis* is one of the hardiest and grows 1–1.2 m (3–4 ft) high. It has white flowers with yellow centres.

Convolvulus cneorum is more tender but is well worth growing in the shelter of a walled garden. The leaves are silver and the pink buds open to white flowers. They look similar to bindweed, which belongs to the same family, but this is not a rampant variety!

Hebes are popular and as they are evergreen they make good background shrubs. There are lots of different shapes and colours to choose from and *Hebe* 'Autumn Glory' is a favourite with its purple stems and dark green leaves. The spiky blue flowers bloom from late summer to early autumn. For ground cover *Hebe pinguifolia* 'Pagei' is useful with tiny grey leaves and white flowers in spring. *Hebe armstrongii* has golden foliage rather like that of a conifer and has clusters of white flowers in spring. Again, they are not totally hardy and may be cut down by frost.

Cytisus (broom) produces a good display of flowers in early summer and will grow in poor soil, preferably slightly acid. *Cytisus × kewensis* has lovely creamy coloured flowers and there is also a white variety, *Cytisus praecox* 'Albus'.

The shrubby *Hibiscus syriacus* is a hardy form which will thrive in a walled garden. It has rich green leaves and showy flowers, in various shades, from summer to early autumn. 'Blue Bird' is blue with a red centre and 'Hamabo' has pale pink flowers with red centres.

I would not suggest hybrid tea roses for a small garden because they look extremely uninteresting for most of the year but in an informal garden a place can usually be found for one or two of the species roses. 'Rosa Mundi' (*R. gallica versicolour*) is a lovely old-fashioned one with striped crimson and white blooms.

Miniature roses are becoming increasingly popular and they can be grown in containers. There are some very pretty ones available including 'Eleanor' (double pink), 'Yellow Doll' and 'Cinderella' (white).

If you want something with an architectural shape you could try the phormiums—New Zealand flax. They are quite tender and will only survive in mild areas but you could grow one in a tub and move it under cover when the weather gets cold. There is a bronze form and one with yellow and green striped leaves.

Yuccas are also an interesting shape with their sword-like leaves, and they look spectacular when in flower. *Yucca filamentosa* has creamy white flowers in summer on a stem up to 2 m (6½ ft) high. *Yucca gloriosa* is a larger plant with pink tinged flowers from late summer to autumn. But both plants will need to be several years old before they flower—*Yucca filamentosa* will usually produce blooms sooner than *gloriosa*.

HERBACEOUS PLANTS

Shade or semi-shade

There are plenty of herbaceous plants that will grow happily in the shade. *Anemone japonica* provides welcome colour towards the end of summer with its pink and white flowers, and plants will spread if left alone. Aquilegias and astilbes both have attractive flowers in subtle shades and astilbes thrive in damp conditions.

Bergenia (elephants' ears) give good ground cover as well as large heads of flowers in varying shades of pink and white. Some of the new varieties such as 'Baby Doll' are less straggly than *Bergenia cordifolia*.

There are several spreading plants that do well in the shade but they need to be treated with caution in a small garden because they are so rampant. These include *Hypericum calycinum* (rose of Sharon) which has bright yellow flowers, lamium (deadnettle) and vinca (periwinkle). It is best to grow them in a bed of their own, perhaps under a tree surrounded by paving. *Lamium* 'Beacon Silver' is an attractive plant with silvery leaves tinged with pink and there are several vincas to choose from, large or small, variegated and with blue or white flowers.

Foxgloves are ideal for informal gardens and they will seed themselves all over the place. You can buy foxgloves in various shades, including yellow, but I still think the common variety is the best.

No shaded garden would be complete without hostas and they look good in groups of at least three rather than planted singly. You could mix plants with different variegations such as 'Thomas Hogg' (green with cream edges), *fortunei picta* (yellow with green edging) and *sieboldiana* (*glauca*) (bluish leaves). The only problem with hostas is that they tend to be attacked by slugs, so put some pellets down if you haven't any pets.

Ferns are also extremely popular and there are some lovely hardy ones that will thrive in a cool moist spot. *Matteuccia struthiopteris germanica* (ostrich feather fern) grows about 1–1.2 m (3–4 ft) high and produces bright green fronds with curled tops. *Adiantum pedatum* is one of the maidenhair ferns and grows 15–45 cm (6–18 in) tall and has light green drooping fronds and purple stalks. For contrast *Cyrtomium falcatum* (Japanese holly fern) has shiny pointed leaves and grows 60–90 cm (2–3 ft) tall. Many ferns will die back in winter, leaving just the crowns visible.

Another 'must' is the euphorbias. My favourite is *Euphorbia polychroma* which grows about 45 cm (18 in) high and has clusters of yellow flowers in early spring. *Euphorbia robbiae* grows slightly taller and also has yellow flowers which are in bloom from late spring to summer. There is a red flowered one, *Euphorbia griffithii* 'Fireglow'.

Geraniums—not to be confused with pelargoniums that are grown as house plants and bedding plants—are easy to grow and flower over a long period during the summer. 'Johnson's Blue' has lovely bright, single flowers and 'Wargrave Pink' has pretty single blooms. There is also a good double variety, *grandiflorum* 'Plenum', with lavender blue flowers.

Brunnera macrophylla has blue flowers rather like forget-me-nots but on taller stems and is an easy plant to grow. Another blue flowerer is *Tradescantia virginiana* 'Isis', an adaptable plant with three-petalled flowers that bloom in summer. There are also purple, carmine and white varieties.

Yellow flowers will brighten up a dark corner and

Mr & Mrs Nicholson have packed plenty of colourful plants into a sunny part of their small yet charming London garden. The bottom half, shaded by a tree, is filled with foliage plants and a trellis lends a hand to the climbers.

Raised beds have several advantages – they add height to the garden, they are easy to weed and can be filled with good quality soil to suit the type of plants you want to grow (courtesy Mr & Mrs D B Nicholson).

trollius, the globe flower, has large buttercup-type blooms and does well in moist soil. *Alchemilla mollis* has attractive foliage that looks particularly good after the rain when the droplets stay on the leaves. It has masses of tiny yellow flowers all through the summer.

Hemerocallis (day lilies) are extremely adaptable plants and very hardy. There are a great many hybrids with a wide range of colours, flowering in summer, and they form clumps of strap-shaped leaves. 'Pink Damask' is the best pink-flowered form and 'Morocco Red' and 'Golden Chimes' are also worth growing.

Pulmonarias are low-growing spreading plants with white spotted leaves that are at their best in a fairly moist shaded position. The drooping funnel-shaped flowers come out in spring and there are blue, pink and white varieties. Symphytum is a similar type of plant that makes good ground cover and has red, pink, blue or white flowers.

Rather more unusual is rheum, the ornamental rhubarb. The variety *Rheum palmatum rubrum* has large purple-red leaves and tall spikes of pinky-red flowers in early summer. It needs plenty of space, growing up to 2.5 m (8¼ ft) high with a spread of 1 m (3¼ ft).

Sun

Oenothera (evening primrose) has large yellow, saucer-shaped flowers that are slightly scented and open in the evening. 'Missouriensis' is a biennial and grows about 10–15 cm (4–6 in) high. *Oenothera fruticosa* 'Yellow River' is a perennial variety which produces masses of bright yellow blooms and reaches 45 cm (18 in). Both flower throughout the summer.

Another yellow flowered plant is *Achillea filipendula* which has clusters of small flowers arranged in flat heads. 'Coronation Gold' and 'Gold Plate' are good varieties and flower all the summer. They are ideal for drying for winter decoration. Also recommended is *Achillea millefolium* 'Moonshine' with silver foliage and yellow flowers.

Moving on to orange flowers there is gaillardia with its daisy-like blooms that last all summer. 'Mandarin' is a lovely cheerful variety with orange-red flowers and 'Ipswich Beauty' is another reliable form. Both grow 75–90 cm (2½–3 ft) tall. There is also an annual gaillardia which is smaller than the perennial variety.

Not all poppies are annuals. *Papaver orientale* (oriental poppy) is a perennial and there are a great many lovely coloured varieties available. They grow about 60–90 cm (2–3 ft) high and usually need staking. 'Pale Face' is a subtle pale pink and there are white, red and orange varieties, some with ruffled edges. If dead-headed they often produce a second show of flowers after the first one in the late spring.

My particular favourites are the sisyrinchiums which deserve to be more widely grown. *Sisyrinchium striatum* is a lovely plant with sword-like leaves and spikes 30–45 cm (12–18 in) high of creamy-yellow flowers which last over a long period from early to late summer. There is also a 15 cm (6 in) high variety, *Sisyrinchium brachypus,* with bright yellow, star-shaped flowers, and a small blue flowered one—*Sisyrinchium bellum*.

The large flowered heleniums are particularly cheerful in a sunny spot. 'Golden Youth' is a lovely bright yellow and 'Moerheim Beauty' has bronzy-red flowers. Some early varieties will give a second show of flowers if they are cut back after the first ones have died off.

The perennial chrysanthemums are useful late summer flowering plants—not the large exhibition types but the smaller, less showy kinds. The Shasta daisies are worth growing and 'Esther Read' is probably the best known with its double white flowers. 'Wirral Supreme' is an improved form and has double white flowers with a yellow centre, it grows about 90 cm (3 ft) high. 'Snowcap' is a smaller variety reaching 60 cm (2 ft).

Asters also flower late in the summer in various shades of blue and pink. *Aster novi-belgii* are the

Michaelmas daisies and among the recommended varieties are 'Marie Ballard' (light blue), 'Patricia Ballard' (rose pink) and 'Royal Velvet' (violet blue). They are either double or semi-double flowers. I prefer some of the single flowered varieties of *Aster amellus*. 'King George' is a lovely lavender blue and 'Pink Zenith' is also pretty. They are longer lasting plants than the Michaelmas daisies and usually trouble free.

Worth a place in any garden are the dianthus or garden pinks. They flower during the summer months and there are old-fashioned and modern varieties. 'Mrs Sinkins' is an old-fashioned white with double flowers and 'Doris' is one of the best known modern ones with very pale pink blooms. There are a great many other varieties, some plain colours, others bi-coloured or speckled and they grow about 25–30 cm (10–12 in) tall, making ideal edging plants.

For the back of the border is cynara (globe artichoke). The flower heads can be eaten if cut when they are still in bud but if left to develop they produce purple thistle-like flowers in late summer. Globe artichokes are perennial plants but are usually short-lived and sometimes succumb to frost.

Echinops (globe thistle) is also best for the background as it grows about 1–1.2 m (3–4 ft) high. The round blue flowers appear in late summer and look good when dried for winter flower arrangements.

ANNUALS

Semi-shade

Annuals will not grow well in full shade but there are some that will tolerate part shade without becoming leggy. The best ones in my opinion are the half-hardy nicotianas (tobacco plants). Even if you don't grow any other annuals these are really worthwhile and provide a lovely show of scented flowers from early to late summer. 'Sensation Mixed' and 'Evening Fragrance' grow up to 90 cm (3 ft) high and there is now a smaller variety 'Domino' reaching 30 cm (1 ft). The flower colours are a mixture of red, pink, mauve, purple and white. 'Lime Green' is a favourite of mine with its unusual yellowy-green blooms.

Impatiens (busy lizzies) do well in semi-shade and so will lobelia. The lobelia is half-hardy and busy lizzies are also usually treated as half-hardy annuals although they can be kept over winter.

Matthiola (night scented stock) is a hardy annual that can be sown outside from early spring to early summer, depending on the weather, and the small lilac flowers provide a lovely fragrance on warm summer evenings. Lunaria (honesty) is a biennial and should be planted in autumn to flower the next summer. The pinky-purple flowers are followed by silvery seed pods which look good dried but if left on the plant the self sown seedlings can be a nuisance.

Another hardy annual is *Iberis umbellata* (candytuft), a low growing plant with white, pink or red flowers, and it does well on most soils.

Sun

There are so many annuals to grow in the sun that it would be impossible to list them all here so I will just mention my favourites.

Eschscholzias (Californian poppies) are cheerful with delicate bright orange flowers in summer and ferny leaves. Some of the new varieties are multi-coloured but they don't look as good.

Rudbeckias also have orange flowers and the single flowered varieties are most attractive. 'Rustic Dwarfs Mixed' grow about 60 cm (2 ft) high and have orangey-brown flowers with brown centres. 'Irish Eyes' is golden yellow and grows 75 cm (2½ ft) high. There is a newer variety called 'Goldilocks' with double or semi-double flowers but I prefer the single-flowered varieties.

Particularly suited to a dry sunny spot are the

A fountain in the pond gives the soothing sound of running water and helps to prevent the water becoming stagnant (courtesy Mr & Mrs W A Batchelor).

The very high wall in this garden (The Greyfriars, Worcester) provides shelter for the climbers and shrubs. The little wooden bridge, flanked by bergenias could be adapted to suit any garden, whether there is water or not (courtesy The National Trust).

gazanias, low growing half-hardy annuals with brightly coloured daisy-like flowers. 'Mini-Star' is bright yellow and there are also mixed colours, all flowering in summer.

Limnanthes douglasii is called the poached egg plant because of its yellow-centred flowers with white edging. It is a hardy annual and can be sown outdoors in spring or autumn.

Mesembryanthemums are small plants with a big name. They are ideal for growing in a raised bed that gets plenty of sun or on walls. They have succulent leaves and brightly coloured daisy-like flowers.

Finally, *Lavatera* 'Silver Cup', is another hardy annual with large rose-coloured flowers during late summer. It grows about 60–75 cm (2–2½ ft) high so will need to go near the back of the border.

The hardy annuals can be sown outdoors in spring, but better results are often obtained by raising them in seed trays in the house or greenhouse, in the way that half-hardy varieties are grown. Alternatively, trays of bedding plants are on sale at shops and garden centres in early summer, but you are not likely to get such a wide choice as when you grow your own.

Bulbs

Semi-shade

There are quite a few bulbs that will flower successfully in semi-shaded conditions and earliest of all are the snowdrops, which turn our thoughts to spring. They look best when planted *en masse* under trees or shrubs and can be mixed with yellow winter aconites which flower at the same time.

Daffodils and grape hyacinths flower later in the spring and also need to be in groups, rather than dotted around singly. There are some lovely small daffodil varieties, called 'triandrus' narcissi, some only growing 15 cm (6 in) high. 'April Tears' has bright yellow,

nodding heads and 'Tresamble' is pure white and scented, growing 40 cm (16 in) tall. Among the taller daffodils there are plenty to choose from, in numerous shades, shapes and sizes. The trumpet daffodils are still the most widely grown but some of the double flowering varieties such as 'Bridal Crown', 'White Cheerfulness' and 'Yellow Cheerfulness' are also popular.

The choice is not so wide among the grape hyacinths (muscari): most are deep blue but there is a white form as well. Scillas are also blue and spring flowering, the small *Scilla sibirica* is well worth growing and so is *Scilla peruviana* (Cuban lily) which flowers in early summer. Bluebells used to belong to this family but they are now classed under the name of *Endymion*. These are suitable for wild gardens but they can become very rampant and difficult to get rid of.

Staying with blue flowers we have the low-growing chionodoxa which appear early in the year with star-shaped flowers. Less well known is 'Pink Giant', only growing 15 cm (6 in) tall despite its name, with pinky-white blooms.

Crocus will grow in semi-shade and provide winter and spring colour as well as those varieties that flower in autumn such as 'Speciosus Conqueror' with sky-blue flowers and 'zonatus albus' (white). Colchicums (meadow saffron) are similar to crocus and they flower in autumn. 'Agrippinum' is an unusual pink and white chequered variety and there's also the very different 'Waterlily' with lilac blooms.

Anemones are firm favourites and will thrive in a sheltered spot in sun or partial shade. The bright blue *Anemone blanda* is particularly appealing, more so than the mixed colours, and the larger 'de Caens' with their typical 'anemone' flowers are also attractive; and then there is *Anemone nemorosa*, the wood anemone, which is suitable for a shaded, wild garden but, like the bluebell, can become a problem. The bright red *Anemone pavonina*, with its creamy centre, is more unusual.

These are some of the most common bulbs but if

you want to grow something unusual you could try camassia (the quamash). They produce tall blue spikes in summer and do best when grown in sun or partial shade.

Fritillarias are also a good choice with their hanging bell-shaped flowers in a variety of colours during spring. The snake's head fritillaries (*F. meleagris*) look good when naturalized in grass and they have chequered blooms in white and shades of pink-purple. The crown imperials (*F. imperialis*) are more showy and suited more to formal situations. They bear their clusters of flowers on tall stems that are topped by a crown of leaves. They are best left undisturbed.

Sun

All bulbs that grow in semi-shade will grow in the sun as well, but there are also a number of bulbs that must have a sunny situation to produce flowers.

You either like tulips or you don't, and I don't! Although I must admit that some of the low growing varieties are appealing and they have the advantage that they don't flop over. 'Franz Lehar' is one of the kaufmanniana hybrids and has bright yellow flowers with a darker centre. *Tulipa tarda* is also attractive, having star-shaped yellow flowers with white tips. It only grows about 10 cm (4 in) high.

The family of alliums include the onion but there are also some decorative varieties such as *Allium giganteum* with large round heads of lilac-coloured flowers on 1.2 m (4 ft) high stems. *Allium ostrowskianum* is much smaller with star-shaped purple pink blooms and I am particularly fond of *Allium moly,* a cheerful bright yellow. All these varieties flower in early summer.

The foxtail lilies (eremurus) are spectacular plants that like to be in a sheltered, sunny position. The flower spikes grow up to 2.1 m (7 ft) high and come in yellow, pink, orange and white, appearing from late spring to summer.

Lilies are also spectacular and in spite of their reputation are easy to grow. There are some fascinating colour combinations—striped and speckled, orange, yellow, white, pink—one to fit every colour scheme.

A similar flower to the lily is the crinum which needs a sheltered site in a warm area. They flower in spring and have handsome trumpet-shaped flowers of white or pink.

For late summer colour you have the nerines which do best in mild areas when planted by a sunny, sheltered wall. *Nerine bowdenii* is the outdoor variety and has bright pink flowers on stems up to 60 cm (2 ft) tall. They prefer to be left undisturbed after planting.

WATER PLANTS

Water lilies (nymphaea) are the best known pond plants and they look very impressive in summer with their exotic flowers. The pygmy varieties are best for a small pond as they only spread about 30 cm (1 ft) across. There are red, yellow, pink and white ones available. Another water plant that floats on the surface is the water hyacinth (*Eichhornia*). They are easy to grow—just pop them on the surface of the water. But they are tender plants and should either be grown as annuals or brought under cover in winter, and kept in moist soil.

The submerged water plants are not as spectacular but the water violet (*Hottonia palustris*) and the water crowfoot (*Ranunculus aquatilis*) are worth growing. Both of these are oxygenating plants so they help to maintain a balanced environment.

If you have a moist area at the edge of your pond there are some lovely plants to choose from. The water forget-me-not (*Myosotis palustris*) has blue flowers in summer and the marsh marigold (*Caltha palustris*) is golden yellow. Spiky, upright plants include the flowering rush (*Butomus umbellatus*) and the sweet flag (*Acorus calamus*).

The bottom of the staircase leads onto a paved patio, bordered by a narrow raised bed (courtesy Mr & Mrs D B Nicholson).

A close up view of the paved area in this garden owned by Mr & Mrs D. B. Nicholson. The combination of bricks and cobbles works very well and the terracotta pot, on a pedestal, makes an interesting focal point.

3

HARD SURFACING

In a small garden paving will be very important because you probably will not have any lawn. A lawn sets off the shrubs and flower beds to their best advantage so you will have to try and create the same effect with hard surfacing. To decide what sort of material you want to use you will first have to look at the house walls and boundary walls or fence to see what will fit in with these. Whether the garden is to be formal or informal will also have to be taken into consideration.

There are many different kinds of paving available and pre-cast slabs are the most widely used. They come in various sizes, shapes and colours and are probably the easiest and one of the cheapest methods of hard surfacing.

Most of the slabs have a smooth surface but there are also textured ones—some made to look like setts, others with a 'riven' or layered look and stable tiles that resemble a bar of chocolate. A smooth surface is necessary on a patio where there is going to be garden furniture and is also best where children will be playing. Non-slip paving is also recommended.

Slabs can be laid in different patterns using different colours, but try to avoid a mottled, disjointed effect, and, if unsure, lay them in line with one another and use one colour.

Stone is much more expensive but is very effective especially next to an old property. It is best to choose a local stone because it will fit in with the surroundings and will also be cheaper. The disadvantage with stone is that it is difficult to lay because of the uneven shapes and thicknesses.

Bricks can look extremely attractive and are used quite widely. Good quality bricks are essential otherwise they will crack and become uneven; walling or facing bricks are not suitable because they are susceptible to frost damage. There are hundreds of different bricks, some hand made and very expensive. Engineering bricks are very good and Staffordshire blues are one of the hardest types if you can get hold of them. They were once used in thousands around ordinary terraced houses and in yards but good quality ones are costly. Brick pavers are also durable and as well as oblong shaped ones, hexagonal and interlocking pavers are available.

The bricks can be laid in all sorts of different patterns, using either the bedding face, presenting the largest surface area, or laid on their side (Fig. 3). They may also be used as surrounds for concrete slabs, if you don't want to cover a large area completely with bricks.

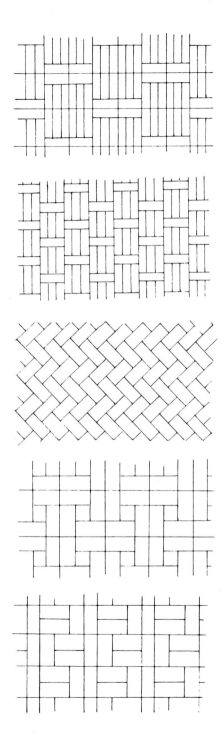

Granite setts are another possibility and these are very long-lasting. They are grey and square shaped and create quite a hard effect. If you have an inspection cover in the garden it is possible to buy a recessed cover so that paving can be set into it and it will blend in with the rest of the surfacing while still being easy to remove if necessary.

Cobbles can either be laid loose or set in concrete and are suitable for areas that will not be walked on very much (Fig. 4). They look good in Japanese-style gardens, especially the larger cobbles. Different sizes are available and they can be laid flat in patterns or laid upright for maximum 'cobbled' effect.

Gravel or shingle is very useful for filling in between paving or stones or as a surface on its own. It comes in various colours and sizes of chipping, the smallest size being easiest to walk on. It is useful as a stop gap between paving and house walls, if the paving is at or above the damp proof course.

It is best to have an edging around a gravel area—bricks or old railway sleepers—to stop the gravel getting on to the flower beds. A fresh layer will be needed from time to time as the gravel consolidates. Shaped edging stones can also be bought—semi-circular or pointed ones.

Fig. 4. Try combining different types of hard surfacing—cobbles set in cement make a paved area more interesting.

Fig. 3. (Left) Bricks can be laid in various ways to produce different patterns—laying them either face down or sideways. Here are five examples.

This part of The Greyfriars garden shows how a low-maintenance garden can be made with the use of hard surfacing. Bricks, cobbles and paving are very effectively combined (courtesy The National Trust).

Steps with a difference – cobbles and old tiles, set in cement, are used in an imaginative way. The everlasting sweet pea in the foreground makes a colourful display (courtesy The National Trust).

For an informal look crazy paving may be laid or gaps can be left between slabs or stone to allow low-growing plants to grow through. Try and get the paving as even as possible otherwise you will be forever tripping over it.

An alternative is concrete laid *in situ*. It is often satisfactory on small areas, once it has weathered a bit, but can look stark and uninteresting on large areas. A strong mix is essential because if it is too weak, i.e. too much sand and gravel and not enough cement, it will break up in frosty weather.

Quarry tiles were often used in old backyards and front courtyards, particularly black and white ones mixed to give a chequerboard effect. There are also some attractive red colours now.

Tarmac is usually thought of as a surfacing for

Fig. 5. A 'stepped' effect will add height to the garden and also provide pockets of well-drained, fertile soil. You can even choose the type of soil according to what sort of plants you want to grow.

driveways, but some of the coloured finishes are suitable for gardens. The easiest method is to buy dry Macadam that just needs to be raked and rolled. It is avialable in red or black, with or without chipping.

Timber decking is very popular now due to continental influences. It looks very attractive but can become slippery in wet weather, although some of the latest products claim to be non-slip.

Drainage is an important consideration because if pools of water lie on the paving they can be a nuisance in warm weather but a potential danger if they freeze in winter. If possible the water should be allowed to drain into the flower beds or if this is impractical, for example if you have raised beds, you will need a drain and soakaway.

When constructing your hard surface area you may want to incorporate a small pool. I think that formal shapes, in brick or concrete, often look better than the moulded fibreglass pools that are seen at most garden centres. If concrete is used it should be water-proofed and reinforced. Brick will need to be rendered with a waterproof facing. The pool could either be flush with the paving or raised above it.

Don't forget that an overflow will be needed, to avoid flooding the garden when it rains, and also an outlet so that the pool can be drained for cleaning.

You may want to use hard surfacing to create a change in level. Slabs and bricks can be made into formal steps and stone also looks very effective when used as random stepping stones. Railway sleepers make good stoppers for gravel treads, although it is best not to use them for the treads themselves as they will become very slippery.

Changes in level can also be made with raised beds. The edges may be constructed of brick, stone, railway sleepers, peat blocks or concrete blocks. The advantage of raised beds is that you can fill them with good quality soil and have a fertile, well-drained medium in which plants will thrive (Fig. 5). They can also be used to cover up an ugly wall or to create more

height. I have seen a very good 'stepped' effect using brick walls with narrow strips of soil in which trailing plants were growing and cascading down over the walls.

Alpines, in particular, grow well in raised beds because they need good drainage. A layer of gravel over the soil surface will prevent the plants from becoming too wet and rotting.

Whatever the type of hard surfacing used it will always look better when it has weathered and when plants have grown up around it. The main problem likely to be encountered is algae forming on paving, making it slippery. There are several cleaning products specially for this purpose and they should be used regularly on areas that are walked on. On parts where you don't often walk the algae can look quite attractive on brickwork and stones.

WALLS AND FENCES

You will probably already have a boundary wall or fence, but you may want a screen somewhere in the garden, to hide something or to provide a private sitting area. Bricks or stone can be used, in keeping with an existing wall, or you may want a more open screen provided by patterned concrete blocks. Most of them look best when there are climbing plants growing up through them, although some of the terracotta shapes are more attractive. Reconstituted stone block also looks quite good.

Trellis will make a screen if covered with climbing plants or you may want to use larchlap or interwoven fencing that can be bought in panels. Choose a good quality fence because the cheaper ones are very flimsy and will not last long. Treatment with wood preservative is essential and nowadays we are spoilt for choice, there are so many makes available.

Wattle fencing is not long lasting but it will fit in well with an informal 'wild' garden.

This boundary wall in Lys de Bray's garden is well hidden with shade-loving shrubs and a variegated ivy clings to the brickwork. The tree stump in the foreground adds interest.

A good example of how a small courtyard or basement entrance can be bright and pleasant. Combinations of hard surfacing and a few plants are all that is needed (courtesy Mr & Mrs W A Batchelor).

4

FEATURES

The finishing touches to any garden are made by the strategic positioning of an ornament, a piece of garden furniture or perhaps even a greenhouse.

There are a great many statues and ornaments for sale now ranging from stone animals to large stone columns and urns. Staddle stones, rather like mushrooms, are popular; they were once used for raising hay barns off the ground. 'Japanese' stones can also be bought for a modern or Japanese-style garden. They come in various shapes and sizes and may be used on their own or in groups.

Several firms sell antique garden ornaments but it is also possible to buy some very good reproductions such as mill stones and stone sundials or lead statues. Depending on what type of garden you have, ornaments can be made into a focal point or tucked away in the greenery. It is very much a matter of taste, after all some people like garden gnomes!

New stone ornaments may look a bit stark at first but will blend in better when they have weathered. One tip, that I have yet to try, is to bury them in the compost heap for the winter. Apparently they come out coated in algae and looking as if they have been around for years!

Sculpture is popular but modern sculpture in part-icular needs to be very carefully sited to look right. It is no good having a sculpture that completely dominates the scene and detracts from the plants, even if it is a focal point. Harmony is the aim and the type of house and style and size of the garden should all be taken into consideration.

Instead of buying an ornament you could create your own features, perhaps with an interesting piece of log or driftwood, or a few boulders. Old tree stumps look attractive with plants growing up them, although you run the risk of honey fungus developing on the dead wood.

Also, if you come across any old water pumps, old gas lamps or farm implements that can be done up they will make quite a feature. And if you really want to create a talking point you could buy one of the old telephone boxes—just right for storing tools in!

Bird baths, feeding tables and nesting boxes will bring plenty of interest, especially if you spend a lot of time sitting looking out at the garden. They are readily available and some of the rustic ones look quite good.

Garden furniture is seen in most gardens and you will want to find something that is attractive and probably also sufficiently hard wearing to be left outside all year—in a small garden there may not be enough room to store furniture under cover. Cast iron and wrought iron will last for years if it is good quality. Some of the ornate cast furniture is too fancy for my liking but there are some attractive plainer designs. Cast aluminium is lighter, and cheaper, than cast iron. Wrought iron was traditionally used for garden furniture, when blacksmiths made them as a side line. It is still available today, although a lot of seats and tables are made from fabricated steel which corrodes much more quickly than wrought iron. There are various metal coatings e.g. plastic ones which can be applied either by dipping or by spraying.

Some of the plastic coated metals are initially attractive but the plastic often peels off and there is not much you can do about that. Only buy top quality plastic coated furniture. All-wood seats are often very attractive and will last well if treated with a wood preservative. Hardwoods, such as teak, mahogany and iroko will last the longest but the cheaper softwoods, for example pine, have a shorter life. Most of the metal seats have wooden slats but there are a few all-metal ones available.

For real style there are the 'Lutyens' type wooden seats based on designs that Lutyens used in his own gardens and in those of Gertrude Jekyll.

Some of the moulded plastic furniture looks good in a modern garden and the top quality ones will stand up to the weather. Many of the patio sets come with parasols as well.

I prefer green and black furniture which blends into the scenery but white is also very popular. A disadvantage with white is that it has to be cleaned regularly to keep it looking smart.

Make sure you try the seats before you buy them—some of the most attractive furniture doesn't seem to have been designed for sitting on!

Permanent seats can be made out of brick or concrete, covering them with cushions when you want to use them. Stone benches, popular in large Victorian gardens, are often available from the same sources as stone ornaments.

Old sewing machine frames make good bases for tables, topped with wood. And blocks of stone could also be used as tables.

Barbecues have taken off in a big way over the past few years and they provide an excellent way of integrating the living area with the garden. There are a lot of free-standing barbecues available, in a wide price range, but these need to be stored somewhere in winter so it is often better to build a permanent one that will fit into the garden without looking obtrusive (Fig. 6).

Brick can be used and if you have brick paving the barbecue could be made with the same material. Keep the barbecue a reasonable distance from the house where it will not set fire to anything if it gets out of hand. A cover could be placed on top of the barbecue when it is not in use and plants could be stood on the cover to disguise it further.

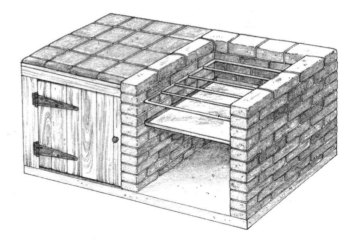

Fig. 6. A permanent barbecue, made out of brick, with storage space for bags of charcoal and utensils, and plenty of room for cooking.

A gazebo is a splendid feature, especially when framed by a canopy of greenery on a carpet of ground cover (courtesy Keith Steadman).

Statues need to be used with care in a small garden but this one, in Mr & Mrs Nicholson's garden, strikes exactly the right balance and makes a fine focal point without being too dominant.

WATER

Most people find water fascinating and even a small pool makes an attractive feature. In a backyard there may not be enough room for anything extravagant and a small square brick pool will often suffice. Stone pools can be bought and they look better than a plastic-lined one. If you have not got room for a proper pond or don't want to have it as a permanent feature you could make a water garden in a half beer barrel. They will remain watertight if the wood is kept wet. Even if you just grow a couple of water lilies in it, the effect will be pleasing.

Still water tends to go green and slimy but this can be avoided by having the correct balance of oxygenating plants. Suitable oxygenators include elodea (Canadian pondweed), hottonia (water violet) and sagittaria (arrowhead). You will need at least 10 plants for every square metre (square yard) of water surface.

The problem will not arise with running water and a simple waterfall can be created down brick steps or over cobbles. Fountains are also very soothing and pumps to circulate the water can easily be bought from garden centres. But bear in mind that they need an electricity supply. If you haven't got room for a pool you could have a fountain coming out of a wall, a bowl-shaped one or even a lion's head.

If you want to do something a little different you could have a mural on one of the walls, perhaps a garden scene to act as an extension to the garden or something on a grander scale as a form of escapism. Or if that idea does not appeal to you don't forget that different effects are created by painting boundary walls in plain colours—green to blend in with the scenery or a brighter, bolder colour to add contrast.

To complete the scene what about some lighting—to illuminate the barbecue on a warm summer evening or simply to light up the garden so that you can look at it from inside? Light shining on to a water feature or statue will create a completely new aspect to the garden. The lamps will need to be made of weatherproof material such as good quality wrought iron. There are many different types of wrought iron lamps, either on stands or for fitting on to a wall. You can either have a modern design or an old-fashioned one, depending on the type of garden, and there are even stone 'Chinese' lanterns available.

As well as lamps for lighting a patio area or path there are also spotlights to illuminate a certain part of the garden. They can be placed unobtrusively among shrub borders and come in several different colours.

Underwater lighting can create an attractive effect, the lamps can either be submerged or floated on the surface. They are sealed units with a waterproof housing to make them safe. Also available are 'light fountains'—the water passes over different coloured lights to produce coloured jets of spray. An added advantage of lighting is that it may deter burglars. It is possible to buy lamps with a built-in light detector so that they will switch themselves on when it gets dark.

Special care must be taken when electrical appliances are used outside and all the fittings and cable should be completely weatherproof and comply with current regulations. It is a good idea to have two-way switches so that the lights can be switched on and off from indoors.

A safer way of using electricity outdoors is to have a transformer from which 12 volt appliances can be used. Lighting systems are sold complete with a transformer and low voltage cable. This means that if there is a fault or a child tampers with the lights they are not lethal. Pool pumps and barbecues can also be run on a 12 volt supply.

If you do run outdoor appliances off a 240 volt mains supply it will be much safer if you use a residual current device, or earth leakage circuit breaker, to give it another name. These can be bought to replace a normal socket outlet. As well as lighting, an electricity supply might be needed for a pool pump or an electric barbecue.

If you do not want to go to the trouble of having an electricity supply run out to the garden there are now modern versions of the old oil lamps that can be bought in a variety of bright colours. They can be put on a table or secured on poles and stuck in the garden or a flower pot. Night flares are also good for an evening barbecue.

You may have room in your garden for a small greenhouse which, if it is a good design, will make a feature in itself. There are several shapes to choose from and probably the best choice if space is limited would be a hexagonal one. There are also domed greenhouses but these don't look as decorative. If you need more space for growing you might want a rectangular shape of which there are many. Red cedar construction looks the best but it needs to be well maintained. Aluminium is an alternative, it doesn't look as attractive as wood but it has the advantage of requiring little maintenance. Lean-to greenhouses and conservatories can be used for growing plants and as an extension to the living area. Some of the Victorian-style constructions look very impressive and there are small versions as well as the grand styles seen on large houses.

If you prefer just to sit and watch your garden rather than participating in greenhouse work you may like to have a summerhouse. I know they are mostly seen in big gardens but there's no reason why they aren't suitable for a small one. Apart from sitting in they can also be a useful place to store a few tools, or furniture in the winter.

On similar lines, but purely for decoration is a gazebo, often made out of fancy wrought iron work; they can even be bought from department stores now. They look delightful with climbers growing up over them and will provide a pleasant place to sit on a hot day.

Another way of adding height is to have a pergola for plants to climb up. It may be made out of timber or metal and can be used to make a covered walkway or sitting area. The construction should not be too big, otherwise the effect might be overpowering in a small space. If you want to be really grand there are pergolas with stone pillars available, but they tend to look better in large gardens.

ROOF GARDENS

Another facet of town gardening is the roof garden, which sounds very romantic but needs a lot of thought before being constructed. The main problem of course is weight, especially if you want to grow trees and large shrubs in borders. An easy alternative is just to have a few plants in pots.

Assuming that you have taken care of the structural problems you then have to decide what sort of plants you want. The garden is likely to be very windy and probably receives plenty of sun. You can choose the type of soil to suit the plants. The growing medium should be as light as possible and, if pots are used, they should also be made from lightweight material.

There aren't really any limits to the sort of plants you can grow. Of course, very big trees would be unsuitable, although it is best to choose tough subjects that can stand up to the wind. The depth of soil is a big factor and you may only be able to have shallow-rooting shrubs or herbaceous plants. If the garden is open you will need some sort of open fencing to filter the wind.

5

PLANTING AND MAINTENANCE

Whatever type of garden you choose it will need some sort of maintenance to keep it looking good. If you don't have a lawn or hedges this cuts down the work considerably, and how many plants you have will be another factor.

Plants in containers need more looking after than those planted in the garden. They need regular watering and feeding in summer and will have to be repotted when they outgrow their pots. This is usually best done in spring, using a good potting compost that is suited to the plant's requirements. Put plenty of crocks in the bottom, for drainage, and firm the soil in well so that there are no air pockets around the roots. It is a good idea to put newly planted containers in a shady spot at first (even the sun lovers) until they have settled in to their new home.

Most shrubs and trees will be bought in containers but bare rooted ones are available in autumn. Soil preparation is important for all types and it is a good idea to dig over the whole border, incorporating peat or compost. Dig a hole big enough to accommodate the roots without them being squashed up and make sure the soil level is the same height as it was when the plant was in its pot. Container-grown shrubs can be planted at any time of the year but they will need special care if planted in summer when they are more likely to dry out.

Mulches are widely used now and they retain moisture and cut down on weeding as well as looking attractive. Forest bark is a rich brown colour and goes well with all types of plants. A 5 cm (2 in) deep layer will be needed to suppress weeds. Make sure that all bare patches of earth are covered and only put the bark down on moist soil. Gravel can also be used as a top dressing in a formal setting.

Another way of cutting down on weeding is to have plenty of ground cover plants. They really are essential if you want a low-maintenance garden and they can be used to under-plant shrubs and trees. It is possible to cover all the soil so the weeds don't stand a chance!

Pruning is a necessary task and it will mostly be a case of cutting out straggly branches and dead wood. Evergreen shrubs require little pruning, unless they become too big and leggy. As a general rule deciduous shrubs that flower on shoots produced in the same year should be pruned in early spring. Growth can be cut back almost to ground level if space is limited. They will then start new growth which will carry the flowers. Those which flower on growth produced in the previous year should not be pruned until after they

If you haven't enough room for a proper pond you could make a small one in a wall, like this one at Greyfriars. Quarry tiles have been used in the recess (courtesy The National Trust).

have finished flowering, and then only old wood should be cut out.

The same rules apply to climbers. Those flowering on current season's growth don't necessarily have to be pruned down to the ground, they can just be thinned out, removing old wood. Clematis have varieties belonging to both groups so it is important to find out which variety you have before pruning, otherwise you might end up with no flowers. Most ramblers and old-fashioned roses flower on shoots produced in the previous year and so should be pruned after flowering. There are differing opinions on when shrub roses should be pruned. On the whole it is best to leave the final pruning until late winter, except in mild areas where it can be done in autumn. Any long straggly growth can be taken off in autumn to prevent wind damage.

Flowers will also need to be dead-headed regularly so that more blooms are produced. Hydrangeas can either be picked and used dried for indoor decoration or they can be left on the plants where they will look attractive during winter and also give extra protection from frost.

Getting rid of garden rubbish is a problem, especially in a built-up area where it is not possible to have a bonfire. Composting can be done on a small scale and the best way to keep it under control in a small garden is to buy a purpose-built compost container that will fit into the garden without looking obtrusive. Alternatively you could make one out of bricks or slatted wood, remembering that it is important to have a good flow of air through the compost if you are going to get good results. Prunings and other bulky rubbish should be chopped up into small pieces. If the compost is managed properly and an activator (to speed up the process) is used then it shouldn't smell unpleasant.

Wood preserving is an important part of the maintenance programme and there are many different products to choose from. The main thing is to use some sort of preservative every year to prevent wood cracking and rotting, and to use one that does not harm plants. Apart from various shades of brown and green there are all sorts of colours, including red and blue.

Pools require a lot of maintenance if they are to remain fresh and pleasant to look at. An annual clear out will be necessary, so it is a good idea to have a small pond otherwise you will have a difficult job getting rid of the old water. Algicides can be bought to clear away green slime but it is far better to have the correct balance of submerged and surface plants. If you are going to keep fish in the pond it is even more important to have clean water.

Whatever type of small garden you have I hope this book will show you how it is possible to design it to suit your needs and to gain pleasure from pottering about in it or just sitting and enjoying the surroundings. Planning a garden is as important as planning the decor for your house, to create the type of environment you want to live in.

CONTAINER GARDENING

INTRODUCTION

Containers in which to grow plants are especially recommended for small gardens as they allow one to pack more plants into the available space.

Also they play a major role in garden design. Containers, in fact, should appear to be part of the overall design and not simply added haphazardly as an afterthought. They should have some definite purpose, a particular role to play.

Containers should be chosen to suit the style of the house and garden. You may decide not to plant some but simply to use them as focal points in a garden.

A collection of planted containers should be capable of providing colour and interest all the year round, particularly important in small gardens where containers often form the major means of growing plants.

This section will, hopefully, inspire you with some fresh ideas. It opens with a brief history of garden containers and then considers their uses in the modern garden.

Some containers are so decorative and attractive that they can be used as garden ornaments in their own right, and this aspect is considered in Chapter 7.

One of the most popular parts of a garden for planted containers is the patio and Chapter 8 describes how to ensure colour and interest there all the year round. It considers first the huge range of colourful temporary plants such as annuals, summer and spring bedding plants and bulbs. Then it looks at the wide range of permanent plants. Many people do not realize that there are many shrubs, conifers, small trees, climbers, roses and hardy perennials that grow well in containers. Of course, these are far less labour intensive than temporary plants, plus they help to ensure year-round colour and interest.

Raised beds and borders, planters and double walls are also classed as containers and have a chapter devoted to them. Some really attractive planting schemes can be created in these, in both sunny and shady positions.

Sinks, whether genuine old stone or suitably modified glazed types, make excellent containers for alpines or rock plants and form attractive features on patios. We explain how to prepare and plant them.

Many people with small gardens like to grow some fruits and vegetables, so in Chapter 10 we suggest what can be grown in containers on the patio. With a little thought, fruits and vegetables can be made to form attractive features in themselves or to combine pleasantly with ornamental plants.

The section is rounded off with preparation of containers, planting and care of plants.

A terracotta urn in classical style. Used as focal points, such containers could be left unplanted but here pelargoniums and trailing ivies have been used to good effect.

6

OLD AND MODERN USES

For thousands of years plants have been grown in containers by many civilizations. The ancient Egyptians, Greeks and Chinese had earthenware pots, and the Chinese also produced handsome ceramic pots. The Romans had a wide variety, both as ornaments and for growing plants. They included them on their roof gardens and even had window boxes.

All kinds of pots, and window boxes, were used in Medieval Europe and they were made of various materials like clay or terracotta, metal and even wattle (woven strips of wood).

Throughout history terracotta clay has been the most widely used material for pots and other containers, no doubt because it has always been readily available and easily worked, even into quite intricate designs. Stone, lead and wood were also widely used. Round or square wooden tubs were once commonly used for growing citrus and other fruits.

We can buy containers today in all of these materials (except wattle). Mass-produced terracotta flower pots date from the early nineteenth century and indeed the Victorians often used them, together with terracotta window boxes. The Victorians had all styles of containers, including very ornate designs of their own. They mass-produced metal window boxes too.

In past centuries some of the most beautiful and highly ornate earthenware urns and pots were produced in Italy, especially in Florence and Venice. Copies of these are very popular today, adding style and elegance to gardens and patios.

Today there is a vast range of ornamental containers to choose from. There are reproductions of many of the classical styles – Greek, Roman, Chinese, Italian, Victorian and so on – and very popular they are too. There are also many modern, twentieth-century styles that are particularly useful for associating with contemporary architecture. For instance, the shallow concrete bowl, which first appeared at the Festival of Britain.

I have already mentioned that most of the traditional materials are still used for making containers today, but there are also containers in various modern materials, like concrete, reconstituted stone, fibreglass and plastics. Terracotta is still widely used and although clay pots are often imported from Italy and Spain, there are some British manufacturers (a trend is towards frost-proof terracotta pots). The U.S.A. imports clay pots from Mexico.

WHY USE CONTAINERS?

Obviously containers have to be used for growing plants if you do not have a garden – for instance, if all your gardening is done on a balcony or perhaps in a basement. But why use containers if you have a garden? There are several very good reasons, mainly to do with garden design.

Firstly, containers can be used as ornaments in their own right, perhaps to create a particular mood or atmosphere in the garden. For example, on a patio one can create a Mediterranean atmosphere by choosing the right styles of containers. Or if you are designing an Oriental garden then the use of Chinese glazed terracotta pots would certainly create the right atmosphere. Likewise a formal Italian-style garden could be embellished with Florentine urns and pots.

A 'rustic' atmosphere can be created in an English cottage or country garden by using wooden tubs and barrels as ornaments. Lead urns and cisterns, as well as stone containers, would also create the right mood.

Containers can be used as focal points to draw the eye to various parts of a garden. For instance, they can be set at the end of a vista or at the bend in a path. They can be used for framing steps and the doors of the house. In other words, ornamental containers can be used just like vases and other ornaments in interior decoration.

Containers, though, are mainly used for displaying plants and therefore are more often than not planted. Even if you have a garden, planted containers are still very useful for they allow you to easily place colour where it is needed. Again the obvious place is on a patio, but you can also introduce colour to other areas, such as porches, driveways, paths, sitting areas, etc.

Hanging baskets and window boxes allow you to bring colour and interest to the house itself, in the same way as wall pots which are fixed direct to the house walls. Hanging baskets can also provide much-needed colour on pergolas, garages and sheds.

Containers can be an integral part of the garden layout, in the form of raised beds and borders, double walls filled with soil for planting, and very large planters. These can all legitimately be classed as containers, for they hold soil in which plants are grown. Generally, raised beds and borders are used to create a variation in height on a flat plot, while double walls are often used as front boundaries, to front a porch and for surrounding patios. Very large permanent planters are often featured on patios; they allow more imaginative planting schemes than conventional containers.

Rock gardens are expensive to build and space-consuming but many people have discovered that an attractive alternative method of growing alpines is to create miniature rock gardens in sinks – either genuine old stone sinks or converted glazed ones.

Often in small gardens the only way to grow fruits and vegetables is in containers on a patio. Fruit trees are, of course, very ornamental in their own right but can be further enhanced by choosing distinctive containers for them.

The growing-bag (a compost-filled plastic bag) enables many people to grow vegetables who otherwise would not be able to do so. They can be used on balconies, on patios and in tiny basement gardens for salad crops, many other small vegetables and, of course, for tomatoes. Of all the many types of container available, the purely utilitarian growing-bags are the most unattractive, but this should not deter you from using them, for they can be disguised so that they harmonize with the surroundings.

The introduction some years ago of the proprietary Tower Pot has enabled many people with only limited space to grow strawberries, for the plants are grown vertically. These containers certainly do not look out of place on the modern patio. Cottage owners can, alternatively, grow lots of strawberries in a small area by planting them in strawberry barrels.

Many people do not realize that there is an enormous range of plants that can be grown in containers – all too often we see nothing but spring and summer bedding plants. Certainly these give lots of colour and should by no means be dismissed, but bear in mind that containers of suitable size allow you to grow small trees, shrubs, climbers, roses, conifers, hardy perennials and other plants in very confined spaces – on patios, in the tiny pocket handkerchief garden, in basements and so on.

Containers also allow you to display various tender plants in the summer, to give a sub-tropical atmosphere, say on the patio; the plants being returned indoors or into the greenhouse before the frosts arrive.

A classical-style terracotta urn acts as a focal point in this garden, drawing the eye to a bed of antirrhinums. Not all containers have to be planted.

A contemporary container on a modern patio. Ideally some containers should be permanently planted. This one contains a very suitable shrub or small tree – a purple-leaved Japanese maple.

7

GARDEN ORNAMENTS

Distinctive and perhaps highly decorated containers can be used as garden ornaments in their own right, without necessarily having to be planted. This idea is often used in large gardens, especially when extensive garden maintenance precludes one from having many planted containers.

When using containers as ornaments one should think in terms of quality: it is not a good idea to use cheap containers, such as plastic imitations of classical designs, as these never appear aesthetically pleasing when standing alone, unplanted. On the other hand they are fine where the container is to be densely planted, for example with trailing bedding plants, which will hide most of the container, and where several are to be grouped closely together on a patio.

In general, however, one should think in terms of the better quality containers. In my opinion it is well worth saving specially for a suitable item. Of course, if finances allow, one could not do better than invest in one or two antique containers. I think invest is the right word, for such containers certainly increase in value over the years – they are, after all, collector's items.

Classical urns, vases and pots are very popular for use as isolated garden ornaments, whether originals or imitations. The more ornate the better, for remember they are for decoration and are meant to be admired and enjoyed for their own sake.

Likely sources of suitable containers include garden centres for imitation classical designs, and antique dealers for originals. There are also several specialist suppliers for both reproduction and antique classical containers, and these would be well worth visiting if they are within easy reach.

CONTAINERS AS FOCAL POINTS

A focal point is an object which draws the eye so that one is tempted to walk towards it and admire it more closely. On reaching the focal point you should, in a well-designed garden, suddenly come across another part of the garden, hitherto hidden from view. Focal points direct attention to various parts of the garden and they provide a sense of unity, linking various parts or areas of the garden. Focal points can create a feeling of distance, too, for usually they are positioned at the ends of vistas or long views: for example at the end of a lawn, at the end of a path or in a far corner of the garden. Focal points can also be positioned wherever a path changes direction, to encourage an exploration of the garden.

Many objects may be used as focal points, including statuary and distinctive plants. Ornamental containers are also ideal for the purpose and indeed are often used, especially in large gardens, but in small ones too.

Among the advantages of using containers as focal points can be included the fact that generally they are relatively easy to move around so that you can, if necessary, position a container in several different places until you are completely satisfied that you have found exactly the right site for it.

Containers which are to be used as focal points must be chosen with great care. Not only should they be distinctive but, most important of all, they should suit the size of the garden. In a large garden you will of course need large containers, perhaps urns, vases and bowls gardens where this has been done, but in my opinion it is rather an eccentric approach.

In a modern town garden there is scope for using modern-looking containers as focal points (Fig. 8).

Concrete tubs, square or circular, could be clustered together, either of different heights or on different levels to create a kind of sculpture. Also in a modern

Fig. 7 A classical stone urn on a pedestal makes an impressive focal-point in a large garden but needs a suitable background such as a group of dark green conifers.

on pedestals to give height (Fig. 7). In a tiny garden more diminutive containers should be used as focal points.

The style must also be chosen with care, for it must suit the style of the garden. It is a bit outrageous, for instance, to have a very modern-looking container in an informal, period or country garden. I do know of

Fig. 8 In a town garden modern-looking simulated-stone containers could be clustered together to create a kind of sculpture. Use such an arrangement as a focal point to draw the eye and ensure it has a suitable background, such as the evergreen shrub *Fatsia japonica*.

Here a dark green hedge makes the perfect background for light-coloured tiered bowls which create an excellent focal point. The bed and containers are planted with summer bedding plants.

This stone bowl on a plinth, in classical style, shows up really well against a dark green yew hedge. Grey-leaved helichrysum and pelargoniums make a tasteful summer display.

garden very plain light-coloured (simulated stone) containers are recommended too, such as urns (those shaped like Ali-baba pots) and vases.

Of course light-coloured containers need a dark background to show them off. In a town garden this might be a fence stained dark brown or it may be a very dark-coloured brick wall – deep red or even grey or blackish. If no suitable background exists, you should consider using a suitable plant as a background: something with dark-coloured foliage. Among the finest shrubs for this purpose are the purple-leaved varieties of the smoke bush, *Cotinus coggygria*, such as 'Royal Purple' with dark wine-purple leaves, or the rich plum purple 'Foliis Purpureis'. *Fatsia japonica*, a very architectural plant with its huge, deep green, shiny foliage, would make a good background too. If you have an acid soil a group of camellias, with their deep green, shiny, evergreen foliage, would make a handsome background for a light-coloured container.

At one time a British supplier was offering blue-glazed Chinese terracotta pots, imitations of products made during the Sung Dynasty (960 – 1280 AD). They were very plain and deep navy blue in colour. If you can find one of these, or something similar, you would have a marvellous item for a focal point in a Chinese or Japanese-style garden. There seems to be a trend towards gardens in the Oriental style, particularly among owners of modern town gardens. They are laid out very simply, not over-planted and, of course, rely on attractive ornaments as well as distinctive plants for creating interest and atmosphere.

Before leaving modern town gardens I should say that containers in classical styles are also often used as focal points: for example, Florentine urns and pots. Combining old with new in this way does seem to work, so do not be put off classical styles just because you live in contemporary surroundings.

However, in an informal rural or semi-rural garden, or the gardens of period houses, the classical styles really come into their own. Highly decorated urns and vases can be made to nestle attractively among shrubs and other plants. Again, do make sure that light-coloured containers have a suitably dark background.

In a country garden this might be an old yew hedge (*Taxus baccata*) with very deep blackish green foliage. Or it could be a laurel hedge (*Prunus laurocerasus*) with large, glossy, deep green foliage. Or maybe you have a group of dark-leaved shrubs which would make a good setting for a container. If you are starting from scratch, consider a group of shrubs such as laurustinus (*Viburnum tinus*), or rosemary (*Rosmarinus officinalis*) both of which have dark evergreen foliage. A bay (*Laurus nobilis*) has attractive aromatic foliage and, grown as an informal shrub, would also make a good background for a focal point.

Warm, orangy, terracotta containers can make delightful focal points in country gardens (Fig. 9). Containers of all kinds can be bought in this material, from classical urns and vases to pots, particularly the fancy or decorated pots in the style of Florentine, Venetian, Minoan and Tuscan earthenware. Traditional English pots are plain, and perhaps not so suitable as ornaments, but they can be ideal for planting for a wide range of subjects.

If you have a deep pocket, why not consider lead containers, which make superb focal points in country and period-style gardens? You can obtain copies of classical designs that come in the form of urns, vases and rectangular or hexagonal cisterns. Lead containers are generally rather small and therefore better suited to the small garden. It is possible, of course, to buy antique lead containers from specialist suppliers or antique dealers.

Of course, terracotta and lead are rather dark colours and so need a light-coloured background. In a country garden this might be a mellow, old stone wall, or maybe a wall of yellow brick. Otherwise create a suitable background with light-coloured foliage plants – perhaps choosing from the huge range of silver- or grey-leaved plants like artemisias, santolinas, lavenders or ornamental grasses such as helictotrichon. The white-striped gardener's garters grass, *Phalaris arundinacea* 'Picta', makes a superb background for terracotta containers. The focal point can be allowed to nestle among the plants but make sure they do not obscure it.

Fig. 9 A terracotta container, such as this bowl and pedestal, preferably in a warm, orangy colour, makes a delightful focal point in a country garden, especially if backed with light-coloured foliage plants such as green and white striped grasses (shown here are *Glyceria maxima* 'Variegata' [left] and *Phalaris arundinacea* 'Picta').

FOR COURTYARDS AND PATIOS

Ornamental containers are ideal for decorating courtyards. The definition of a courtyard is an area enclosed by walls (or buildings) but open to the sky. In warm countries, where the courtyard is more popular, it is used as a cool, shady place to sit, away from the heat of the day.

Traditionally courtyards are decorated with statuary, ornamental containers, pools and fountains. Statuary and containers can be as elaborate as desired and ornate classical styles of urns, vases and pots can be used. Stone, or simulated stone, containers may be more appropriate for a courtyard where subtle or neutral colours are called for. We are aiming for a 'cool', restful atmosphere.

Courtyards are sometimes paved with marble, especially so in Mediterranean countries, so why not consider square or rectangular planters made of marble? These would certainly provide elegance in any courtyard.

White-glazed clay bell pots would also help to create the right atmosphere in a courtyard. They can be used out of doors – although it might be better to take them inside for the winter if you live in an area subjected to hard winters. They look equally good indoors where they can be used as containers for potted plants. Lead containers such as cisterns and urns would also be a good choice for courtyards.

Of course you may want to plant some of your courtyard containers, particularly marble planters and the larger glazed pots. Large-leaved foliage plants would be a good choice like *Fatsia japonica*; the hardy palm, *Trachycarpus fortunei*; and hostas or plantain lilies. The oleander, *Nerium oleander*, with pink or white flowers

What a superb focal point for a large garden – a huge copper tub planted with standard fuchsias which give colour throughout the summer.

If the background is plain, wall containers and hanging baskets can be a kaleidoscope of colours, provided, for example, by summer bedding plants like begonias, impatiens, lobelia and helichrysum.

in summer, is a good container plant but is tender and needs to be protected from frosts, which means over-wintering it indoors or in a greenhouse. Another attractive flowering plant for courtyard containers is the white arum lily or *Zantedeschia aethiopica*. It also has bold foliage. Hardy ferns of all kinds could be grown in containers. None of these plants will actually hide the containers so you can still enjoy the latter for their own sake.

The patio will probably feature mainly planted containers, rather than urns, vases, tubs, etc, used as ornaments in their own right. However, large patios and terraces are sometimes surrounded with stone balustrades. The entrance to the terrace or patio, which may be by means of steps, is traditionally flanked by stone pillars each of which is topped with an ornate stone urn, which may or may not be planted, according to taste. There may also be stone pillars at intervals along the balustrade and these, too, traditionally support stone urns. Bear in mind that such a patio or terrace is really only suitable for large gardens – in a small garden it can look rather ostentatious.

FRAMING WITH CONTAINERS

Containers can be used for framing certain features of the garden and house. Pairs of identical containers are used for this purpose. For instance, many people flank the front door of their house, or porch, with distinctive containers. With a modern house, usually something fairly plain is called for, such as large English terracotta pots, or concrete or simulated stone planters. Invariably one will want to plant these: clipped bay trees look good, perhaps trained as pyramids, or maybe each container could be planted with a pyramid-shaped conifer.

The front door of the country cottage could be flanked with terracotta pots or even with oak half barrels, suitably varnished and with the rings painted black. Each of these could contain a topiary specimen in yew (*Taxus baccata*) or box (*Buxus sempervirens*) – very appropriate for a cottage garden.

Steps, such as those leading to a terrace, patio or sunken garden, could be flanked in a similar way with containers. Gates, too, could have twin containers on each side, as could garden arches.

BALCONY CONTAINERS

Window boxes, hanging containers and wall pots are admirable for balconies, but the balcony gardener will also want some suitable containers for the floor. Here one should choose lightweight tubs, urns, pots, troughs, etc and also use a lightweight compost for filling them – the all-peat potting composts are ideal.

A wide range of containers is available in plastic and fibreglass and although some may not be as attractive as those in, say, reconstituted stone or terracotta, nevertheless they can be well hidden with trailing plants.

Planting ideas will be found in Chapter 8.

8

COLOUR ON THE PATIO

One of the most popular parts of a garden for planted containers is the patio. Here one can use the wide range of tubs, urns, vases, pots, troughs and bowls; again, as emphasized earlier, choosing styles to suit the style of the house and garden. Also, the plants used should be appropriate for the particular setting: for instance, bold, modern-looking kinds for the contemporary patio, olde-worlde kinds for the informal cottage garden.

With a good collection of containers one can, by careful choice of plants, ensure colour and interest all the year round, using a combination of permanent plants and temporary kinds like spring, summer and autumn bedding. Provided you are able to, containers can be moved around to give different effects at various times of the year. For instance, many people like to plant containers with spring bedding plants such as wallflowers, forget-me-nots and double daisies, plus spring bulbs. But these look decidedly dreary throughout the autumn and winter and would be better placed in a spare part of the garden, out of site, until the plants are coming into flower, when the containers can be moved on to the patio. Tender summer bedding plants could be planted in containers under glass, to get them established, and again they could be moved out on to the patio when in full bloom – ideally, after hardening off in a cold frame. Permanent tender plants can be placed on the patio for the summer, perhaps to give a Mediterranean or sub-tropical effect, and moved back under cover (indoors or into a frost-free greenhouse or conservatory) before the autumn frosts commence. In very cold parts of the country many permanent, nor-mally hardy plants would be better over-wintered in a cool, frost-free greenhouse or conservatory as they are liable to suffer outside in severe winters. (A useful piece of equipment for moving containers is the two-wheeled sack trolly – rather like the trollies used by railway porters.)

It is important to choose containers of suitable size for plants. Depth is especially important to allow plants to root deeply and to prevent rapid drying out of the compost. With the majority of containers available the depth is perfectly adequate – it is, of course, generally in proportion to the diameter of the container. There are some containers, though, whose depth is not in proportion to the diameter and these are the modern shallow concrete bowls. However, these are widely used in modern settings, mainly for bedding plants which do not mind dryish conditions, but a close eye should be kept on the compost as it can rapidly dry out in warm conditions.

So what is a suitable size for patio containers? Whether you want to grow temporary or permanent plants, we are thinking in terms of containers with a diameter of at least 30 cm (12 in). These will hold several bedding plants, or single small shrubs, perennials, conifers, etc. But you can have more effective bedding displays with larger containers – say with diameters of 45–60 cm (18–24 in). These sizes of container are also recommended for larger permanent plants like shrubs, conifers, small trees and so on. If containers are much larger than this they really cease to be portable and come in the category of permanent 'planters', which are discussed in Chapter 9.

One of the most popular parts of a garden for planted containers is the patio. Here, traditional designs have been used in a period setting.

Raised beds as well as other ornamental containers can ensure plenty of colour on and around a patio if generously planted with bedding and other summer flowers.

TEMPORARY PLANTS

Temporary plants are used to give seasonal colour on the patio and include the obvious spring, summer and autumn bedding plants, as well as tender shrubs, perennials and succulents, and hardy annuals.

Modern formal settings

In a modern formal setting modern, simple containers are the most appropriate. For example, concrete or reconstituted-stone tubs, large plain pots in orange or buff terracotta and large shallow concrete bowls. Modern concrete, reconstituted stone or terracotta troughs are also very attractive in such a setting.

TENDER SHRUBS AND PERENNIALS

Although tender shrubs and perennials are grown permanently in containers, they have to be moved into a frost-free greenhouse or conservatory, or indoors, for the winter. They are useful for giving a sub-tropical effect on the patio throughout the summer and can be grouped with colourful summer bedding plants.

The oleander, *Nerium oleander*, is a Mediterranean shrub which makes a good tub plant. It has lanceolate, leathery, evergreen foliage and red, pink, cream or white flowers in summer and autumn. It makes quite a large shrub and needs plenty of sun.

Citrus fruits are excellent tub plants and eventually make fairly large shrubs. They are grown as bushes or dwarf pyramids. Most people like to grow the various oranges, such as the sweet orange, *Citrus sinensis*, and the Seville orange, *C. aurantium*. The white flowers are deliciously scented. Plenty of sun needed.

Abutilon striatum 'Thompsonii' is a striking foliage shrub with large yellow-mottled leaves and orange flowers. It makes a fairly large shrub for a sunny spot. Sometimes small plants are used as temporary bedding plants to give foliage interest among flowering kinds.

An extremely useful tub plant is the New Zealand cabbage palm, *Cordyline australis*, with very long, narrow, greyish green leaves. It will take sun or partial shade and makes an imposing single specimen, or very often small plants are used as a centrepiece for tubs of summer bedding plants.

The aromatic, grey-leaved *Eucalyptus globulus* is a fast grower and will quickly become too large for a container, but it can be used for a few years to help create a sub-tropical effect on the summer patio.

Of the succulent perennials, the century plant, *Agave americana* 'Marginata', is a striking subject for the modern patio with its rosette of stiff sword-shaped leaves edged with yellow. It is slow growing and needs plenty of sun.

Small pots of *Echeveria glauca* dotted among tubs of summer bedding plants look attractive. This plant has rosettes of greyish foliage and is also a sun lover.

Indian shot, or *Canna × generalis*, is a tender perennial which grows from fleshy rhizomes. The plant becomes dormant in winter and is rested in dry compost. It is restarted into growth in early spring by repotting, resuming watering and increasing temperature. The bold foliage may be green, bronze or purple and in summer spikes of exotic, highly colourful lily-like flowers are produced, creating a truly tropical effect in a sunny spot.

ANNUALS FOR FOLIAGE EFFECT

There are several tender plants which are treated as annuals (discarded at the end of the season) which can be used for foliage effect on the patio during the summer. They can be grown on their own or used as centrepieces in tubs of summer bedding plants. The castor-oil plant, *Ricinus communis*, creates a tropical touch with its huge palmate leaves, which may be plain green or, in some of the newer varieties, heavily flushed with bronze. It likes the sun and is raised from seed in early spring – as indeed are all plants recommended here.

Coleus, with their multi-coloured foliage, are all too often thought of only in terms of greenhouse or conservatory pot plants, yet they are successfully grown outside during the summer – they can be used among summer bedding plants if desired, or mass planted in containers of their own.

Among the most highly coloured foliage plants are the amaranthus, particularly some of the newer strains like 'Flaming Fountains', 'Illumination' and 'Red Fox', with red or multicoloured foliage.

SUMMER BEDDING PLANTS

The contemporary patio and its surrounding architecture call out for brightly coloured summer bedding plants. But this does not necessarily mean a kaleidoscope of colours creating an over-fussy effect, which is perhaps better for the patio around the country cottage. As with window boxes, you may find that using single or perhaps two contrasting subjects creates more impact, especially if the colours are co-ordinated with those of the house. Indeed, some of the ideas for window boxes, outlined in Part 3 of this book, could well be used for patio troughs (in reconstituted stone or terracotta). Patio tubs are often planted with tallish subjects in the centre surrounded with trailing plants.

I like a simple mix of flowering and foliage plants, such as red or orange zonal pelargoniums with silver-leaved *Senecio cineraria*; or bush fuchsias with the grey-leaved *Helichrysum petiolatum*. The popular wax begonias, *Begonia semperflorens*, with pink, red or white flowers, actually look very good with trailing small-leaved ivies – an ideal combination for a shady part of the patio (Fig. 10).

Also suitable for shade are the bedding varieties of busy lizzie, or impatiens, and the mimulus hybrids. I prefer to use these alone in containers and generally plant them in strawberry-type terracotta pots (the ones with holes in the sides for planting) which results in domes of colour.

Dwarf bedding dahlias are excellent for tubs and troughs, either single or mixed colours. They flower throughout summer and into the autumn. Petunias are also popular plants for tubs, troughs, etc where they are usually allowed to cascade over the edges, the centre of the container having taller, bushier plants such as zonal pelargoniums. The small-flowered multiflora petunias are best as they are more rain-resistant than the large-flowered kinds.

Very well suited to shallow concrete bowls are bed-

Fig. 10 A summer scheme for a modern patio, using concrete tubs. Flower colour is provided in one tub by the wax or bedding begonia, *Begonia semperflorens*; this being surrounded by trailing small-leaved ivies which can stay in the container the year round. Contrasting foliage is provided by the century plant. *Agave americana* 'Marginata' (*left*) and by the castor-oil plant, *Ricinus communis*.

ding plants which revel in hot dry conditions. These include the daisy-flowered gazania hybrids, in shades of yellow, orange, pink, etc, and the multi-coloured Livingstone daisy, *Mesembryanthemum criniflorum*. You could provide height in the centre of the bowl with a century plant, *Agave americana* 'Marginata'.

If you need autumn colour on the patio consider some tubs of charm chrysanthemums with myriad small flowers in various colours. These could be planted in the containers in early summer, relegated to a spare part of the garden for the summer and moved on to the patio when in flower.

In this garden an unusual copper container has been used to draw the eye to a particular part. It is planted with fuchsias and pelargoniums.

In this patio collection the temporary summer bedding plants have a background of permanent evergreen shrubs which help to show to advantage the various colours.

SPRING BEDDING PLANTS AND BULBS

These are planted in the autumn and as they are by no means attractive until they come into flower they should, ideally, be stored in a spare part of the garden until spring.

The usual spring bedding plants for tubs, etc, are double daisies, wallflowers, the Siberian wallflower and forget-me-nots. Dwarf spring bulbs can be combined with any of these, such as the greigii and kaufmanniana tulips and hyacinths.

You might like to consider, too, the winter-flowering pansies, like the 'Universal' strain – these really do flower in winter, often peeping through a covering of snow.

An observation I have made with bedding plants in containers (whether summer or spring kinds) is that a better effect is created if the containers are grouped together, rather than scattered around singly.

Cottage-garden and country settings

Here more traditional containers like wooden tubs and troughs, and half barrels, make suitable containers. Urns, pots and vases in classical styles look good, too, and particularly in association with period-style houses.

Choose plants to suit the style of the garden. Often old-fashioned plants and flowers look more at home on the patio of a country cottage.

BEDDING PLANTS

What better for a country cottage than tubs full of ornamental tobacco or nicotiana? Choose good modern strains, particularly those which are scented in the evening like 'Evening Fragrance' and 'Nicki Formula Mixed'. As these come in mixed colours I feel that no other plants are needed.

Ivy-leaf pelargoniums will also make a good display and could be combined with that favourite cottage-garden plant, heliotrope.

Other summer bedding plants that deserve a place on the cottage patio are ageratum, useful for edging tubs, trailing lobelia, *Nemesia strumosa*, petunias and verbena hybrids. Annual pinks and carnations are considered 'essential' cottage-garden plants, as are violas and pansies.

It is more appropriate in this setting to have a glorious mixture of plants in the tubs and troughs, so do not be afraid to combine several kinds of plants. Spring bedding plants and bulbs can include all of those recommended above.

HARDY ANNUALS

Some of the hardy annuals are recommended for cottage-garden tubs and troughs, sown direct where they are to flower. The pot marigold or *Calendula officinalis* should be in every cottage garden, and this is true also of nasturtiums. Choose the dwarf bushy kinds for containers, rather than the climbing types. Have tubs full of dwarf sweet peas, too, but make sure they never go short of moisture.

PERMANENT PLANTS

There is a surprisingly wide range of permanent plants for containers, including shrubs, conifers, small trees, climbers, roses and hardy perennials. The woody plants – the shrubs, trees, conifers and climbers – provide a 'framework' and background for containers of temporary plants and they help to provide an established, mature atmosphere. One can create pleasing seasonal groups, too, such as spring-flowering shrubs with spring bedding plants and bulbs (Fig. 11). Containers of colourful summer bedding plants could be given a background of evergreen foliage shrubs or mixed with roses and hardy perennials for contrast in colour, form and texture.

Containers for most of these subjects must, of course, be sufficiently large – 30 cm (12 in) diameter for small shrubs, etc, and for perennials; and 45 – 60 cm (18 – 24 in) in diameter for larger specimens. Very

Fig. 11 Permanent plants in tubs can be used in seasonal groups. Here a camellia is surrounded by terracotta urns containing daffodils and tulips – a most pleasing combination for the spring patio.

important is adequate depth. Generally, the plants recommended here look best in tubs or large pots, rather than troughs and containers such as narrow-necked urns.

Permanent plants make for labour-saving gardening, so this may be important, and furthermore they really do help to ensure year-round interest and colour on the patio.

Modern formal settings

Again, plants should suit the setting, and containers, too, as discussed earlier. So let us start with plants that can be used to furnish patios in contemporary settings.

SHRUBS

I suggest a combination of flowering and foliage shrubs. Also specimens clipped to regular shapes, such as bay (*Laurus nobilis*), box (*Buxus sempervirens*) and hollies (ilex) trained into pyramids, standards, etc, which make useful accent specimens on the patio – perhaps to frame a door or steps.

Other foliage shrubs include the 'architectural' *Fatsia japonica*, with large, palmate, glossy evergreen leaves which make a good background for more colourful plants. It takes semi-shade. Equally dramatic is *Aralia elata* with massive deciduous compound leaves.

Pieris formosa forrestii is really grown for its foliage, although in spring it produces trusses of white bell-shaped flowers. The young leaves of this evergreen are spectacular – glowing red in colour. It needs lime-free compost, shelter and ideally partial shade.

The gold-splashed leaves of *Elaeagnus pungens* 'Maculata' will provide a bright splash of colour all the year round, as will those of *Euonymus japonicus* 'Aureopictus'. Here the leaves are golden, edged with green. It will take partial shade. Small-growing euonymus are the *E. fortunei* varieties, which also take shade, like golden-variegated 'Emerald and Gold'.

Some of the small or slow-growing hollies make excellent tub plants, including the silver hedgehog holly, *Ilex aquifolium* 'Ferox Argentea', whose very spiny leaves are edged with white. The dwarf *I. crenata* 'Golden Gem' has tiny oval, golden leaves.

Ivies are shade-lovers and extremely useful for the edges of containers, when they will cascade down the sides. The small-leaved *Hedera helix* varieties are best, including such well-known kinds as 'Adam', white-edged leaves; 'Buttercup', deep yellow foliage; 'Glacier', silvery grey; and 'Goldheart', yellow-splashed leaves. The plain green ivies like 'Caenwoodiana', 'Green Ripple', 'Ivalace' and 'Sagittifolia'

The walls of this house are colourful from bottom to top as various types of container have been colourfully planted, with climbing roses and nasturtiums adding to the effect.

These wall baskets are being used in a similar way to conventional hanging baskets, having been attractively planted with pendulous begonias for summer colour.

83

make an excellent foil for brightly coloured flowers, such as summer bedding.

The dwarf viburnum, *V. davidii*, has large, deep green, deeply veined leaves and, if several plants are grown together, crops of turquoise berries.

In mild sheltered areas it is worth growing in a tub the hardy palm, *Trachycarpus fortunei*, with large fan-shaped leaves and a shaggy brown trunk. It helps to create a sub-tropical effect, as do the yuccas with their sword-like foliage, such as *Y. gloriosa, Y. filamentosa* and its variety 'Variegata', and *Y. flaccida* 'Ivory'. These all eventually produce spikes of bell-shaped flowers.

The Japanese maples, varieties of *Acer palmatum*, are noted for their brilliant autumn leaf colour and should be grown in a sheltered, partially shaded spot. Some have purple summer foliage, such as 'Atropurpureum' and 'Dissectum Atropurpureum'.

Coming on to flowering shrubs, dwarf rhododendrons and azaleas grow well in tubs; they need lime-free compost and ideally a position in dappled or partial shade. *Rhododendron yakushimanum*, with white flowers, and its coloured hybrids, are outstanding, as are the early flowering, purple, 'Praecox', white, fragrant *R. mucronatum*, and deep red 'Elizabeth'. Dwarf evergreen azaleas like white 'Palestrina', pink 'Rosebud' and crimson 'Hinodegiri' are simply 'made' for tubs.

Camellias look good all year round with their deep green glossy foliage and produce their flowers in many shades of red, pink and also white, in late winter and spring. Varieties of *C. japonica* and *C. × williamsii* are recommended. Grow in lime-free compost in a partially shaded position, which does not receive early morning sun.

Heathers are useful for grouping around larger shrubs, especially the varieties of winter-flowering *Erica herbacea* (*E. carnea*).

Try also the dwarf laurel, *Prunus laurocerasus* 'Otto Luyken', with handsome evergreen foliage and spikes of white flowers in spring; and the dwarf evergreen *Skimmia reevesiana* with red berries in autumn/winter.

CONIFERS
Small-growing conical, globular or prostrate conifers make ideal accent plants for the formal patio. Try the following: *Chamaecyparis lawsoniana* 'Ellwoodii', a grey-green cone; *C. l.* 'Ellwood's Gold', tinged with yellow; *Chamaecyparis pisifera* 'Boulevard', a steel-blue cone; *Juniperus × media* 'Mint Julep', arching, spreading habit, rich green; and *J. × media* 'Blaauw', with partially upright branches and grey-blue foliage.

SMALL TREES
Small ornamental trees are useful for giving height and dappled shade on the patio. Try the following: *Malus floribunda*, with pale pink flowers in spring, followed by yellow fruits; *Prunus* 'Amanogawa', with pale pink cherry blossom in spring; the weeping *Pyrus salicifolia* 'Pendula' with silver willowy leaves; the golden-leaved *Robinia pseudoacacia* 'Frisia'; *Salix caprea* 'Pendula', a weeping willow with yellow catkins; and *Sorbus* 'Joseph Rock' with yellow autumn berries and good autumn foliage colour.

CLIMBERS
Climbers can be trained to patio or house walls, trellis screens or over a pergola. The large-flowered clematis hybrids look good on the modern patio, especially when combined with climbing roses. They like their roots in shade and their 'heads' in sun.

The ivies are also recommended: I have already described some varieties of *Hedera helix* (see page 41) but consider also the large-leaved, variegated *Hedera canariensis* 'Gloire de Marengo' and *H. colchica* 'Dentata Variegata'.

For autumn colour on a shady (or sunny) wall try the Virginia creeper, *Parthenocissus tricuspidata*. One of my favourite climbers for tubs is the ornamental grape vine, *Vitis* 'Brant', which looks superb growing over a pergola, bearing crops of edible black berries and displaying good autumn leaf colour. It needs plenty of sun.

ROSES
Many kinds of roses can be grown in containers. The obvious choice is the huge range of miniatures, which attain no more than 45 cm (18 in) in height, flowering

profusely in summer with tiny blooms like scaled-down versions of large-flowered (hybrid tea) and cluster-flowered (floribunda) roses.

The low-growing cluster-flowered varieties are ideal, too, for the modern patio: there are lots of varieties like 'Anna Ford', orange-red; 'Kerry Gold', deep yellow; 'Marlena', crimson; 'Regensburg', pink and white; and 'Topsi', orange-scarlet.

Small-growing climbing roses suitable for tubs include 'Aloha', salmon-pink; 'Copenhagen', deep scarlet; and 'Golden Showers', bright yellow. Try a combination of climbing roses and clematis – some stunning effects can be created.

HARDY PERENNIALS

A selection of flowering and foliage perennials will help to create contrast in shape and texture. For the modern patio try to choose distinctive or 'architectural' plants, like *Acanthus spinosus* with bold, deeply divided foliage and spikes of mauve and white flowers. Or *Agapanthus* 'Headborne Hybrids' with strap-shaped foliage and heads of lily-like flowers in shades of blue.

Euphorbia wulfenii is a stately plant that will thrive in partial shade, with greyish foliage and large heads of green-yellow flowers.

Any of the ornamental grasses are suitable for containers, useful for providing contrast in foliage shape. Suitable for shade are the lenten roses, *Helleborus orientalis*, with palmate evergreen foliage and pink, purple or white cup-shaped flowers very early in the year. The day lilies, hemerocallis hybrids, produce their lily-like flowers throughout summer and into autumn. They come in a wide range of colours. The hostas with their large, bold leaves, in many shades of green and yellow, and variegated, are essentially foliage plants but spikes of mauve, lilac or white flowers are produced in summer. There are no finer foliage plants for shade than the hostas.

Rodgersia pinnata 'Superba' has large, palmate, bronze leaves and produces pink flowers in summer. It will grow in partial shade and looks good near a pool.

If you want to create a Mediterranean atmosphere on your patio try the following perennials: *Beschorneria yuccoides* has greyish green yucca-like evergreen leaves and tall stems of red-bracted flowers; the red hot poker, *Kniphofia caulescens*, has dramatic glaucous grassy foliage and in autumn spikes of salmon-red flowers; some of the eryngiums are truly dramatic plants, like *E. agavifolium* with rosettes of spiny sword-shaped leaves, and *E. bromeliifolium* with rosettes of jagged-edged strap-shaped leaves.

The phormiums, or New Zealand flaxes, have sword-shaped evergreen leaves and the modern dwarf forms are ideally suited to containers. Try such colourful varieties as 'Cream Delight', 'Maori Sunrise', 'Sundowner' and 'Yellow Wave'. These four subjects need a warm, sunny, sheltered position and are better suited to milder parts of the country or overwintered under glass in cold areas.

DWARF BULBS

Remember that dwarf or miniature bulbs, such as muscari, chionodoxa, scilla, crocuses, miniature daffodils, snowdrops, bulbous irises, and so on can be planted permanently around shrubs, trees, climbers and roses to provide spring colour.

Cottage and country settings

The patio in the cottage or country garden calls for more informal plants, even old-fashioned kinds, to reflect the planting of the main garden.

SHRUBS

There are several flowering shrubs suited to tubs which look at home in the cottage garden, including the smaller hardy fuchsias like the *F. magellanica* varieties 'Pumila', red and violet, and 'Variegata' with cream-edged leaves and red and purple flowers. There are lots of hybrids, too, like 'Alice Hoffman' (red and white), 'Margaret' (crimson and violet), 'Mrs Popple' (red and violet) and 'Tom Thumb' (red and violet). All will take partial shade, as will the varieties of *Hydrangea macrophylla*, which have large mop-headed flowers in

Terracotta containers come in all shapes and sizes and really look at home in any situation. They contrast well with the neutral colour of paving.

A traditional wooden tub is a good choice of container for a patio in a country garden. This one is planted with 'cool' blue campanulas or bellflowers and pansies.

blue, pink, red or white. Use an acid compost if you want blue flowers.

The Mexican orange blossom, *Choisya ternata*, is an evergreen with handsome foliage and highly scented white flowers in spring and summer. It needs a sheltered sunny spot. Also an evergreen, with yellow-edged leaves, is *Daphne odora* 'Aureomarginata' with very fragrant red-purple flowers in spring. Needs full sun.

Some of the smaller hebes make good tub plants in a sheltered sunny spot and have evergreen, often elegant foliage, as well as a profusion of flowers in summer and autumn. Of the vast range, I can particularly recommend *H. × franciscana* 'Blue Gem'; 'Marjorie', light violet and white; 'Mrs E. Tennant', light violet; and *H. rakaiensis*, white.

Many of the 'modern' conifers look ill at ease in informal gardens, but yews are a good choice. For a tub try the pillar-like Irish yew, *Taxus baccata* 'Fastigiata', which is happy in shade.

TREES

The crataegus or thorns look at home in country gardens, and for a tub I would especially recommend *Crataegus oxyacantha* 'Paul's Scarlet', with double scarlet flowers in late spring. Try also *Cotoneaster* 'Hybridus Pendulus' whose white flowers are followed by crops of red berries. It is an evergreen, and should be bought as a grafted plant on a 1.8 m (6 ft) stem, when it will make a weeping specimen.

CLIMBERS

'Old fashioned' scented climbers are called for here, like jasmines and honeysuckles. The summer jasmine, *Jasminum officinale*, has deliciously scented white flowers in summer. The yellow blooms of the winter jasmine, *J. nudiflorum*, are not scented, but it is well worth growing for winter colour, particularly on a shaded wall.

The honeysuckles like their heads in the sun but their roots shaded. A good scented one is the early Dutch honeysuckle, *Lonicera periclymenum* 'Belgica', with yellow and reddish-purple flowers in spring and summer.

ROSES

Especially suitable for cottage-garden tubs are the polyantha roses, low-growing shrubs varying in height from 30 – 90 cm (12 – 36 in) and producing clusters of small blooms throughout summer and into autumn. Try 'Baby Faurax', pale violet; 'Ellen Poulsen', rose-pink; 'Little White Pet', double, white; 'Paul Crampel', orange-scarlet; 'The Fairy', rose-pink; and 'Yvonne Rabier', double, white.

'Ballerina' is a small modern shrub rose but looks superb in the cottage garden over a very long period, with its huge clusters of small, pink, white-eyed flowers.

Of the climbing roses, there is an old China rose (introduced 1839), called 'Pom-Pon de Paris', which attains no more than 1.8 m (6 ft) in height and bears tiny but well-shaped pink flowers in the summer. A couple of feet taller is 'Crimson Shower', a summer-flowering rambler with small crimson rosette–like flowers.

PERENNIALS

Some of the perennials recommended for modern patios can be used in cottage and country gardens, including hostas and hemerocallis; plus such typical cottage plants as lady's mantle, *Alchemilla mollis*, with mounds of yellow-green flowers in summer, suitable for partial shade; the shade-loving bergenias with their large leathery evergreen leaves and pink, red or white flowers in spring; the peach-leaved bellflower, *Campanula persicifolia*, with spires of blue flowers in summer, suitable for partial shade; the 'Russell Hybrid' lupins, which flower in early summer and come in many colours; and even delphinium hybrids, both tall and dwarf, with stately spires in blue, purple or white.

9

MINI-GARDENS

In large permanent (non-portable) containers like raised beds, planters, raised borders and double walls, it is somewhat easier than with smaller containers to create attractive planting schemes, for one has more space. Indeed such containers can be thought of as conventional beds when it comes to planting.

Raised beds, borders and so on can, if desired, be devoted to collections of plants, perhaps alpines or maybe lime-hating plants (especially recommended if you garden on alkaline soil and desperately want to grow such charming plants as dwarf rhododendrons, camellias, heathers and other acid-loving plants). Certainly each container can be a mini-garden.

RAISED BEDS AND PLANTERS

These terms are really synonymous and refer to large raised structures, which may be any shape desired if you build them yourself. Very often they are included as features on patios, but can be used in various parts of the garden, being particularly popular with owners of very small town gardens, as they help to create different levels in what are invariably flat sites. Large square, rectangular or circular planters can be bought, if you do not wish to construct your own; they come in various materials and are simply placed where desired on the patio.

In a very modern setting circular concrete sewer-pipe sections make excellent planters. If space permits you could, perhaps, have a group of three. The sections can be set in cobbles or granite setts and then painted with masonry paint to match the house. Make sure the base is not in very close contact with the ground for excess water must be able to escape.

If you wish to make your own beds they can be constructed from ornamental concrete walling blocks, in brick or stone finish to match the house and patio. Alternatively you can use ordinary bricks (again to match the house), natural stone, timber railway sleepers, or even tree sections. The last three are particularly good choices for rural gardens.

As mentioned earlier, build to any shape desired – square, rectangular, L-shaped or even triangular to fit a corner. As with any container, depth is important to allow the plants to root deeply and to ensure the compost does not dry out rapidly. A good depth is between 45 and 60 cm (18 and 24 in). The walls of beds built with ornamental concrete walling blocks, bricks or stone should be topped with coping stones, either imitation concrete or natural stone. Home-made beds or planters can, if desired, incorporate a seat, simply by setting large paving slabs over part of it.

Beds can be built directly onto an existing paved area, but if you are building a new patio it is wasteful of slabs to lay them where the planters are to be. In this instance the planters can be built on concrete footings. In any event, there must be drainage holes at ground level around the sides of the planter, to allow excess water to escape.

After constructing the beds place a 7.5–10 cm (3–4 in)

These raised beds have been built from imitation railway sleepers and from vertical 'logs' which are supplied in rolls. Both are ideally suited to natural or country gardens.

A modern raised bed constructed from ornamental concrete walling blocks, which resemble natural stone. Such beds often feature on or around patios.

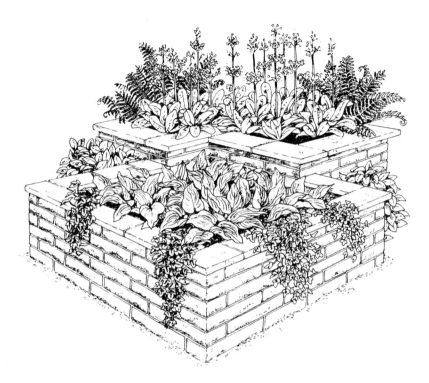

Fig. 12 Raised beds constructed of ornamental concrete walling blocks in stone finish. These beds are suitable for all kinds of plants. Here is a planting scheme for a shady spot: hostas or plantain lilies, trailing ivies, candelabra primulas and ferns. There are many other shade-loving plants that could be included in this scheme.

layer of rubble or pebbles in the bottom to act as a drainage layer, top this with a 2.5 cm (1 in) layer of rough peat or leafmould and then fill with soil or compost. If you need a large volume of soil then, for reasons of economy, buy in a quantity of good-quality topsoil – a light to medium loamy type. Remember that if you want to grow lime-hating plants the soil must be acid: with a ph of below 6.5. As most lime-haters like a humus-rich growing medium, mix plenty of peat or leafmould with the soil before filling the planter.

Planters can, alternatively, be filled with a soil-based potting compost, (but not for lime haters). If you wish

to grow alpines then a very gritty, well-drained compost should be used. You can either use light topsoil or proprietary compost, but add to a given volume one-third of coarse horticultural sand or grit. These ingredients should be lime free.

Planting ideas

SHADY AREAS

Raised beds or planters can be placed either in shady or sunny positions and plants chosen accordingly. For instance, if the bed is in shade you could have a delightful collection of peat-garden plants, grown in an acid, peaty compost.

Choose small-growing peat-garden plants, such as dwarf rhododendrons. There is a vast range of these but some of my favourites, which I can particularly recommend, are *Rhododendron impeditum*, a small mound of tiny leaves studded with purplish blue flowers; the prostrate *R. forrestii repens* with scarlet bell-shaped blooms; *R. campylogynum* with waxy bell-shaped flowers in pink or purplish shades; and *R. keiskei* with trusses of lemon-yellow funnel-shaped flowers in early spring.

Good companions for the rhododendrons are the cassiopes, small evergreen shrubs with white bell-like flowers in spring. Well-known species are *C. lycopodioides* and *C. tetragona*. A prostrate, spreading, evergreen shrub which can be allowed to spread over the edge of the planter is *Arctostaphylos uva-ursi* with white urn-shaped blooms in spring, followed by red berries. Small-growing gaultherias should be considered, like *G. trichophylla*, an evergreen with deep pink urn-shaped flowers in spring followed by attractive blue berries.

Lithospermum diffusum is stunning in the intensity of its blue flowers. Try to obtain the variety 'Heavenly Blue'. The flowering period is early summer to mid-autumn. *Phyllodoce aleutica* is a heath-like evergreen with globular, greeny yellow flowers in spring and early summer. Small-growing vacciniums are a good choice, too, like the prostrate, creeping, *V. praestans* with white or reddish bell-shaped flowers in early summer followed by red berries and brilliant autumn leaf colour.

There are two new dwarf pieris which would also be suitable: *Pieris japonica* 'Little Heath', a rounded evergreen shrub with small creamy white variegated leaves and pink-flushed new growth; and *P.j.* 'Little Heath Green' with glossy, bronze-tinted foliage. Surprisingly, these pieris do not produce flowers – they are essentially foliage shrubs.

If you want a more general planting scheme for a shady spot, then try the classical combination of hostas or plantain lilies, with their bold, 'blue', green, yellow or variegated foliage, candelabra primulas, meconopsis or blue poppies, and ferns (Fig. 12). These could be planted around a 'framework' of Japanese maples, varieties of *Acer palmatum*, noted for autumn leaf colour. Winter and spring interest could be provided by Lenten

roses (*Helleborus orientalis*) and small bulbs like snowdrops (galanthus) and miniature daffodils (*Narcissus cyclamineus* and *N. bulbocodium*). Spring-flowering miniature cyclamen are recommended too.

SUNNY POSITIONS

In a position which receives plenty of sun why not consider a collection of alpines or rock plants? You could have a miniature rock garden – or perhaps a better description would be a scree bed.

A natural scree is a drift of broken rock at the bottom of a rock face – it does not contain much soil and is therefore very free draining. It makes a home, though, for many choice alpines. Similar conditions are easily created in a raised bed or planter. This feature looks particularly good in a modern setting. Do use a very well-drained compost: 10 parts stone chippings or pea shingle, 1 part loam, 1 part peat and 1 part coarse horticultural sand. Add a little organic slow-release fertilizer such as bonemeal.

A few well-shaped pieces of rock can be bedded into the compost before planting; and after planting the surface of the compost can be covered with a layer of stone chippings (if you cannot obtain these, use pea shingle which is readily available from builders' merchants).

Although many rock plants or alpines will flourish in these conditions, I suggest trying some of the more choice plants, such as *Androsace, Calceolaria, Daphne, Dianthus, Draba, Gentiana, Hebe*, miniature *Iris, Leontopodium* (edelweiss), *Lewisia, Phyteuma, Saxifraga* (of which there is a huge selection), *Sedum, Teucrium* and *Veronica*. Variation in height can be created with dwarf conifers, like junipers and pines.

Also for a modern setting, a bed of heathers and dwarf conifers can be recommended. This would be a truly labour-saving bed and by choosing a good selection of heathers you could have colour all the year round. You will need an acid or lime-free compost or soil, with plenty of peat added.

Dwarf conifers can include the deep gold *Thuja occidentalis* 'Rheingold'; the greyish or bluish green *Juniperus chinensis* 'Pyramidalis'; bright yellow *Chamaecyparis pisifera* 'Filifera Aurea'; bright green

Picea glauca 'Albertiana Conica'; and silvery blue *Chamaecyparis pisifera* 'Boulevard'.

Now to the choice of heathers for year-round colour. For winter and spring use any of the varieties (which most appeal to you) of *Erica herbacea* (also known as *E. carnea*), and *Erica × darleyensis*. For summer and autumn colour plant varieties of *Calluna vulgaris* (not forgetting some of the superb coloured-foliage varieties for additional winter interest); *Erica cinerea; Erica tetralix; Daboecia cantabrica; and Erica vagans.* Once the heathers have established and formed a dense carpet they will suppress annual weeds. The only attention they need (apart from watering in dry weather) is a light trim after flowering to remove dead flower heads. I would suggest mulching this bed with sphagnum peat to help prevent the surface of the soil from drying out.

RAISED BORDERS

A good way of creating different levels in a small flat garden is to have raised borders. The only ways in which these differ from raised beds or planters is that they are obviously longer (for instance, it may be desired to run the border the length of the plot) and generally they are not so high – a height of 30 cm (12 in) may well be sufficient to create the desired effect. Indeed, if any higher there is a danger the height will not be in proportion to the length. Do not make the borders too narrow – a width of at least 90 cm (3 ft) is recommended.

Construction and filling is the same as for beds and planters, and generally it is not necessary to have a layer of drainage material in the base. But if the garden soil is very poorly drained it should be improved by digging deeply and adding plenty of coarse grit or shingle, before starting to build.

To avoid repetition, suffice it to say that planting ideas for borders are the same as for beds. Of course, there is a much wider range of plants that could be used: there is no reason why climbers should not be planted and trained up the back wall or fence. Shrubs, provided they are not too large, would be suitable, so long as they are happy with the normal garden soil, for remember that due to the shallow depth of the border they will root down into the soil below. Hardy perennials, bulbs, alpines, bedding plants and hardy annuals are all suitable for raised borders.

DOUBLE WALLS

A double wall for planting is rather like a narrow raised bed. It is often used as a boundary for the front garden, as a feature in front of a porch and for surrounding a patio. The height of the wall will depend on its use: for instance, if it is to form the front boundary it may need to be at least 90 cm (3 ft) high, but slightly lower, if desired, in front of a porch or around a patio. A good width is about 60 cm (2 ft).

Suitable materials for construction include ornamental concrete walling blocks in brick or stone finish to match the house, bricks, or natural walling stone. With the latter you could, if desired, build a dry-stone wall so that trailing plants can be grown in the sides. With a dry-stone wall the joints are not mortared but filled with soil for planting. The stones should be laid at random but interlocked to ensure strength. If desired, plants can be inserted as building proceeds.

Each wall should be built on a substantial strip foundation consisting of well-rammed hardcore topped with concrete. Depth of each about 10 cm (4 in). With long walls it is recommended that cross ties are inserted every 1.2 m (4 ft), extending from one wall to the other, to ensure extra strength. These can consist of iron bars or, in the case of dry-stone walls, long pieces of stone.

The walls should be finished off with coping and then filled with soil or compost, above a layer of drainage material, as described for raised beds (see page 89). Also, do not forget to leave drainage holes along the sides at ground level. Unless sufficient drainage holes are provided, the soil or compost in the wall could become waterlogged, leading to deterioration of the plants.

On a patio a collection of containers looks best grouped together, rather than scattered around indiscriminately. This collection of terracotta ware even includes old chimney pots.

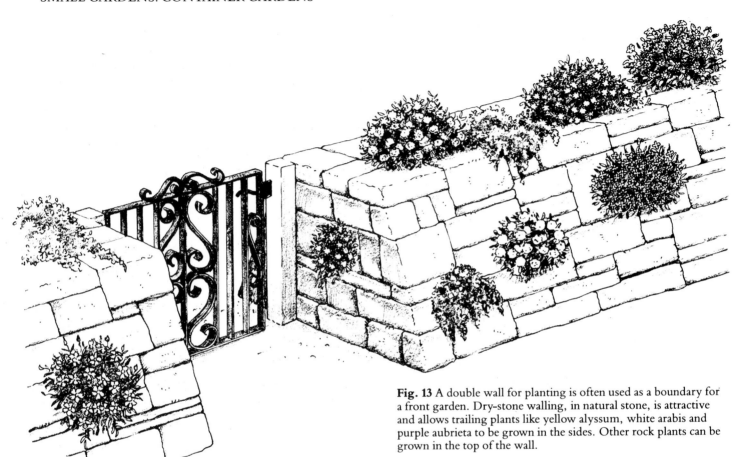

Fig. 13 A double wall for planting is often used as a boundary for a front garden. Dry-stone walling, in natural stone, is attractive and allows trailing plants like yellow alyssum, white arabis and purple aubrieta to be grown in the sides. Other rock plants can be grown in the top of the wall.

Planting ideas

If you want lots of summer colour, perhaps around a patio or in front of a porch, then of course any of the summer bedding plants can be used as described in previous chapters. These can be followed with spring bedding and bulbs. But if you want planting schemes which are a bit out of the ordinary (and indeed labour-saving) then there is a wide range of attractive perm-anent plants that you could choose from.

Rock plants immediately spring to mind. I have already recommended some for raised beds (see page 93), but some of the more popular, showy kinds could be used if you want lots of colour, like the ever-popular yellow *Alyssum saxatile*, blue, purple, red or pink aubrieta, and white arabis (Fig. 13). I know that this particular scheme is very much over-done, but if you want plenty of colour in spring it takes a lot of beating.

Other rock plants you could use include trailing campanulas with blue flowers, like *C. portenschlagiana*, which can be planted in the sides of a dry-stone wall; the rock pinks or dianthus; rock roses or helianthemums whose single-rose-like flowers come in a wide range of bright colours; the white perennial candytuft or *Iberis sempervirens*; lewisias, which are ideal for planting in the sides of a dry-stone wall, as are the sempervivums or houseleeks; and the creeping thymes, or varieties of *Thymus serpyllum*.

Dwarf bulbs could be planted with the rock plants, such as tulip, crocus and dwarf allium species. These, and the alpines, need plenty of sun.

There are lots of dwarf shrubs which enjoy a sunny spot, including the brooms. Try *Cytisus × beanii* with yellow flowers, and *C. × kewensis*, with sheets of cream blooms, both at their best in late spring. Then there is *Genista lydia* with masses of golden flowers at that time of year. *Daphne arbuscula* is a small evergreen shrub which bears scented pink flowers in early summer. Try some dwarf berberis, too, like the *B. thunbergii* varieties 'Atropurpurea Nana', purple foliage' and 'Kobold' with shiny green leaves. *B. buxifolia* 'Nana' forms an evergreen mound and bears yellow flowers.

Small perennials which would enjoy the dryish conditions of the double wall, and which need full sun, include *Anthemis cupaniana* with attractive greyish foliage and a long succession of white daisy-like flowers in summer and through to autumn. The red valerian, *Centranthus ruber*, can be planted in the sides of a dry-stone wall. It flowers continuously from early to late summer, carrying panicles of deep pink or red flowers, set against glaucous foliage. There is also a white-flowered form, 'Albus'.

The stems of the spurge, *Euphorbia myrsinites*, will trail over the edge of the wall and are clothed with attractive bluish-grey foliage. In the spring acid-yellow flowers are produced. *Oenothera missouriensis* has a similar habit of growth, and throughout summer it bears large saucer-shaped yellow flowers.

The herbaceous potentillas relish sunny, dryish conditions and produce attractive single-rose-like flowers in spring or summer. A particularly attractive species is *Potentilla tabernaemontani* which forms an evergreen mat, studded in spring with yellow flowers.

The stonecrops or sedums will certainly be at home in a wall, and if it is dry-stone can be planted in the sides. Try species like *S. acre*, yellow flowers; *S. album*, white; *S. cauticolum*, red; *S. spathulifolium* and its varieties 'Purpureum' with purple foliage and the grey-leaved 'Cappa Blanca'; and *S. spurium* with deep pink flowers.

The Californian fuchsia, *Zauschneria californica*, is a somewhat unusual and desirable plant which bears red fuchsia-like flowers in summer and autumn, set against greyish-green foliage.

SINK GARDENS

Sinks make excellent containers for alpines or rock plants, and they form attractive features on both formal and informal patios. One can, in fact, create miniature rock gardens in these containers.

The old shallow stone sinks are worth searching for, but are not easily found these days, for they are scarce collectors' items and demand a high price. The alternative is to convert a white glazed sink so that it resembles stone (Fig. 14). You should be able to pick up one of these quite easily from a scrapyard or local builder for they are frequently discarded with the boom in fitted designer kitchens. Perhaps this is more practical, anyway, for a white glazed sink has a greater depth than the old-fashioned stone versions, so there is less risk of the compost drying out rapidly during warm weather.

A glazed sink is covered with hypertufa, which is a mixture of cement, sand and peat. When this has hardened and has become well weathered it looks like natural tufa rock. Before you apply a hypertufa mix the sink has to be treated with a PVA adhesive, to ensure the hypertufa sticks to the glaze. This adhesive, which is used in the building trade, is available from DIY and hardware stores. Brush it on the outside of the sink and part of the way down on the inside. When it has become tacky (before it completely dries) apply the hypertufa mix.

The hypertufa mix consists of 2 parts sphagnum peat, 1 part sand and 1 part cement – parts by volume.

An old stone sink, attractively planted with alpines or rock plants, makes an unusual feature on a patio. Note the raised bed behind, built with dry-stone walling.

This raised bed for alpines has been built up with dry-stone walling, which makes an ideal home for various trailing plants. Plants could be set in the sides as building proceeds.

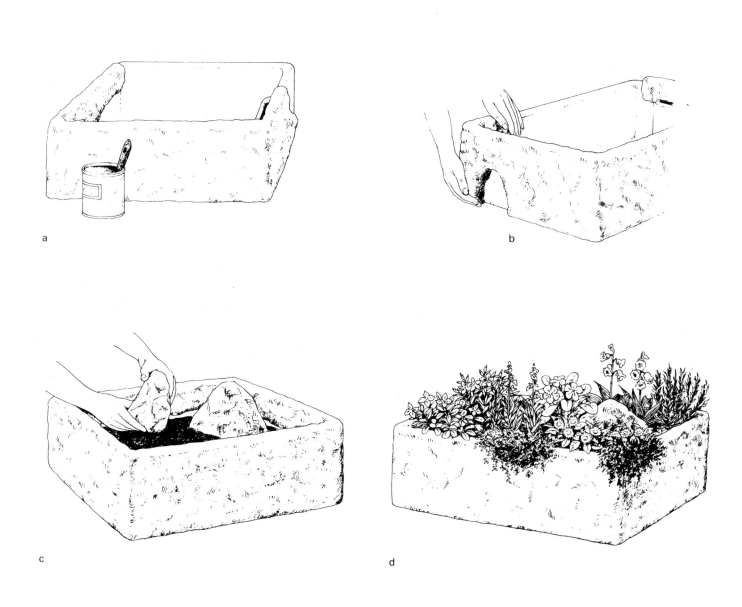

Fig. 14 Converting a white-glazed sink so that it resembles stone. First treat with a PVA adhesive (*a*) then, before it completely dries, apply a hypertufa mix (*b*) which consists of peat, cement and sand.

Fill with gritty compost and add a few pieces of rock (*c*), then plant with alpines of restrained habit (*d*).

Add sufficient water to make a stiff but pliable mix. Then spread it about 12 mm (½ in) thick all over the treated parts of the sink, firmly pressing it into place with your fingers. Leave a fairly rough texture to resemble natural stone.

The hypertufa will take at least two weeks to harden thoroughly, after which the sink should be filled with a solution of permanganate of potash, and left for at least 24 hours, which will remove any harmful chemicals from the cement. Afterwards wash out the sink thoroughly.

Before filling the sink with compost decide where you want it on the patio – choose the sunniest spot – and then stand it on two rows of bricks, two courses high, to raise it slightly above ground level. The bricks can be bonded with mortar for stability. Place over the bottom of the sink a 2.5 cm (1 in) layer of 'crocks' (broken clay flower pots) to act as drainage. Put a large piece over the drainage hole. Cover the crocks with a thin layer of coarse peat or leafmould. Then fill to within 2.5 cm (1 in) of the top with potting compost. A soil-based type is best for alpines. Add to this one-third extra of coarse horticultural sand or grit to ensure really good drainage. The sand or grit should be free from lime.

Before planting, bed a few pieces of natural rock into the compost to create a mini rock garden. Set rocks to about one-third of their depth into the compost.

Choosing plants

First plant one or two dwarf conifers to give height and contrast in form. The most suitable is the tiny Noah's ark juniper, *Juniperus communis* 'Compressa', with greyish-green prickly foliage.

For the edges of the sink use trailing alpines like *Phlox douglasii*, a mass of lilac flowers in the spring; and the pink, early summer flowering *Aethionema armenum*. The spreading, silvery-leaved *Raoulia hookeri* (also known as *R. australis*), will 'soften' the edges of the sink as it becomes established.

Fill in with more alpines, choosing those of restrained habit so that they do not take over the entire container. Suitable kinds include the thrift, *Armeria caespitosa*, a mound-forming plant studded with pink flowers in the spring; the rose-pink, early summer flowering rock pink, *Dianthus neglectus; Geranium cinereum*, spring flowering, pink blooms; *Gypsophila caucasica*, white flowers in early summer; saxifrages like the white, spring flowering *S. × burseriana*; and the cobweb houseleek, *Sempervivum arachnoideum*, whose rosettes of succulent leaves are covered with white webbing, like spiders' webs.

When planting is completed cover the surface of the compost with a thin layer of stone chippings or pea shingle. This will create an attractive appearance and help to ensure good drainage around the plants.

10

DESIGN IDEAS FOR UTILITY PLANTS

Many people with small gardens like to grow some fruits and vegetables and often opt for cultivation in containers on the patio. Certainly many crops are suited to container growing and although essentially utility plants, nevertheless they can, with a little thought, be made to form attractive features in themselves or to combine pleasantly with ornamental plants.

FRUITS

Apples, pears, plums, cherries, peaches, nectarines, grapes and citrus fruits can all be grown in containers as dwarf trained forms.

In my opinion all of these trees are attractive in themselves, especially when in flower and fruit, and therefore no apology should be made for including them on a patio. They can be enhanced by growing them in classical square wooden tubs, painted white (Fig. 15). Diameter and depth should be 45–60 cm (18–24 in). Containers should be filled with a soil-based potting compost, making sure there is a good layer of drainage material in the bottom, such as crocks or broken clay flower pots.

Fruits need a warm, sunny, sheltered spot. Take care with watering to ensure the compost does not dry out, nor becomes excessively wet. Feed once a week in the spring and summer with a high-potash fertilizer. Fruits should be thinned out to ensure the trees do not carry an excess. Fruit trees require regular pruning but

Fig. 15 Dwarf pyramid apple and bush fig in classical square wooden tubs. Both would enhance any patio, as would the grape vine growing in a classical terracotta vase. The grape vine is very amenable to training and for container work is conveniently grown in the form of a standard, as shown here.

Herbs and scented-leaved plants are generally attractive and deserve a place on the patio, ideally planted in dumpy or bowl-shaped containers rather than tall pots.

as this is quite an involved subject and varies according to the type of fruit and the form in which it is grown, a specialist fruit book should be consulted.

Choosing fruits

Most of the fruits described here are trained as dwarf bush trees or dwarf pyramids and they should be obtained on dwarfing rootstocks to keep them small. With apples and pears you have to grow several varieties to ensure cross-pollination of the flowers, otherwise few if any fruits will be produced. If space is very limited you could grow a 'family' apple or pear tree – which has several varieties grafted onto it.

Apples on dwarfing rootstock M9 or M27 should be bought, and grown as dwarf bush or dwarf pyramid trees. Make sure the varieties cross-pollinate each other. For instance, you could grow together the varieties 'Cox's Orange Pippin', 'Greensleeves', 'Discovery', 'Ashmead's Kernel' and 'Egremont Russet', all good popular varieties.

Pears are grown in the same forms as apples. Again grow at least two varieties to ensure cross pollination: the popular 'Williams' 'Bon Chretien' with 'Conference'; or 'Doyenne du Comice' with 'Beurre Hardy'. All are good well-known varieties.

With cherries buy a self-fertile variety such as 'Stella' which needs no other variety to pollinate it. It should be bought on the dwarfing rootstock 'Colt' and grown as a dwarf pyramid or bush.

Also with plums, buy a self-fertile variety, like the highly popular 'Victoria'. It should be on the dwarf rootstock 'Pixy' and grown as a dwarf pyramid or bush.

Peaches and nectarines are grown as dwarf bush trees. Remember that the flowers, which appear early in the year, have to be pollinated by hand by dabbing the centre of each flower in turn with a soft artist's brush to transfer the pollen.

Citrus fruits, like the sweet orange, *Citrus sinensis*, and the Seville orange, *C. aurantium*, can be grown as dwarf pyramid or bush trees. Remember that these are tender trees and need to be kept in a frost-free greenhouse or conservatory over the winter. Figs must also be overwintered under glass to protect the young developing fruits from frost. Grow figs as bush trees.

The grape vine is very amenable to training and for container work is conveniently grown as standard: that is, a single permanent stem with most new growth being produced at the top. The overall height is about 1.8 m (6 ft). All the shoots which form the 'head' are cut back to within one or two buds of their base each year in early winter.

Strawberries can make an attractive feature on a patio, especially if grown in proprietary Tower Pots on the modern patio; or in strawberry barrels on the cottage patio. The Tower Pot basically consists of a tall cylinder with planting pockets in the sides, while the strawberry barrel is an ordinary timber barrel with 5 cm (2 in) diameter holes drilled in the sides, about 20 cm (8 in) apart, in a staggered formation. The roots of the strawberry plants are inserted through the holes as the barrel is being filled with compost. Finish off with several plants in the top, too.

VEGETABLES

Many vegetables can be grown successfully in growing-bags on the patio, but these containers are far from attractive. They are long – approximately 1.2 m (4 ft) – plastic bags filled with peat-based compost and are generally 'decorated' with the maker's name and other lettering. They are temporary containers, being discarded at the end of the season. Holes are made in the tops of the bags for planting.

Fortunately the bags are easily hidden by surrounding them with pots of colourful summer bedding plants. It pays to grow a few extra plants, individually in 12.5 cm (5 in) pots, specially for hiding growing-bags. Choose bushy or trailing bedding plants for the purpose, which will also hide their own containers, like trailing petunias, verbena, lobelia, alyssum and ivy-leaved pelargoniums. Bedding impatiens can also be recommended as they make very bushy growth.

The majority of vegetables like plenty of sun so bear this in mind when siting growing-bags.

Choice of vegetables

It is sensible, wherever possible, to grow attractive-looking vegetables on the patio – those which contribute colour or some other pleasing feature. Then they will not look too much out of place in this essentially ornamental area.

I consider **beetroots**, with their purple foliage, quite attractive plants and they look good with colourful summer bedding plants. Choose the round-rooted varieties, thinning seedlings to 10 cm (4 in) apart.

Rhubarb chard, a leaf beet, has striking red stems which, together with the leaves, are cooked and eaten. A growing-bag will hold four or five plants.

I also like the ferny foliage of **carrots**, the early varieties of which are well worth growing on the patio. Thin seedlings to 5 cm (2 in) apart each way.

Red chicory, 'Rossa de Verona', has very attractive reddish foliage which is used in salads. A growing-bag will hold about four plants.

For salads, and providing an attractive foil for brightly coloured summer bedding, choose **curled endive**, with green curled foliage. Also with very attractive deeply cut foliage is the non-hearting lettuce 'Salad Bowl'. Here one picks the individual leaves as required. There are lettuces available with reddish foliage. Again, a growing-bag will comfortably hold four or five plants of endive or lettuce.

Tomatoes can be highly decorative, especially if you buy seeds of a mixture of ornamental kinds, which include miniature plum-, currant- and pear-shaped kinds with red and yellow fruits. There are several varieties of cherry tomato and yellow-fruited and striped tomatoes, all of which create colour on the patio. Three to four plants can be accommodated in a growing-bag.

Asparagus peas are highly ornamental with their profusion of red flowers. These are followed by winged pods which are picked and cooked whole, while they are young – absolutely delicious when served with butter. Plants should be spaced about 20 cm (8 in) apart each way.

Climbing French beans are more productive than dwarf varieties and particularly attractive is the aptly named variety 'Purple Podded'. Plants can be spaced 10–15 cm (4–6 in) apart.

Runner beans can also be grown in growing-bags and make a good display when in flower with their red, white or pink flowers, according to variety. Plants can be spaced 10–15 cm (4–6 in) apart.

Climbing vegetables can, of course, be trained to a wall or fence, using netting or a trellis panel as a support. Tall tomatoes can be supported with a proprietary growing-bag crop support, as bamboo canes cannot be used in growing-bags.

There are several other vegetables which are ideally suited to growing-bags, although to be honest they could not, by any stretch of the imagination, be called decorative. Nevertheless you may wish to grow them: they include radishes, spring or salad onions, outdoor cucumbers, dwarf early peas and dwarf French beans.

HERBS

Most herbs are fairly or very attractive and therefore deserve a place on the patio, ideally near the kitchen door where they can be easily picked when preparing meals.

Herbs deserve to be grown in attractive containers and I would particularly recommend dumpy or bowl-shaped terracotta pots, either decorated or plain (Fig. 16). In any event the containers should not be too tall as most herbs are quite short plants. Terracotta is particularly suitable for herbs as it is a porous material and does not result in the compost remaining wet for long periods, which is anathema to herbs, which like very well drained and well-aerated compost.

Terracotta troughs would also make good containers for herbs and so, too, would window-boxes, perhaps in the same material, or constructed of wood.

Warm orangy terracotta containers can make delightful focal points in country gardens. This one is planted with zonal and ivy-leaved pelargoniums for summer colour.

This large stone container makes a striking focal point in this garden and has been planted with the popular summer bedding plants heliotrope and fibrous-rooted begonias.

Fig 16 Herbs deserve to be grown in attractive containers, such as these classical-style bowl-shaped pots, and trough, in terracotta. Seen here are a clipped bay (*a*), sage (*b*), thyme (*c*), chives (*d*) and mint (*e*). An attractive group, ideal for placing conveniently near the kitchen door.

Parsley pots – those terracotta pots with holes in the sides – can certainly be used for parsley, but they are probably not suitable for many other types of herbs. In fact, I don't use them for herbs at all, much preferring to grow summer bedding plants in them.

Herbs must be grown in the warmest, sunniest spot available on the patio (with the exception of mint which will thrive in shade or semi-shade, although it will not object to sun).

I have already mentioned that herbs like well-drained conditions and this means crocking the pots well and then filling them with a soil-based compost. I generally like to add some extra coarse lime-free, horticultural sand or grit to this, particularly if a bit on the heavy side, to keep it open and well drained and aerated.

A collection of herbs is an idea for a patio planter – they would certainly help to provide a Mediterranean atmosphere.

Choice of herbs

There is a wide range of herbs available for culinary use but you may find the following most useful.

Mint, of course, is virtually essential if you want mint sauce for lamb and wish to flavour new potatoes. It grows well in shade, needs plenty of moisture and should be planted about 15 cm (6 in) apart each way. It is best confined to a pot as it is a vigorous grower: it could get out of hand in a planter.

Parsley is also a much-used herb and is raised annually in spring from seeds which, it is worth noting, are very slow to germinate. Thin out seedlings to 15 cm (6 in) apart each way.

The leaves of **chives** are used to impart onion flavourings to dishes. Space small clumps about 15 cm apart each way. Lift and divide them every couple of years or so.

Sage can be raised from seeds or young plants bought in spring. The leaves are used for flavouring meats. If you want more than one plant, set the plants 30 cm (12 in) apart each way.

Thyme, which is used for flavouring meats and poultry, can also be raised from seeds, sown in spring, or young plants can be bought, setting them 20 cm (8 in) apart each way.

Rosemary makes quite a large shrub eventually and therefore only one plant is usually needed. The leaves are often used in meat casseroles, and are particularly good for flavouring lamb.

The sweet bay is a large evergreen shrub and makes

an attractive clipped specimen in a wooden tub. The leaves are used in all kinds of cooking. It is not too hardy and in cold areas would be better overwintered in a frost-free greenhouse or conservatory.

Fennel is a very attractive perennial plant with ferny foliage. It grows up to 1.8 m (6 ft) in height and is therefore better suited to the back of a planter or raised bed.

The leaves are used mainly for flavouring fish. Generally a single plant is sufficient. It will thrive in sun or slight shade and prefers moist soil.

Oregano or wild marjoram is a perennial with pinkish flowers in summer. The leaves are used in all kinds of dishes – especially Italian and Provencal. Plant about 20 cm (8 in) apart each way.

Pairs of identical containers are often used for flanking steps. These beautiful terracotta pots in a traditional style contain standard conifers underplanted with trailing plants.

In this garden pairs of stylish terracotta pots are used to 'frame' a formal garden pool. They are planted with pelargoniums and grey-leaved helichrysum.

11

PREPARATIONS AND CARE

To ensure that plants establish and grow well containers should be properly prepared and a suitable compost used to fill them. Compost must be changed regularly for both temporary and permanent plants as it gradually deteriorates. Permanent plants may, of course, outgrow their containers and need moving on to a larger size. As with plants in beds and borders, regular feeding is needed in the growing season. And regular watering will be needed – perhaps once or twice a day in warm weather. One should not simply forget plants in the winter; at this time they are at their most vulnerable and they could suffer or die if the compost remains frozen solid for long periods. All of these aspects of container preparation and care are discussed in this chapter. As you can see, container growing is not exactly labour-saving, but nevertheless can be very rewarding.

POSITIONING AND SITING

From the design point of view positioning and siting of containers has been covered in detail in previous chapters, but some thought should also be given to the practical aspects of placing containers.

Try to avoid siting containers in wind tunnels, as may occur in the gaps between houses. Wind rushes through these gaps and can cause damage to plants, such as foliage scorch; and large leaves can be torn. Also, wind contributes to rapid drying out of compost. At all costs avoid placing hanging baskets in windy places – for the obvious reason that they will be rocked around by the wind. If this happens, the plants are likely to be damaged.

I have already covered the subject of sun and shade and recommended many plants for both situations. Just a reminder here, then, to choose plants accordingly – plants which like the sun will not grow or flower well in shady conditions and often produce very weak growth. Many shade-loving plants can suffer scorched foliage if subjected to too much sun.

If drips from window boxes are liable to be a problem (for example, with boxes on the balconies of flats and apartments) then place drip trays under them to catch surplus water. Do make sure that containers are not in very close contact with the ground for this can impede the drainage of surplus water and result in saturated compost, which can cause roots of plants to rot. And make sure that a seal of soil does not build up around the base of containers, which again effectively prevents drainage of water. It's a good idea to very slightly raise containers above the ground to allow drainage, only a fraction of an inch – say about 6 mm (¼ in) – so that it is barely noticeable. This can be achieved with pieces of wooden lath, but make sure they do not cover drainage holes nor protrude beyond the container.

DRAINAGE MATERIALS

All containers for plants such as tubs, urns, pots and window boxes must have drainage holes in the base to allow excess water to escape. Before filling with compost and planting, these drainage holes must be covered with a layer of drainage material. Traditionally 'crocks' or broken clay flower pots are used. Large pieces are placed over the holes and then a layer of smaller pieces placed over these. Total depth should be at least 2.5 cm (1 in).

There is one pot manufacturer in Britain who actually supplies purpose-made crocks – made from fired ceramic material. Alternatives to crocks are large shingle and horticultural aggregates.

The drainage layer must be covered with a thin layer of rough organic material to prevent compost from washing down and blocking it. Suitable materials are rough leafmould or peat, or pulverized bark.

Composts

On no account fill containers such as tubs, urns, pots, window boxes and hanging baskets with ordinary garden soil as it may not be sufficiently well drained and aerated. Far better to use a proprietary or home-made potting compost, which will also contain a good balance of fertilizers. Certainly large planters, raised beds, double walls, etc, can be filled with good-quality topsoil, ideally a light to medium loamy type, as a large volume of potting compost can be quite expensive to buy. I have already given some recommendations of composts for various types of plants but let us go into the subject in a bit more detail.

There are two basic types of potting compost that we can use in containers – the type containing loam (or soil) and the soilless or all-peat composts. Soilless composts are very light in weight and ideal for hanging baskets and window boxes, although they can be used in other types of container, too. Ericaceous plants like rhododendrons and heathers, and camellias,

flourish in them, although bear in mind that they may not adequately support large heavy plants. For lime-hating plants you should, of course, use an acid or lime-free compost (generally sold as ericaceous compost).

You should also bear in mind that soilless composts must not be firmed too much, plant foods are quickly leached out so more regular feeding will be needed; they should not be allowed to dry out as it is very difficult to wet them again; and that they are inclined to hold more water than soil-based composts, so if you are very heavy-handed with the watering can the compost may become too wet.

The heavier soil-based composts are ideal for large heavy plants, especially permanent kinds. Again use a lime-free compost for lime-hating plants. This type of compost drains well, contains a good supply of air for the plants' roots and is able to hold on to its fertilizers for much longer than soilless composts. If a soil-based compost dries out it is not too difficult to moisten again, and there is little risk of saturating the compost with water.

It generally works out cheaper to mix your own composts and this is especially worth while if you want a large volume. Here are some standard formulae:

SOIL-BASED POTTING COMPOST
   7 parts loam
   3 parts peat
   2 parts sand
   Parts by volume and all mixed together very thoroughly.
   To every bushel (8 gallons or 36 litres) of this mix add 113 g (4 oz) of potting base fertilizer and 21 g (¾ oz) ground limestone or chalk.
   Most plants, however, prefer a slightly richer compost, so add to each bushel 226 g (8 oz) of potting base fertilizer and 42 g (1½ oz) ground limestone or chalk.
   An even richer compost, ideal for most large permanent plants like shrubs, trees and fruits, can be made by adding to each bushel 340 g (12 oz) of potting base fertilizer and 63 g (2¼ oz) ground limestone or chalk.

The front entrance to this house has been considerably brightened up with a traditional wooden tub and hanging baskets overflowing with fuchsias and petunias.

Wall-mounted containers are invaluable as they can be used to provide colour wherever desired around the house. These contain pelargoniums, fuchsias and lobelia.

You can buy loam in bags from garden centres. Try to obtain a light or medium loam, which should have been partially sterilized by the producer, and ideally slightly acid, with a pH of 6–6.5. For lime-hating plants it must be more acid than this – pH 5–5.5.

The ideal peat is granulated sphagnum-moss peat which is bought in bags or bales from garden centres. The sand should be a horticultural type, free from lime and quite coarse.

If the compost is for lime-hating plants omit the ground limestone or chalk from the mix.

SOILLESS POTTING COMPOST

3 parts peat
1 part sand (or alternatively, use vermiculite or per-lite)

Add to this mix a proprietary potting-base fertilizer (acid for lime-haters), the amount being as indicated by the maker.

This mix is suitable for lime-hating plants; or it can be modified if desired: for example, you could incorporate 1 part of acid loam and 1 part of leafmould, and omit the base fertilizer, but this modification is optional.

PLANTING TECHNIQUES

Before planting, wet the rootball of the plant if it is dry, as afterwards it is difficult if not impossible to wet it and the plant may not establish. The easiest way to wet a dry rootball is to stand the plant, complete with its nursery container, in a bucket of water almost up to the rim of the container, for an hour or so.

To plant a single plant in a tub, pot, etc, first place a layer of compost in the bottom, over the drainage material. This must be of sufficient depth that when planting is complete the top of the rootball is 12 mm (½ in) below the level of the new compost and there is a 12–25 mm (½–1 in) watering space (according to size of container) at the top. This layer of compost should be firmed moderately if soil-based, or lightly if soil-less.

Carefully remove the plant from its nursery container, avoiding root disturbance. If in a pot the easiest way to remove it is to invert the pot and tap the rim on a solid object so that the rootball is loosened and slides out. If the plant is in a flexible polythene bag simply slit this down one side and underneath and peel it off. Place the plant in the centre of the tub, etc, and trickle compost all round it, at the same time firming moderately if soil-based and lightly if soilless. Firm with your fingers.

If you are planting several plants in containers, such as spring or summer bedding plants, then it is easiest to fill the container with compost first and then make a planting hole for each, say with a trowel.

Bedding plants are often planted bare-root – in other words, lifted from trays or boxes, with very little soil around the roots. Do ensure the roots do not dry out before planting, so only lift a few plants at a time. Holes for bare-root plants must be sufficiently deep to allow the roots to dangle straight down to their full extent – roots crammed into shallow holes can result in the plants failing to grow well. Planting depth should be the same – in other words, do not plant more deeply nor more shallowly.

After planting, water the plants heavily as this helps to settle the compost around them.

Before planting wire hanging baskets first line them inside with sphagnum moss, with one of the proprietary basket liners or with a piece of polythene with drainage holes in it. Black polythene is least conspicuous. You can then insert plants through the wires in the sides of the basket to provide a ball of colour. Plants should be inserted as the basket is being filled with compost. Carefully push the roots through and cover them with compost. Do not forget to leave a good watering space at the top – about 2.5 cm (1 in). To make a hanging basket more stable when planting stand it on a flower pot of suitable size.

When planting growing-bags make holes in the top as directed by the makers. Do not make drainage holes in the bottom (you will have to be careful with watering to avoid having saturated compost). It is essential to stand growing-bags on a completely level surface.

CHANGING COMPOSTS

When growing plants in tubs, urns, pots and similar containers, and in window boxes and hanging baskets, you should periodically give them a fresh supply of compost, for potting composts deteriorate eventually, with drainage and aeration becoming poor and plant foods depleted.

Potting on

Single plants are best started off in small containers and potted-on (or moved on) to containers two sizes larger before they become pot-bound (container packed with roots). This is better than putting a small plant in a very big container as then it will have a large volume of compost around its roots which may then remain very wet with possibility of root-rot. Of course, if you are starting off with a large plant then it would be more practical to give it a large final-size container to start with.

The best time of year for potting-on is in early spring and the technique is as described under Planting Techniques for single plants in containers, on page 73.

Re-potting

Single permanent plants in large final tubs, pots, etc, should ideally be re-potted every other year to give them a fresh supply of compost. Again early spring is the best time.

It will take two people to handle a large plant. Firstly, the container should be placed on its side. Then one person taps the rim of the container with a block of wood. At the same time the second person gently and steadily pulls the plant. Hopefully the rootball should slide out. If it doesn't insert a long thin blade all round the inside, between container wall and rootball. Then try again.

Reduce the soilball in size by carefully teasing away about 5 cm (2 in) of compost from the sides, bottom and top. If necessary roots can be pruned back by this amount.

Then scrub out the container with water to remove all traces of compost and allow it to dry thoroughly. In the meantime keep the rootball of the plant covered with wet sacking to prevent drying out.

Finally replace the plant in its container, using new compost, which must be worked right down to the bottom. There should be no air spaces.

In the years between re-potting, or if you find you are unable to re-pot, topdressing can be carried out in spring. Remove about 2.5 cm (1 in) of old compost from the top and replace with the same depth of new compost.

Other techniques

If containers are used only for temporary plants like spring and summer bedding it is advisable to completely change the compost every two years or so – certainly before it starts to deteriorate.

With hanging baskets which are used for temporary plants it is usual to discard the compost at the end of each season.

Eventually hanging baskets and window boxes which contain collections of small permanent plants will become overgrown and that is the time for complete replacement – of compost and plants. Plants need not necessarily be discarded: they could be planted in the garden.

The same advice applies to sink gardens. Remember that small perennials and alpines can often be split or divided into smaller portions, so you do not necessarily have to buy new plants. Double walls may need rejuvenating every so often when they become overcrowded.

Raised beds and borders and large planters can be left for several years, just as beds in the garden. It should not be necessary to disturb shrubs, trees, roses, climbers, etc, but every three of four years it is a good idea to lift and divide any perennials and groups of bulbs. With the former this is best done in early spring; while bulbs are lifted, separated and replanted when they are dormant.

FEEDING

Once plants are established and well rooted into the compost a feeding programme can commence. For instance, with subjects planted in spring you can start feeding in summer. With autumn-planted subjects feeding can commence in the following spring.

Only apply feeds during the growing seasons – that is, spring, summer and early autumn. On average, plants in containers can be fed every two weeks, but if pot-bound weekly feeding would be better.

Use a compound general-purpose or flower-garden fertilizer containing the major plant foods nitrogen, phosphorus and potash. Liquid feeding is preferable for container-grown plants and certainly the most convenient means of applying foods. A fertilizer high in potash (for example, 10 per cent nitrogen, 10 per cent phosphorus and 27 per cent potash) is useful for flowering and fruiting plants.

Granular general-purpose or flower-garden fertilizer is best for raised beds, borders and large planters, applying an annual topdressing in spring and lightly forking it into the soil surface.

WATERING

Do not wait until the compost becomes bone-dry before watering as plants can suffer from this: flower buds and foliage can drop. Various plants, like camellias, rhododendrons, fuchsias and conifers soon react to dry compost by dropping leaves and/or flower buds. So regularly inspect containers, testing the compost surface for moisture content with your fingers. If it is drying out on the surface then apply water. Alternatively you could test the state of the compost with a soil-moisture meter.

Apply enough water so that it actually drains out of the bottom of the container; then you know that the compost has been moistened right the way through. Do not apply any more water until the surface is starting to dry out again (too much water can be harmful).

In warm weather containers should be checked once or twice a day for water requirements, and indeed may need watering once or twice, especially hanging baskets. Do check containers in winter, too, for although they dry out slowly the compost can still become dry.

If you have many containers to water you may find a watering lance useful, attached to the end of a hosepipe. With one of these it is an easy matter to water hanging baskets.

If you are away a lot in the spring and summer you may need to consider an automatic watering system. Ideal for containers is the drip system with many thin tubes 'sprouting' from a main hose. The thin tubes are positioned over the compost in the containers. Such a system can be fed either from an elevated water reservoir or from the mains water supply via a header tank with ballcock valve.

If you grow lime-hating plants beware of 'hard' or limy tap water. Occasional use of this does no harm but regular use can result in chlorosis of the leaves (the foliage turns yellow). Instead, try to collect and use rainwater.

WINTER PROTECTION

Many modern containers are frost-proof (that is, they are not damaged by frost), including many terracotta types. However it is the plants that we have to worry about in winter, for they can be severely damaged or

Citrus fruits, like oranges, look good in white tubs, but bear in mind that they need to be overwintered in a frost-free conservatory or greenhouse.

killed if the compost remains frozen solid for a prolonged period.

To help reduce this problem wrap containers thickly with straw, held in place with wire netting. Alternatively put plants in a cool but frost-free greenhouse or conservatory for the winter, particularly those which are liable to be damaged like camellias, African lilies (agapanthus) and hardy fuchsias.

In cold parts of the country which are subjected to hard winters it certainly pays to overwinter plants under glass – certainly most evergreens will not withstand compost which is frozen solid over a long period. I have found that spring bedding plants and bulbs suffer too, or may be killed, if left out all winter in cold areas.

In cold parts of the country it pays to grow as many very hardy plants as possible if you do not relish taking all your containers under glass, and to insulate the containers as described above. Tough evergreen plants include many of the dwarf junipers, the yew *Taxus canadensis*, dwarf varieties of *Thuja occidentalis*, dwarf varieties of *Prunus laurocerasus*, and varieties of ivy, *Hedera helix*.

In very hot areas the compost in containers can heat up excessively and so wherever possible the containers should be shaded in some way, perhaps with plenty of foliage trailing over them.

WINDOW BOXES

INTRODUCTION

The third part continues the theme of containers by looking in detail at window boxes and hanging baskets. These provide an obvious means of creating more growing space in small gardens, as well as ensuring welcome colour around the house.

Once again the emphasis is on colour and interest all the year round.

There are numerous window boxes available, so this section opens with choosing, taking into consideration materials and colours. Of course, you may wish to make your own, in which case full details are given. The information on positioning and fixing window boxes should be carefully followed.

Then follows advice on creating pleasing planting schemes, both temporary and permanent, taking into consideration variations in height, scale, form and colour. There is advice, too, on choosing plants which will cope with air pollution and shade.

Chapter 13 considers the use of temporary seasonal plants for the four seasons. Boxes are at their most colourful in summer, but it is surprising just how much colour can be provided in autumn, winter and spring with bulbs and, in the latter season, with spring bedding plants.

Chapter 14 advises on permanent planting schemes for window boxes, using such plants as small evergreen shrubs and conifers, rock plants and hardy perennials. Again we consider planting schemes for all four seasons.

As with other containers, it is possible to grow fruits, vegetables and herbs in window boxes, as will be seen in Chapter 15. One cannot be quite so adventurous with fruits, though, and the most practical to grow are strawberries. Good crops of tomatoes and other vegetables are easily achieved.

It is impossible to discuss window boxes without also including hanging baskets. Chapter 16, therefore, deals with these, from siting to planting, particularly in conjunction with window boxes.

It is mainly summer-flowering plants that are used in baskets. A good selection is recommended, plus how to arrange them effectively.

This section ends on a practical level by discussing suitable growing composts for window boxes and the need for good drainage. There are further tips on window-box growing, such as planting techniques, watering and feeding. Then we explain how to prepare, plant and look after hanging baskets.

Plants in window boxes and hanging baskets may not escape attacks from pests and diseases (indeed, even slugs and snails may find their way into them!), so the final chapter deals with these problems, plus cultural troubles and physiological disorders.

An oasis of colour and greenery on a city street: note the window boxes and baskets arranged so that they drape the frontage with a cascading ribbon of flowers and foliage, crossing and breaking up the hard architectural lines.

12

PLANNING AND DESIGN

THE CONTAINERS

The first step towards creating handsome window garden displays is, naturally, to choose your containers; and there is a vast range available, from highly ornate troughs to the simplest of wooden boxes.

Like many gardeners, I prefer my plants to be the main attraction, rather than their containers; so for preference I would usually go for something fairly simple and plain which won't fight with the flowers for attention. It's all a matter of personal taste, but do remember that a highly decorated or brightly coloured box may appeal when seen in the store but look very unnatural and clash with the flowers when planted up.

It's also best if the window boxes don't clash too much with the style of the building, either. The one situation where you could perhaps get away with having very intricately designed and ornamented containers would be where the architecture is equally ornate; for example, in a Spanish style, against which more intricate boxes wouldn't seem so out of place.

However, something plain and more utilitarian, with clean lines and a neutral colour, would better suit the vast majority of buildings (particularly modern ones) as well as setting the plants off to better effect.

Colour

Speaking of colour, you can of course select or paint containers to match the paintwork of your windows, and this can look very effective, but bear in mind that white boxes will need annual repainting and regular cleaning (particularly in urban areas), otherwise they'll quickly become dirty and unsightly.

Boxes may also be chosen or painted in a colour to blend with the walls (e.g. brick-red, stone hues, or to match coloured rendering or painted walls) and this is especially effective where the containers are to be fixed on brackets just below the windows, rather than actually on the sills.

If in doubt, play safe and opt for subdued tints like dark green, beige, brown or plain varnished timber, all of which will offset plants and flowers well. Bear in mind also, if you're hand-painting, that a matt finish generally looks more subdued and blends in better than a high-gloss paint (unless you're matching it to existing glossy paintwork.)

Material

Plastic troughs are light to handle and should have a long life provided they're made from good heavy-duty material; very thin and flimsy poor quality plastics may quickly become brittle in sunlight, making them prone to cracking and breakage.

Be wary when buying decorative metal containers as well. Wrought iron and steel may be robust but can quickly start to rust unless well coated with paint or plastic against the elements, and no-one wants unsightly rain-washed rust stains disfiguring the house; particularly where the walls are white or of a very pale colouring.

Glass fibre is a good choice, tough and very long-lasting, and unglazed eathenware pottery troughs look very classy.

I really don't think you can beat good old-fashioned

timber; it's comparatively inexpensive (especially if you build your own boxes); it lasts well if treated inside with preservative; it's easily painted to suit your requirements and looks particularly good when clear varnished to make a handsome feature of the wood grain. If you can obtain rough-cut planks complete with bark edgings, or a bark-covered facing timber, these will give your window gardens a particularly attractive rustic look: lovely on an older house, and an interesting natural contrast to an ultra-modern frontage or a large picture window.

Size

The box should be as large as the window ledge will allow. The more planting compost it holds, the longer it'll take to dry out between waterings, which means less work and worry; and of course you'll be able to squeeze in more plants in greater variety for a really marvellous display.

Shallow containers should be avoided wherever possible, as these dry out fastest of all and therefore demand very frequent watering. Anything shallower than 15 cm (6 in) is likely to cause trouble, and 20 cm (8 in) or more is better.

You needn't settle for a very narrow box even if the window sill is shallow; your container can project out a little way from the sill without looking odd, and on an extremely narrow ledge a wide box can be supported at the front with wall brackets (see 'Positioning and fixing' below).

POTS AND REMOVABLE LINERS

There are two basic ways to use window boxes; simply filled with growing compost and planted up, or as containers to hold removable liners or pot-grown plants (Fig. 17). The first option is the most straightforward, but the second does allow for quicker and simpler seasonal changes and alterations to the display.

Boxes with removable liners certainly make life easy for the window-gardener. When the spring display starts to fade, for example, the inner liner containing the spring flowers is easily removed, speedily making way for a fresh liner full of plants for summer, and so on through the seasons. Even permanent displays of perennial plants may, in this way, be moved around from one window box to another for variety and a change of scene; or permanent plantings may be removed for ease of weeding, replanting and other maintenance tasks.

Having said that, window boxes with removable liners are probably most useful to someone with a garden, yard or glasshouse space where liners full of seasonal plants may be continually grown on in readiness for a quick change-over. In an apartment, with no facilities for this kind of conveyor-belt planning and preparation, removable liners aren't as much of an asset.

Growing pot plants free-standing on window ledges is always hazardous, with every strong gust of wind (or careless movement when watering) likely to send them crashing to the ground—a very real danger in the case of high windows, when the risk of broken heads below must be taken into consideration. They'll be perfectly safe, however, in a securely fixed window box and will offer the same quick-change benefits as removable liners; in fact, even more so.

Plunge material

Pot plants may be simply placed in the window box, but they're better plunged in a water-retentive material like peat or one of the newer lightweight man-made plunging materials. This will help to keep the individual pots cool and moist, reducing the need for hand-watering.

Note that the plunge material should be watered at the same time as the pots, so that it acts as a reservoir of moisture which can be taken up through the bases of the pots; dry plunge material may actually draw water out of the pots, having the opposite effect to the one desired.

Fig. 17a. With removable liners to fit your window boxes, changing the plants for colour in different seasons becomes a simple matter. Buy two liners per box, and you can always have the next season's flowers growing on in advance, ready for a quick change-over.

If the plunge material is deep enough to just cover and hide the rims of the pots, so that the plants appear to be growing in the box, the effect will be that much more attractive.

Making your own

Home-made timber boxes couldn't be simpler, demanding little in the way of carpentry skills, and they can of course be tailored to fit your individual windows.

Inexpensive softwood (e.g. pine) is quite acceptable and long-lasting if treated with preservative and given

Fig. 17b. Using a box to hold pot-grown plants is a versatile method of window gardening. Swopping plants around for seasonal interest is quick and easy.

a fresh coat of paint or varnish annually. Varnished hardwood boxes look very classy and have a long life but are naturally far more costly.

A very simple straight-sided 'ammunition box' shape is perfectly good and easy to construct, but sloping the front out a little towards the top by cutting the end-pieces at an angle (Fig. 18) produces a slightly more pleasing effect. An angled front piece allows for a larger planting area of compost at the top of the box, and a larger surface area for catching valuable rain-water. It also permits trailing plants and flowers to cascade over the front in a freer and more attractive way.

Don't forget to drill drainage holes in the base, preferably about 2 cm (¾ in) in diameter so that they won't become blocked up with compost; and nail or screw a small strip of timber to each end of the base to act as feet and raise the box off the ledge, again to ensure free drainage of excess water.

Lovely effect here; the rich violet-purple flowered *Clematis* 'Jackmanii Superba' trained across the cottage, growing around and framing the hanging basket with its contrasting splash of hotter colours.

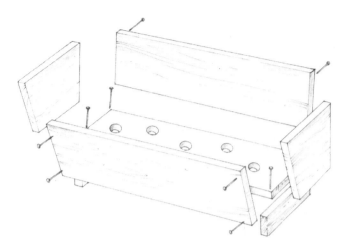

Fig. 18. Constructing a home-made window box: use timber 1.9–2.5 cm (¾–1 in) thick. Be sure to drill large drainage holes in the base, and tack strips of timber under the base to raise it off the window ledge.

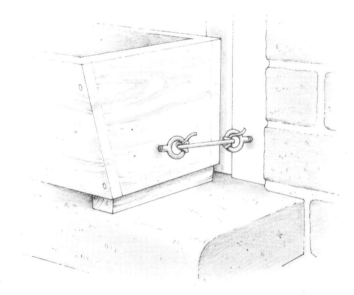

Fig. 19. Make sure that window boxes are safely secured, particularly on high ledges. The easiest way is to screw eye-hooks into each end of the box, attaching these with wire to eye-hooks screwed into the window frame.

Treat the inside of the box with a couple of coats of preservative, using one that's recommended by the manufacturer as not harmful to plants (e.g. those containing copper napthenate; your local garden or hardware store should be able to advise on available brands.) Store-bought wooden window boxes should have been pretreated in this way, but it's worthwhile checking; and, in any case, only one coat may have been given, so an extra treatment won't do any harm. Emptying, cleaning and reapplying preservative once a year when replanting will help to ensure many years of useful life from your boxes.

Protect the outside of home-made containers with a couple of coats of exterior quality varnish or paint, taking care to work this thoroughly into the joints. Sand down any rough surfaces before painting. Repaint or varnish annually for long life.

POSITIONING AND FIXING

Where the box can be placed on the window ledge, this obviously makes thing very easy, but even here, it's best to secure the container to ensure that it can't be accidentally knocked to the ground; and this is particularly important, as a safety factor, with high windows. Eye-and-hook catches may be fitted to the ends of the box and the sides of the window, or simple eye-hooks screwed into the window frame and box may be connected by strong wire (Fig. 19).

Should the window ledge be rather narrow, an overhanging box may be secured by attaching metal brackets to the base at the front, bending these around the sill and fixing them to the wall below (Fig. 20).

Where the ledge is virtually non-existent, the box will have to be attached with brackets to the wall just below the window. This is also where the box will have to be located if the window opens outwards, making it impossible to place anything on the ledge outside. Alternatively, under ground-floor windows, boxes may be supported on wooden legs (Fig. 21).

Don't be put off the idea of window gardens if this is the situation that you face. It's not at all difficult, using an ordinary power drill with a masonry bit, screws and wall plugs, to fit suitable brackets; and if you can't tackle it yourself, any handyman should be able to do the job for you quickly and inexpensively.

Using wall brackets, it's equally easy to fit hanging baskets above and alongside windows, to add yet another interesting dimension to your window gardens; but more on that later.

As to aspect, sunny windows are the ideal sites for box gardens, since the majority of plants do best with

Fig. 20. On a narrow ledge, the box may be allowed to overhang provided it is secured with brackets and timber blocks to the wall beneath.

Fig. 21a. Where the ledge is extremely narrow, or where there is no ledge at all, a box may be fixed with brackets to the wall just below the window.

Fig. 21b. Alternatively, boxes may be raised up on supports to the level of a ground-floor window, where the ledge is very narrow.

In a shady situation like this basement, shade-loving impatiens varieties (busy lizzies) thrive.

Imaginative use of the ledges over bay windows transforms this frontage in summer. Always make sure that window boxes and pots on a street front are well secured.

plenty of sunlight. If you're planning just one or two window boxes, choose your sunniest windows. However, even the gloomiest sunless situations can be brightened up, using a selection of shade-loving and shade-tolerant plants (see 'Plants for Shade' at the end of this chapter).

PLANTING SCHEMES

The first thing to decide, after buying or constructing the containers, is the type of planting schemes that you want: whether seasonal 'bedding' with spring flowers followed by a fresh set of plants for summer colour, and so on through the year; or fairly permanent planting schemes, comprising evergreen perennials for year-round interest; or herbs, fruits and vegetables.

Naturally, if you're planning more than one window garden then you can go for a variety, some with seasonal plants and some for permanent effects. It's quite possible to mix temporary seasonal flowers for summer with such things as herbs, small fruit plants and vegetables all in the same box.

What you decide will depend on various factors—how much work you're prepared to put in on emptying and refilling the boxes for different seasons; whether you'd prefer to just plant up the once, with things for a long-lasting effect; whether you want to grow fresh produce for the kitchen, and so on. Frequent replanting with temporary plants does involve more work, but means lots of bright colour. Permanent plantings tend to be rather less colourful, with a show of flowers one month, a gap, some more colour later, and with handsome evergreen foliage playing a major role.

The one strong recommendation that I'd make is to be adventurous and try as many different types of planting schemes and as many different types of plants as possible—variety being the spice of life, after all.

Whatever you're going to grow, the most important thing is to spend plenty of time on planning and design before you pick up a trowel, and before you buy a single plant; just as you would before setting out to create a full-size garden. The points to bear in mind are indeed virtually the same as those that apply to larger-scale gardening.

The first point, and probably the most important, is to plan for a constant succession of colour and interest, ideally right around the year. With seasonal replantings—a fresh set of temporary annuals, bulbs and suchlike for spring, summer, autumn and winter—this is easily achieved, but it does involve planning ahead; making out lists well in advance, of plants and bulbs to be bought, and seeds to be sown, in readiness for a quick change-over at the end of each season's display.

The best way is to work out, on paper, a series of planting schemes for the whole year. This will then, at least, act as a basic planting timetable on which you can elaborate or improvise if you wish, as each season comes around and replanting time approaches.

With permanent displays of perennial plants, it means choosing attractive evergreens for constant foliage interest, preferably with contrasting leaf shapes and tints. It also means trying to select your plants so that you'll have at least some flowers in each season.

There's a limit to what can be done in a small container, but even in a tiny window box it should be possible to include at least one plant for spring flowers, another for summer, one for autumn and yet another for winter. It also helps to select plants which bloom over a long period within their appointed season. We'll be looking at plant selection for different times of year and for long-flowering later. For now, some more basic guidelines on good design.

Height

As in any garden, variations in height, scale and form are essential for an interesting and eye-catching effect. The last thing you want to end up with is a box boringly filled with plants all of the same height and habit of growth. Think of the window box as a garden bed or border, and plan for as much variety as possible.

One or two tall 'spot' plants are essential, as focal points for the whole arrangement. In a garden border, these would be towards the back, with smaller plants grading down towards the front. But in a window box the approach has to be rather different. You don't want to block the view and the daylight from the window too much, so the best place for the tallest things is at the sides, with the rest of the plants getting gradually smaller towards the centre. You could place two tall plants of the same type and height, one at each side of the window, but even here it's that bit more interesting if you can get a little extra variation into the design.

A classic arrangement would be to place a very tall plant on one side as the main focal point, grading down to smaller plants and then up again a little to a medium-tall specimen on the other side. In this arrangement, as in a well structured painting, the eye is caught by the tallest plant to one side, and then drawn in towards the centre of the feature by the curving downward line; an effect that's natural and pleasing to the eye.

Much depends on the shape and size of the window, of course. A very wide window, for example, could accommodate tall plants (and possibly a number of them in a group) on both sides, without blocking out the view and daylight excessively.

Naturally, a very long window box could accommodate additional slight 'ups-and-downs' of height variation between these two extremities. However, plants towards the centre should still not be too tall, and certainly not taller than those to the sides—the aim should always be to enhance and 'frame' the window with flowers and foliage, not to obscure it with a tall mass in the middle.

A very narrow window, on the other hand, might only be wide enough to take a single tall plant to one side, with the other plants grading down in height towards the opposite corner.

Climbing plants are also useful for adding height towards the sides of the box, supported on canes or perhaps on a narrow wooden or plastic trellis attached to the inside of the window. Very tall, narrow windows in particular cry out for perennial or annual climbers to scramble up them (Fig. 22); and in such a situation, you'll often find that climbers make better 'height' plants, clinging close to the side of the window and cutting out less light than a tall, bushy plant.

Large windows which are both tall and wide offer the greatest possibilities for exciting displays using all of these elements; climbers scrambling all the way up the sides, tall bushy plants inside these, curving down to ever smaller things, and possibly a few more medium-height plants for added variety (see Fig. 23 for the effect of height variations).

Fig. 22. A climbing plant trained on canes or a trellis to one side of the window will add greatly to the character and appeal of your window box garden. It will add extra height to the display without blocking the window excessively.

Simple timber boxes are an excellent choice; a natural setting for the flowers, neutral in colour and perfect for buildings with a period character that might be spoiled by the intrusion of modern plastic containers.

More town houses with this kind of summer floral display would be a welcome sight on our streets.

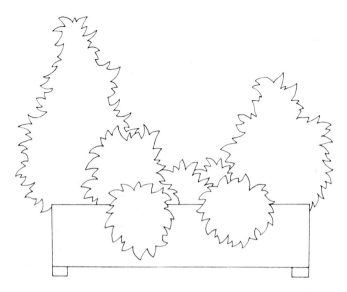

Fig. 23. A classic window box planting design; using a tall focal plant to one side, grading down to smaller plants in the centre (to avoid blocking the light and view through the window) and finally rising up again at the other end to a medium-height plant; the whole arrangement forming a pleasing curve.

Trailing plants

Trailers are just as vital, spilling out of the box and cascading downwards; and without at least one trailing plant, no window garden could be complete. They add an exotic 'jungly' touch and (equally important) they help to balance the feature, offsetting the height of the taller plants and climbers above; a window garden without trailers tends to look top-heavy, and (vice versa) one with trailers and no tall plants can appear bottom-heavy.

Speaking of climbers and trailers, it's interesting to experiment with mixed plantings for unusual effects. For example, two different types of climbing plants may be placed close together to scramble up through one another. Perhaps an ivy with handsome glossy foliage, and a sweet pea to twine up through this, the

flowers peeping out from amongst the ivy leaves. Or, in a permanent planting of evergreens, you could use two different types of ivy, one with dark green leaves and the other a golden or silver variegated variety; or one large-leaved and the other with small leaves. Remember that ivies can be used both as climbers and as trailers.

With trailers, the same sort of mix-and-match principle may be tried. Put one trailing plant at the front of the window box and a second (different) one just behind it, to grow through the first plant so that their trailing leaves or flowers cascade out of the box intertwined.

Colour

With flowering plants, try to match the flower colour so that they go well together, otherwise the whole effect will be spoiled.

Don't forget that foliage plants can also play an important role, not just in permanent evergreen plantings but also in seasonal arrangements where variegated leaves, silver foliage and other colourful leaf tints may greatly add to the overall effect. More on these later.

On a more general point, in larger-scale gardening, groups of plants of the same type massed together often look better than a patchwork mixture made up of single plants of different kinds. This principle, too, can sometimes be applied to window boxes, bearing in mind the limitations of space. The smallest window gardens may only offer space for one tall focal plant or climber, one or two smaller bushy things and a single trailer, but where space permits, in large boxes, arranging the plants in groups of two or three of the same kind and colour together does produce a very bold and pleasing effect.

You'll have noted from some of the above design suggestions that much depends on the size and shape of the window, and on the size of the box, much the same as in a garden, where layout and planting are often greatly influenced by the shape, size and situation of the plot.

So let's now take a look at other ways in which window garden displays can be designed to suit, and to enhance, different types of situation.

Site of container

For a start, what difference does it make to the planting scheme whether the window box sits on the ledge or is fixed to the wall beneath? I've already mentioned placing low-growing plants towards the centre of the display, to avoid blocking the window too much. Bearing this in mind, it's obvious that these central flowers can be taller in a box fitted below the window than in one sitting on the ledge; and all the plants could be that little bit taller if you so wished.

Indeed, a 'low-slung' box just below the ledge will allow a wider range of plants to be grown, bringing in the possibility of taller things that might not suit a window-ledge box. Should you have a hankering for certain types of taller flowers, say tall growing bulbs like lilies for summer, then it might well be a good idea to purposely site the container under the ledge (Fig. 24).

There is, however, an important point that affects this question of plant height greatly, and which hasn't yet been mentioned: whether the window is exposed and windy or well sheltered. Naturally, a window garden in a particularly windy situation is best planted mostly with very short, sturdy things that will stand up to constant buffeting without flopping over or snapping off at the stem. This applies particularly to windows above the ground floor, and especially to high windows facing the wind funnels of canyon-like city streets.

Ground-floor windows tend to be less windy, since wind speeds are always slower at lower levels and there's usually more wind shelter around. Here taller plants and bulbs should be safer, except in a very exposed position.

Plants for air pollution

In city areas subject to heavy and frequent air pollution, it pays to include at least some really tough, pollution-tolerant plants in the window display.

Fig. 24. Fixing a box with brackets below a window will often allow quite tall plants to be used; these sturdy 'Mid-Century' hybrid lilies, for example. If you wish to grow taller plants, you might like to site your box in this position deliberately, whether you have a window ledge or not.

Plants which will stand heavy air pollution include: *Iberis* (candytuft), both the annual *I. umbellata* varieties, and the perennial rock garden species and varieties like *I. sempervirens*; ivies for foliage interest, as climbers and trailing plants; *Dianthus* (pinks); primroses and poly-anthus primroses; dwarf *Euonymus fortunei* varieties, like 'Silver Queen' for colourful foliage; dwarf rhododendrons or evergreen azaleas; and virtually all bulbs (spring, summer, autumn and winter flowering).

Colour effects

Flower and foliage colours should also, to some extent at least, be selected with the situation and surroundings

Tubs are also useful when it comes to decking the house with summer colour; especially where paving or concrete makes it impossible to plant at the base of a wall.

Pot holders are an excellent alternative to hanging baskets, and these black-painted iron fixtures are perfectly in keeping with the period character of the cottage.

in mind. Most importantly, the colours shouldn't blend in with the background too much. To take an extreme example, white flowers are unlikely to stand out and show up to best effect if they trail over the edge of the window box with a brilliant white painted wall as a background.

In general, pale flowers and light foliage tints look best contrasted against a darker background; yellows, pinks and whites against dark brick or stone, for example. And vice versa: deeper colours like hot reds, blues, purples and violets stand out better against a light background, like a white or pastel colour-washed wall. This is worth bearing in mind particularly when choosing plants to trail over the edges or front of a box, and with plants to grow up the sides of the window.

Darker coloured flowers also tend to show up best in sunny situations, where sunlight streaming through their petals will light them up and really bring them to life; in shade, they may look duller and less lively. The best flower colours for brightening up gloomy shady windows are the gleaming paler ones.

Plants for shade

Speaking of shade, sunless window gardens do require more thought than sunny ones, since so many plants grow too weakly and spindly or refuse to flower properly in shade. As a general guide, the following is a selection of plants which will tolerate or do well in this kind of situation. For further information, see the plant lists.

Bulbs, corms and tubers: tuberous anemones, tuberous begonias, *Chionodoxa, Colchicum*, crocus, hardy cyclamen, *Eranthis, Galanthus, Hyacinthus, Ipheion, Narcissus, Scilla*.

Annuals: *Begonia semperflorens, Calceolaria* (slipper flower), *Impatiens* (busy Lizzie), *Lobelia, Malcolmia* (Virginia stock), *Mimulus* (monkey flower), *Nemophila* (baby blue eyes), *Viola* (pansy).

Perennials and dwarf shrubby plants: *Hedera* (ivies), *Primula* (primroses and polyanthus), fuchsias, ferns, dwarf rhododendrons, dwarf evergreen azaleas, *Lysimachia nummularia* (creeping Jenny).

13

USING TEMPORARY SEASONAL PLANTS

Summer is the season that most people associate with window box displays more than any other time of year; and this is indeed when they're at their best, brimming over with the brilliant, long-lasting colour of exotic-flowered annuals and tender bedding plants like fuchsias and pelargoniums, but it would be a shame to leave the boxes bare and empty for the rest of the year.

Exactly how the planting timetable for the year is worked out depends to some extent on whether plants and bulbs are being grown direct in the boxes, or in removable liners and pots. Using liners and pots inside the boxes does allow more flexibility, as I've already mentioned. Let's go through the seasons and see what we can use to brighten up our windows, and when.

Fig. 25. An example of a well-planted seasonal display for summer, with a balanced mix of tall plants (fuchsia, *left*, calceolaria, *centre* and pelargonium, *right*) lower, bushy plants (sweet alyssum and impatiens, *right centre*) and trailers (lobelia, *left* and nasturtium, *right*).

SUMMER

Annuals are the mainstay of the summer display (Fig. 25), backed up by one or two frost-tender perennials and perhaps some of the neater summer bulbs.

Sowing time for annuals to flower in summer is from late winter to early spring. Hardy annuals may be sown direct into the box; but they get off to a faster start, make larger plants and flower earlier if sown in pots or trays under·cover, to be planted out once growing strongly. Half-hardy annuals must be sown in warmth and planted out after the spring frosts are over (except in areas with a very mild, frost-free climate). A glasshouse is invaluable for seed-sowing and growing-on, but it's quite possible to raise seedlings indoors on a windowsill.

Alternatively, young annual plants may be bought from market stalls, gardening stores and nurseries in late spring or early summer, ready for immediate planting. However, the range available is usually limited, and you can choose from a wider and more exciting selection if you raise your own from seed.

Annuals

Many annual plants are too large for window boxes, but the following is a selection of suitable types:

TRAILING PLANTS
Alyssum maritimum, *Lobelia*, *Impatiens* (pendulous varieties), *Lathyrus* (sweat pea), *Petunia*, *Thunbergia* (black-eyed Susan), *Tropaeolum* (nasturtium).

NEAT, BUSHY PLANTS
Ageratum, *Anchusa capensis* 'Blue Angel', dwarf *Antirrhinum* (snapdragon), *Begonia semperflorens*, *Lobelia*, *Calceolaria* (slipper flower), dwarf bedding dahlias, *Alyssum*, *Dimorphotheca* (star of the veldt), *Eschscholzia* (Californian poppy), *Gazania*, dwarf *Godetia*, *Iberis* (candytuft), dwarf bushy *Impatiens*, *Limnanthes* (poached egg plant), *Malcolmia* (Virginia stock), *Mesembryanthemum* (Livingstone daisy), *Mimulus*, *Petunia*, *Nemophila* (baby blue eyes), *Nemesia*, dwarf *Nicotiana* (tobacco plant), dwarf annual phlox, *Salvia*, dwarf *Tagetes* (African and French marigolds), dwarf *Zinnia*.

Some of the above are available in taller varieties or strains suitable for adding height to the display, notably the salvias, *Antirrhinum*, bedding dahlia, *Godetia*, *Nicotiana*, *Tagetes* and *Zinnia*. But many of the taller annuals may be tried as feature plants.

CLIMBERS
Lathyrus (sweat pea), *Ipomoea* (morning glory), *Cobaea* (cathedral bells), *Eccremocarpus scaber* (Chilean glory flower), *Thunbergia*, *Nasturtium* (climbing varieties).

Perennials

Tender glasshouse-type perennials, like the fuchsias and pelargoniums, may be planted direct into boxes, or they may be grown in pots, to be plunged or placed in the box for the summer. In all but the warmest frost-free areas, these plants must be kept on an indoor windowsill or in a heated glasshouse during winter. Growing them in pots as mentioned above makes this seasonal move easier; but even when they're planted direct into the boxes, it doesn't take long to simply knock some of the growing compost off their roots in

late autumn and pot them up for the winter.

Young, bushy plants may be bought, along with annual seedlings, from market stalls, gardening stores and nurseries in late spring and early summer. They shouldn't be planted out in the window gardens until all danger of late spring frost is over.

Most may be propagated from cuttings of non-flowering shoots in spring or early summer. Pelargoniums and dwarf dahlias may also be raised from seed sown in heat during late winter, to flower the same year.

Speaking of raising tender bedding perennials from seed, dwarf dahlia seed is often sold as a half-hardy annual; but the tuberous roots are perennial and can be lifted and stored frost-free in pots of compost during winter, to flower again in future years.

Long-flowering dwarf dahlias suitable for window boxes are available in double and single flowered strains; go for the neatest types that don't grow above 30 cm (12 in).

Begonia semperflorens, usually sold as an annual, can also be potted up and kept indoors or in a frost-free glasshouse during winter.

Pelargoniums

Pelargoniums are probably the all-time favourites for summer colour in window boxes, and their hot reds and bright candy pinks are unbeatable for a truly eye-catching show. All have handsome foliage, often attractively marked with red-purple or other tints. Tall varieties are stunning 'height' plants, and the newer miniature strains of pelargonium are particularly suitable for even the smallest window box; some produce dainty small flowers, others are as large in bloom as the tallest strains and varieties.

The ordinary bedding pelargoniums are easy and flower freely over a long period. The rather fancier regal or show varieties with their jagged-edged leaves and ruffled flowers are better as indoor or greenhouse plants except in the warmest areas.

Luckily the ivy-leaved *Pelargonium peltatum* is as easy

The exotic, large-flowered petunias are ideal for window gardens, particularly the pink, violet-blue and red 'Cascade' strains.

to grow and as free-flowering as the bedding varieties. This is a superb trailing plant with lovely ivy-like foliage and flowers of red, pink, white or mauve. The variety 'L'Elegante' is particularly attractive, with its small white flowers and cream-edged leaves.

Fuchsias

Fuchsias are equally valuable in the window garden. They can be grown as neat bushy plants by pinching out the top shoots, or as taller pyramids and standards by nipping out side-shoots. The trailing varieties, also, are marvellous at the front of a box.

When grown as tall pyramids or short standards, the fuchsias are, in my view, the best flowers of all for adding height and acting as focal plants in the summer display. Like the pelargoniums, they bloom over a very long period, from mid-summer to late autumn, with quite a variety of flower shape and colour.

The single-flowered varieties are the most elegant, and some of the best are: 'Bon Accord' (lilac and white); 'Brutus' (red and purple); 'Madame Cornelissen' (red and white); 'Mission Bells' (red and purple); 'Rufus the Red' (deep salmon-red) and 'Ting-a-Ling' (pure white).

Good doubles include 'Alice Hoffman' and 'Snowcap' (both red and white); 'Tennessee Waltz' (pink and lilac), and 'Dollar Princess' (red and lilac).

All of the above varieties produce large, rounded flowers, but there are others with long, tubular flowers which dangle in elegant clusters; of these, 'Thalia' is a popular choice for its dark green foliage and orange-red blooms; well worth looking out for.

As for trailing fuchsias, the following are excellent: 'Cascade' (purple-red and white); 'Swingtime' (scarlet and white, double-flowered); and 'Marinka' (red and purple).

Bulbs, tubers, corms

Of the summer-flowering bulbs, tubers and corms, many are too tall for the window garden, but a few are very suitable.

Most popular of all are the tuberous begonias which flower through to autumn. Some of the large-flowered double *Begonia × tuberhybrida* varieties are tallish plants which can be used to add height to the display. The dwarfer and smaller-flowered varieties look good as a box edging, and so do the graceful trailing *B. × tuberhybrida* 'Pendula' types. The tender tubers can be started into growth indoors in late winter but should not go outside until all danger of spring frost is past. Lift in autumn and store frost-free in dry growing compost.

The poppy-flowered 'De Caen' and the double-flowered 'St Brigid' anemone strains are also popular. For a long season of colour, plant the tubers in small batches from early to late spring.

Freesias specially treated for outdoor summer flowering are offered by bulb growers these days, and their rich fragrance wafting in through an open window is a delight. Plant a handful of corms in spring, and they'll bloom in late summer (earlier if you start them off indoors or under glass in late winter).

Another low-growing summer bulb that I like very much is *Tigridia pavonia* (tiger flower). This is superb at the back of a display where its large and exotic iris-like blooms appear over a long period throughout late summer; usually sold in a mixture of colours ranging from glowing reds, through yellow and mauve to glistening white, all with eye-catching red and purple tiger-markings in the centre.

Most large-flowered gladioli are far too tall for any window garden, but it is possible to use the very smallest hybrids, like the dainty 60 cm (2 ft) *Gladiolus nanus* varieties. Two or three corms planted to sprout up the side of a tall window, for example, would add height and long-lasting colour to the display, and also contribute attractive sword-shaped foliage to contrast with bushier plants. These small varieties would also suit a box slung beneath a window ledge, where taller plants are more easily accommodated without danger of blocking the window too much.

The same comments apply to the sumptuous lilies: most are too tall, but in a low-slung box or as focal plants to the side of a large window, some of the lowest-growing ones would make a stunning feature. For example, there might be a place for a bulb or two of the upright-flowered 'mid-century' hybrids like the popular nasturtium-red 'Enchantment' or the lemon-yellow 'Connecticut King' which grow to between 60 and 90 cm (2 to 3 ft). There are also some very lovely large-flowered and sweetly scented dwarf *Lilium auratum* hybrids coming onto the market. Bred to be grown as sturdy pot plants, these brilliant red and pink flowers are ideal for the window box, where they'll add a truly exotic touch to the whole effect.

Trailers

Now for some attractive trailing foliage plants for the summer window garden: ivies are excellent, of course, plain-leaved varieties providing a dark green foil to set off the colourful flower display, or gold and silver variegated forms for added effect. The silver grey-leaved *Helichrysum petiolatum* is very elegant, providing a good contrast with darker foliage, as does the ferny-leaved silvery-white *Senecio maritimus*.

Various trailing house plants may also be used in the summer window box, including *Chlorophytum comosum* 'Variegatum' (the white variegated spider plant), *Saxifraga stolonifera* (mother of thousands) with its round silver-veined leaves, purple on the undersides, and the stripy-leaved *Zebrina pendula* and tradescantias (wandering Jews).

The most popular bushy plants for bright foliage colour are the flamboyant *Coleus* varieties, instantly recognizable by their nettle-like leaves, strikingly splashed and zoned in all shades of yellow, green, pink, red and maroon-purple. And, of course, in a shady window box ferns are especially useful.

AUTUMN

Most annuals will continue flowering into the autumn, often only stopping when the first frosts arrive; and they'll bloom longer and more generously if the dead flower heads are regularly nipped off, to stop them running to seed. The same goes for most of the tender perennials, particularly the fuchsias, which are especially useful for late colour; but, of course, these tender plants should be removed before frosts threaten, if they're to be kept for the following year.

Bulbs

As autumn advances, however, the display does start to fade. Yet it's a simple matter to revive the window garden by popping in a few autumn-flowering bulbs to provide added colour and interest. These should be planted in late summer or as early as possible in the autumn, and most will spring into growth and start to push up flower buds almost immediately. If they're left unplanted until late autumn, then they tend to start sprouting in the dry state, and the resulting flowers are usually thin, malformed and very disappointing. Rather than risk getting them in this condition from the store or the mail-order company, be sure to buy or order as early as possible.

You can simply poke holes in the growing compost between the summer plants which are still colourful enough to be left, and pop the bulbs in; and any plants that have finished flowering or are starting to look unsightly may of course be removed to make more room.

Be sure to water the window garden heavily after planting bulbs; they'll have to compete with existing plant roots in the box and may flower poorly if the compost is dry. It's also a good idea to give them some liquid fertilizer. By the time the bulbs are up and starting to flower, you'll probably find that more of the summer plants are going over and can be carefully removed to make way for them (cut annuals off at the base, leaving the roots, so as not to disturb the bulbs.)

If you're using pots inside the window box, or removable liners, then of course special displays of autumn bulbs can be planted up and grown on in advance, ready for a quick change-over when the bulbs start to come into flower.

The most spectacular of all the autumn bulbs are the

All the ingredients of a classical arrangement: a tall plant hugging close to one side of the window, lower-growing pelargoniums in the centre, all balanced by the trailing lobelias below.

Single-colour plantings can prove just as effective as a rainbow mixture: a selection of all-white flowers with silver foliage plants perhaps, or reds and pinks as in this grouping of pelargoniums.

colchicums, commonly referred to as 'autumn crocus' although they're actually quite different (except for a basic similarity in flower shape) from the true autumn-flowering crocus. Most of the species and varieties commonly available from stores and mail-order catalogues produce huge goblet-shaped flowers, much larger and showier than true crocus. These emerge leafless from the soil, usually many blooms to a corm, so that even one or two will make an eye-catching display.

You should find *Colchicum byzantinum* and *C.* 'Lilac Wonder' on sale in local stores, and these both produce a long succession of large and very bright lilac-pink flowers, but there are many more to be had from mail-order suppliers, some of them even better than these old favourites. The most flamboyant of all is the large double-flowered pink variety aptly named 'Waterlily'. *Colchicum speciosum* is another beauty, with large tulip-shaped blooms that may be either lilac-rose, deep mauve-red or pure white. The variety 'The Giant' is the largest-flowered, with white-throated violet-pink blooms, and 'Violet Queen' is attractively chequered lilac-pink and deep violet-purple.

As for the true crocus, there are a fair number that bloom in autumn, but probably the best of all is the large-flowered *Crocus speciosus*. Various colour forms are available from good bulb catalogues, all shades of lilac-blue, sometimes very close to a true sky-blue, a wonderful sight when even a handful of corms are clumped together. There's also a stunning white form. Like the colchicums, *C. speciosus* produces a succession of many flowers from each corm over a fairly long period. Other autumn crocus to look out for in the catalogues include the violet-flowered *C. medius* and the rosy-lilac *C. kotschyanus* (formerly *C. zonatus*).

Autumn-flowering hardy cyclamen are the other main standby for this time of year, and the ever-popular *Cyclamen hederifolium* (formerly *C. neapolitanum*) is lovely in a window garden where its small nodding pink flowers can be admired at close quarters; and keep an eye out for the equally beautiful white form, *C. hederifolium album*.

Finally, a bulb or two of the hardy *Nerine bowdenii* would enhance any autumn window garden, with its large clusters of bright pink funnel-shaped flowers.

Naturally, all of these need to grow on after flowering, during the winter and the following spring, if they're to bloom again in the future. With pots or removable liners, this is no problem; they can simply be removed to make way for winter and spring flowers. If they're planted direct into the window box, they'll have to be carefully lifted and either planted out in the garden or potted up, so as not to hinder further seasonal plantings.

WINTER

This is the most difficult season in the window garden, as it is in gardening generally. In areas with a very mild climate, tender perennials and annuals can be had in flower almost the whole year round; but in most areas you have to rely on dwarf winter-flowering bulbs and a few neat winter-flowering perennials, dwarf shrubby plants and evergreens for attractive foliage.

Evergreen perennials and dwarf shrubs are best used for permanent displays, since they resent frequent disturbance and replanting. However, if you're using pots or removable liners in the window box then you can, of course, introduce this kind of winter display quite easily; simply have these plants growing on in pots or liners, ready for the seasonal change over.

If planting direct into a window box full of compost (without a removable liner) one or two pot-grown perennials or dwarf shrubs may be plunged in the growing medium to bulk out the winter show.

These kinds of 'permanent' plants will be discussed in more detail later. For now, here are a few suggestions that are particularly useful for incorporating into the winter window garden, either for flower or ever-green foliage effect (see later comments and plant lists for details). *Erica carnea* and *E. × darleyensis* varieties (winter-flowering heathers); dwarf conifers (for added height, shape and foliage colour); ivies (plain-leaved and variegated); colourful-leaved sempervivums (houseleeks) and sedums (stonecrops); the shrubby

Euonymus fortunei 'Silver Queen' (creamy-white variegated leaves); and *Carex morrowii* 'Evergold' (a neat evergreen golden-leaved grass).

Bulbs and corms

Apart from these, however, much can be done to brighten up the winter window garden with a few small bulbs and perhaps some tough winter-flowering pansies. The bulbs—and the pansies, and also any of the temporary perennial plants for winter listed above—should be planted in autumn, of course, somewhat later than the autumn-flowering bulbs. Using pots and removable window box liners, they can follow on from the autumn bulbs. Growing direct in the box, they'll have to be planted amongst the autumn bulbs as these start to sprout and flower; and at this time more summer plants may be removed to create further free space.

The hardy *Cyclamen coum* is superb, often pushing up the first of its dainty, nodding ruby-red or carmine-pink blooms in time for Christmas or the New Year, and continuing in flower for months. The glossy green or silver-zoned leaves are also very pleasing to the eye.

Snowdrops look good with the winter-flowering cyclamen. *Galanthus elwesii* is a particularly large and early-flowering species (often double the size of the ordinary snowdrop); you'll find this in the better bulb catalogues, or sometimes in stores and markets offered as 'large single snowdrops'. *G. nivalis* (common snowdrop) is easily obtained from local stores, and mixing single-flowered bulbs with the doubles adds variety and creates a very attractive effect.

If you're going to plant snowdrops with *Cyclamen coum*, then complete the picture with the golden buttercup-flowered *Eranthis hyemalis* (winter aconite); all should flower together and make a real picture.

The dwarf bulbous irises are also marvellous for winter colour, and particularly for adding a touch of brilliant blue to the display. *Iris reticulata* in its various colour forms is the most popular choice. The bulbs sold in stores and markets are usually either the ordinary deep purple-blue, or mixed colours ranging from purple-red to pale blue. Better still, order named varieties from the better bulb catalogues, since bold clumps of the same colour always look better than the 'bitty' effect produced by a mixture. The varieties 'Harmony' and 'Joyce' are two of the best, both large-flowered deep sky-blues with contrasting orange and yellow crests to the falls; 'Cantab' is a delightful clear pale china-blue; 'Clairette' is an eye-catching bicolour, pale blue with darker blue falls; 'J.S. Dijt' is sweetly scented and a rich red-purple; and 'Violet Beauty' is a large-flowered deep violet-blue.

Striking as the *I. reticulata* varieties are, *I. histrioides* 'Major' is my all-time favourite. The flowers are larger and more robust than any of the above, standing up to winter weather well, and they're the clearest sky-blue imaginable. For contrast with all these blues, try the bright lemon-yellow *I. danfordiae*.

Some of the early-flowering dwarf rock garden narcissi are also excellent for a splash of yellow in the winter window box; try the golden *Narcissus bulbocodium* (hoop petticoat daffodil) which should flower around the same time as the cyclamen, irises, snowdrops, etc.

If you fancy some very early-flowering crocus, look out for the dainty lilac-blue species *Crocus laevigatus* 'Fontenayi' in specialist bulb catalogues; like the cyclamen, it starts doing its thing as early as Christmas and the New Year. The numerous varieties of *C. chrysanthus* start their display in late winter; 'Blue Pearl', 'Cream Beauty', 'E.A. Bowles' (butter-yellow) and 'Snowbunting' (white) are some of the best. These produce many flowers to a corm, so even a small clump makes an eye-catching show, and they continue in colour right through to spring.

Of course, there are many more dwarf bulbs ideal for the window garden, and some of these bloom from late winter to spring, while others join the larger bulbs in boosting the main spring display. Indeed, it's difficult to tell when late winter ends and spring begins where bulbs are concerned, but the rest of the dwarf rock garden type species and varieties will probably be better listed under spring flowers.

Fuchsias, petunias, pelargoniums and lobelias mingle in a froth of summer colour.

Boxes on high ledges, like hanging baskets, are mainly admired from below; so a predominance of colourful trailing plants, as here, is an excellent idea.

Pansy

To end the winter planting suggestions, that popular old bedding favourite, the pansy must be mentioned. Most strains and varieties bloom from spring onwards (and more on these later) but even more useful are the winter-flowering types. They can be raised from seed sown in spring or early summer, to be planted out when they start to bloom in late autumn, and they should continue right through the winter to spring. Usually they are sold as selected red, yellow, violet-blue and white seed strains, or mixed. Alternatively, buy ready-grown plants in autumn from stores or markets.

SPRING

This can be almost as colourful a season as summer, using a combination of bulbs chosen for a succession of flowers from one month to the next, plus a selection of early-flowering bedding plants (Fig 25 a).

Once again, as in the other seasons, growing plants and bulbs in removable liners or pots allows more flexibility. Displays of dwarf spring bulbs, daffodils and tulips may be grown on to replace the winter display; or set-pieces can be planned, like daffodils and primroses for early colour, followed by a show of later-flowering tulips.

Where pots or liners are not used, the larger spring bulbs will have to go into the window box with the dwarf winter-flowering bulbs in autumn, to provide a succession of colour from winter through to spring.

Ideally, the spring bedding plants (e.g. primroses and polyanthus) should also go into the box in autumn. However, you can always pick up a few of these from the market or store in spring, and pop them in for a quick boost to the display.

Bulbs

Virtually all spring bulbs are suitable for window gardens, but where daffodils and tulips are concerned, the smaller species and varieties are best; they stand up to

Fig. 25 a. Spring bulbs and bedding plants arranged into a classic window garden layout, using *Narcissus* 'February Gold', primroses and polyanthus, pansies, forget-me-not, *Narcissus* 'Baby Moon', crocus and *Tulipa praestans* 'Fusilier'.

wind and weather better, they're short enough for the smallest window display, and you can squeeze more of them in for a greater variety of colour and form.

Of the daffodils, I'd particularly recommend the shorter-growing *Narcissus cyclamineus*, *N. triandrus* and *N. jonquilla* hybrids. The following are especially good: 'February Gold', a shapely little trumpet, very early flowering and one of the best choices; 'Tete-a-Tete', with two dainty yellow trumpets to each stem; 'Jack Snipe', creamy-white with a primrose cup; the elegant triandrus hybrids 'Liberty Bells' and 'Silver Chimes' with their nodding, small-cupped blooms; the highly fragrant *N. jonquilla* (sweet jonquil) and *N. jonquilla* 'Baby Moon'. These are all between 20 and 30 cm tall (8 to 12 in).

As for tulips, the 'rock garden' species and dwarf hybrids are ideal; and my first choice for a truly stunning effect would be the multi-flowered *Tulipa prae-*

stans 'Fusilier'. This little beauty grows to just 23 cm (9 in) but produces a bunch of up to five bright scarlet blooms on each sturdy stem. The following are also excellent, none of them growing to more than 25 cm (10 in): *T. tarda,* white with a yellow centre; *T. kauf- manniana* varieties (waterlily tulips); and the *T. greigii* hybrids with their handsome maroon-red striped leaves.

Hyacinths have also long been popular spring win- dow box flowers, and there's a wide range of colour varieties to choose from these days, from bright pinks and reds, through lavender-blues and mauves to cream and white. They're particularly useful since they bloom over such a very long period.

Of the smaller spring bulbs, the chionodoxas (glory of the snow) and scillas (squills) are invaluable for a welcome touch of blue to offset the dominating yel- lows and reds of the daffodils and tulips. Spring wouldn't be spring without the crocus, of course. The large-flowered dutch crocus are very bold and bright, but I feel that the smaller species and varieties suit window gardens better. I've already mentioned the chrysanthus varieties as flowers for late winter, but they will continue well into spring. Look out also for *Crocus sieberi* 'Violet Queen'. *C. ancyrensis* ('Golden Bunch'), *C. biflorus* and *C. minimus* in the catalogues.

Other small bulbs suitable for the spring window garden include the blue, white, pink and red forms of *Anemone blanda,* the long-flowering violet-blue *Ipheion uniflorum,* and the blue and white muscaris (grape hyacinths).

Bedding plants

The most popular spring bedding plants, and deser- vedly so, are the primroses and polyanthus; marvell- ous for a bright splash of early colour, and the ideal foil to spring bulbs. They bloom over a very long period, helping to fill any gaps in the bulb display, and their lush, fresh foliage hides the bare stems of taller bulbs perfectly.

Although they're perennials, primroses and polyan- thus are seldom used as permanent plants in window

boxes, since the leaves are unexciting and often rather untidy once flowering is over. But they're wonderful as temporary plants, to be potted up or planted out in the garden for the summer, to be used again the follow- ing year. If they've made large clumps, they can be divided up after flowering or in the autumn; this both increases your stocks and keeps them growing and flowering strongly. You can raise them from seed sown in early spring to flower the following year, or buy ready-grown plants in autumn.

Pansies are also popular for spring colour. The winter-flowering types previously discussed will often continue flowering into spring, but you can also buy plants in autumn which have been raised specifi- cally for a spring display. You can raise these and the other popular spring bedding plants from seed your- self, sowing in late spring or early summer to flower the following year, but it's quicker and easier to buy them in ready-grown.

Other suitable spring bedding plants include double-flowered *Bellis* varieties (daisies), dwarf *Cheiranthus* (wallflowers) and *Myosotis alpestris* var- ieties (forget-me-not).

Naturally, to complete the seasonal window box calendar and come full circle, the spring bedding plants and bulbs must be removed to make way for the summer display. Winter and spring bulbs will still be growing at this time, so these must be either potted up or planted out in a corner of the garden, to finish their growth period before being dried out ready for replanting in autumn; don't dry out the bulbs until the foliage yellows and starts to die back.

SPECIAL EFFECTS

Colour schemes, as I said earlier, are mainly a matter for personal choice and imagination. But there are some classic designs that always look good and are worth mentioning with regard to seasonal planting schemes; particularly those for summer, where there's a wide choice of flower colours to play with.

Single-colour planting schemes can look very classy

A lovely traditional 'cottagey' mixture with lots of hot reds and warm pinks.

No ledge to this bay window, so the owner makes sensible use of the level window-roof instead.

indeed. For example, white flowers plus silver and grey foliage plants; such things as *Senecio maritimus* and *Helichrysum petiolatum* for silvery foliage, with white petunias, snow-white sweet peas and white sweet alyssum. All-yellow plantings are also very effective.

Alternatively, groupings of similar colour types work well: like the warm colours, yellows, oranges and red together, contrasted with dark green foliage plants; or cooler tints like blues, mauves, pale pinks and white, with silver and variegated foliage. Blues, whites and silvers always go well together, and grouping pale blue, pink and lilac pastel shades, with a touch of white, also produces a pleasing effect.

Having said all that, I do like a good old cottage-garden mixture of colours as much as any carefully devised scheme. Try both, for variety.

SEASONAL PLANTS
Summer

FOLIAGE PLANTS
Chlorophytum comosum 'Variegatum' (spider plant); tender perennial trailer; leaves striped white and green. (HB)
Coleus varieties; tender bushy perennials; leaves zoned in bright shades of red, pink, purple, green and yellow.
Ferns; both hardy outdoor types and tender pot-plant types may be used; good choice for very shady window boxes.
Hedera species and varieties (ivies); hardy perennial climbers and trailers; plain green, silver and gold variegated. (HB)
Helichrysum petiolatum; frost-tender perennial trailer; silver-grey. (HB)
Saxifraga stolonifera (mother of thousands); tender perennial trailer; silver-veined leaves. (HB)
Senecio maritimus; bushy half-hardy annual; deeply cut foliage, silvery-white. (HB)
Zebrina pendula (wandering Jew); tender perennial trailer; leaves striped cream and green. (HB)

FLOWERING TRAILERS
Alyssum maritimum (sweet alyssum); hardy annual; white or lilac flowers; 'Tiny Tim' and 'Snowcloth' are low, trailing white varieties.
Begonia×tuberhybrida 'Pendula'; tender tuberous-rooted perennial; 'Golden Shower', 'Red Cascade' and 'Pink Cascade' are good. (HB)
Fuchsia; tender perennial; usually red-and-purple or red-and-white; 'Cascade', 'Swingtime' and 'Marinka' are good trailing varieties. (HB)

Impatiens (busy Lizzie); tender perennial usually treated as half-hardy annual; pink, red, mauve and white; the 'Futura' varieties are the best trailers. (HB)
Lathyrus odoratus (sweet pea); hardy annual; although usually treated as a climber, will also make a good trailer. (HB)
Lobelia erinus 'Pendula' varieties; half-hardy annual; e.g. 'Red Cascade'. 'Sapphire' (deep blue) and 'Cascade Mixed' (red, blue, pink, lilac and white). (HB)
Pelargonium peltatum (pendulous geranium); tender perennial; ivy-shaped leaves, red, pink or mauve flowers; also variegated-leaved, white flowered variety 'L'Elegante'. (HB)
Petunia; half-hardy annual; pink, red, lilac, mauve, purple and white; choose trailing varieties like 'Blush Cascade' (pink) and 'Ruby Cascade'. (HB)
Thunbergia alata (black-eyed Susan); half-hardy annual; black eyed yellow or orange flowers; a climber that also looks good when allowed to trail. (HB)
Tropaeolum majus (nasturtium); hardy annual; yellow, orange or red; best trailing varieties include 'Golden Gleam', 'Orange Gleam' and 'Scarlet Gleam', all semi-double. (HB)

BUSHY FLOWERING PLANTS
Ageratum houstonianum (floss flower); half-hardy annual; fluffy blue, pink or white flower, 15–25 cm (6–10 in) according to variety.
Alyssum maritimum (sweet alyssum); hardy annual; white or lilac, 8–15 cm (3–6 in); both bushy and trailing varieties available. (HB)
Anchusa capensis 'Blue Angel'; hardy annual; blue flowers, 23 cm (9 in).

Antirrhinum majus (snapdragon); half-hardy annual; yellow, orange, red or pink, dwarf varieties 15–20 cm (6–9 in).

Begonia semperflorens (fibrous-rooted begonia); tender perennial, usually treated as half-hardy annual; red, pink or white, often with bronze-tinted foliage, 15–30 cm (6–12 in) according to variety. (HB)

Begonia×tuberhybrida (tuberous begonia); tender tuberous perennial; large double rose-like blooms, red, orange, yellow, pink and white, 25–45 cm (10–18 in). (HB)

Calceolaria (slipper flower); half-hardy annual; yellow, orange or red, 15–30 cm (6–12 in).

Dahlia (dwarf bedding varieties); tender tuberous perennials, usually treated as half-hardy annuals; single or double flowers, red, yellow, orange, pink or white, 30–60 cm (1–2 ft).

Dimorphotheca aurantiaca (star of the veldt); hardy annual; yellow, orange, pink and white daisy flowers, 30 cm (1 ft).

Eschscholzia (Californian poppy); hardy annual; orange, red and yellow poppy flowers, 15–30 cm (6–12 in).

Fuchsia; tender perennial; elegantly dangling red, white, red-and-purple or red-and-white flowers; height depends on training, generally 30–60 cm (1–2 ft). (HB)

Gazania; half-hardy annual; yellow, orange and red daisy-like flowers, 23–30 cm (9–12 in).

Godetia grandiflora; hardy annual; large funnel-flowers, crimson, pink, mauve and white, 23–38 cm (9–15 in).

Iberis umbellata (candytuft); hardy annual; fragrant white, pink or red flowers, 23–38 cm (9–15 in).

Impatiens (busy Lizzie); tender perennial usually treated as half-hardy annual; pink, red, mauve and white, 15–30 cm (6–12 in). (HB)

Limnanthes douglasii (poached egg flower); hardy annual; white blooms with egg-yolk-yellow centre, and ferny foliage, 15 cm (6 in).

Lobelia erinus; half-hardy annual; red, blue, pink, violet and white, 10–20 cm (4–8 in). (HB)

Malcolmia maritima (Virginia stock); hardy annual; strongly scented, white, mauve, pink and red, 15–20 cm (6–8 in).

Mesembryanthemum (Livingstone daisy); half-hardy annual; white, pink, red, orange and yellow daisy flowers, 10 cm (4 in).

Mimulus (monkey flower); half-hardy annual; red, orange and yellow trumpet-flowers, 15–30 cm (6–12 in). (HB)

Nemesia strumosa; half-hardy annual; red, cream and yellow, 23–30 cm (9–12 in).

Nemophila menziesii (baby blue eyes, Californian bluebell); white-centred sky-blue flowers, 15 cm (6 in).

Nicotiana alata (tobacco plant); half-hardy annual; various colours, 30–60 cm (1–2 ft).

Pelargonium (geranium); tender perennial; handsome leaves and red, pink, lilac or white flowers, 20–45 cm (8–18 in) according to variety. (HB)

Petunia; half-hardy annual; large funnel-shaped flowers (doubles and singles), red, pink, mauve, lilac, blue and white, 15–30 cm (6–12 in). (HB)

Phlox drummondii; half-hardy annual; many colours, 15–30 cm (6–12 in).

Salvia splendens; half-hardy annual; dark green leaves and large spikes of bright red flowers, 23–45 cm (9–18 in).

Tagetes (dwarf French marigolds); double and single yellow, orange and red marigold flowers, 15–30 cm (6–12 in).

Viola (pansy); various colours, 15–23 cm (6–9 in). (HB)

Zinnia; half-hardy annual; large daisy-like flowers, single or double, wide range of colours, 15–60 cm (6–24 in) according to variety.

CLIMBERS

Cobaea scandens (cathedral bells); half-hardy annual; large purple-blue bell flowers.

Eccremocarpus scaber (Chilean glory flower); half-hardy annual; orange tubular flowers.

Hedera (ivies); hardy perennials; see foliage plants.

Ipomoea (morning glory); half-hardy annual; 'Heavenly Blue' is the most popular variety, a deep sky-blue flower.

Lathyrus odoratus (sweet pea); popular hardy annual; needs no description from me, but look out for the strongly-scented 'old-fashioned' strains.

Thunbergia alata (black-eyed Susan); half-hardy annual; black-eyed orange, yellow or creamy-white flowers.

Tropaeolum majus (nasturtium); hardy annual; the climbing varieties are as easy to grow as the bushy trailing nasturtiums; red or yellow flowers.

BULBS, CORMS AND TUBERS

Anemone 'de Caen'; hardy tuber; single poppy flowers, red, pink, mauve, blue and white, 15–25 cm (6–10 in).

Anemone 'St. Brigid'; hardy tuber; double flowers, same colour range and height as above.

Freesia; tender corm; specially treated corms for outdoor summer flowering available from catalogues; normally sold as mixtures of yellow, red, violet and lilac-blue.

Gladioli; tender corm; short-growing types, like the 'Nanus' hybrids, white, pink and rose-red, up to 60 cm (2 ft).

Lilium (lilies); hardy bulbs; short-growing hybrids like 'Enchantment' (nasturtium-red) and 'Connecticut King' (yellow), 60–90 cm (2–3 ft).

Autumn

Colchicum (often incorrectly called autumn crocus); hardy corm; large lilac-pink, mauve-pink, rosy-purple and white goblet-shaped flowers (like giant crocus), 15–20 cm (6–8 in).

Crocus kotschyanus (*C. zonatus*); hardy corm; lilac-pink, 10 cm (4 in).

C. medius; hardy corm; violet flowers, 8 cm (3 in).

C. speciosus; hardy corm; large flowers in shades of lilac-blue, or white, 13 cm (5 in).

Cyclamen hederifolium (*C. neapolitanum*); hardy tuber; nodding pink or white flowers, 10 cm (4 in).

Nerine bowdenii; hardy bulb; heads of pink flowers, 30–45 cm (12–18 in).

Winter

EVERGREENS

Hedera (ivies); see 'Foliage plants' (Summer).

Erica carnea and *E.* × *darleyensis* varieties (winter heathers); *Sedum* and *Sempervivum*; *Euonymus fortunei* varieties; and *Carex morrowii* 'Evergold'; see 'Plants for Permanent Display' for details.

BULBS, CORMS AND TUBERS

Crocus chrysanthus varieties; hardy corm; yellow, cream, blue and white, 8 cm (3 in).

C. laevigatus 'Fontenayi'; hardy corm; lilac-blue, 8 cm (3 in).

Cyclamen coum; hardy tuber; nodding ruby-red or rose-pink flowers, 8 cm (3 in).

Eranthis hyemalis (winter aconite); hardy tuber; yellow buttercup flowers, 10 cm (4 in).

Galanthus nivalis (snowdrop); hardy bulb; single and double flowered forms, 13 cm (5 in).

G. elwesii (Turkish snowdrop); hardy bulb; large flowered species, 15–20 cm (6–8 in).

Iris danfordiae; hardy bulb; lemon-yellow, 8 cm (3 in).

I. histrioides 'Major'; hardy bulb; sky-blue, large flowers, 10 cm (4 in).

I. reticulata varieties; hardy bulb; blue, violet and purple-red, 13 cm (5 in).

Narcissus bulbocodium (hoop petticoat daffodil); hardy bulb; golden-yellow, 10 cm (4 in).

BUSHY PLANTS

Viola (winter-flowering pansy strains); hardy annual; various colours, 10–15 cm (4–6 in).

Spring

BULBS, CORMS AND TUBERS

Anemone blanda; hardy tuber; blue, pink, red and white, 10 cm (4 in).

Chionodoxa (glory of the snow); hardy bulb; blue flowers, 13 cm (5 in).

Crocus; hardy corm; various kinds, including *C. sieberi* 'Violet Queen' and *C. minimus* (violet-blue).

Hyacinthus (hyacinth); hardy bulb; rose-red, pink, lavender-blue, mauve and white, 20–30 cm (8–12 in).

Ipheon uniflorum; hardy bulb; violet-blue, 15 cm (6 in).

Muscari (grape hyacinth); hardy bulb; blue, 15 cm (6 in).

Narcissus (daffodil); hardy bulb; short-growing cyclamineus, triandrus and jonquilla hybrids, 15–30 cm (6–12 in).

Tulipa; hardy bulb; rock garden species and dwarf kaufmanniana and greigii hybrids, 10–20 cm (4–8 in).

BEDDING PLANTS

Bellis perennis (daisy); hardy perennial; double and single varieties, white, pink and red, 8–15 cm (3–6 in).

Cheiranthus (wallflower); various colours, dwarf varieties 15–30 cm (6–12 in).

Myosotis alpestris (forget-me-not); hardy biennial; blue flowers, 15–30 cm (6–12 in).

Primula (primrose and polyanthus); hardy perennials; various colours, 10–25 cm (4–10 in).

Viola (pansy); various colours, 10–15 cm (4–6 in).

Masses of trailing plants here, for a luxuriant 'jungly' effect: silver-leaved *Helichrysum petiolatum,* lobelias, ivy-leaved *Pelargonium peltatum,* and the trailing red-and-white fuchsia 'Cascade'.

14

PERMANENT PLANTING SCHEMES

Some 'permanent' perennial plants may be used in temporary seasonal planting displays; particularly foliage plants like the ivies. However, the major role for these types of plants is in creating window gardens for a year-round effect without the bother of seasonal replanting. With this kind of display, the only work involved is watering, plus occasional weeding and feeding; with perhaps some periodic cutting-back of any plants that grow too large and threaten to swamp their neighbours.

The main aim with a permanent planting scheme should be to use evergreens for year-round interest; preferably with as wide a variety of leaf shape, growth habit and foliage colour as possible. At the same time, try to include plants to flower in every season, even if you can only squeeze in one for each season. See Fig. 26 for an example of a permanent planting scheme for year-round interest.

All the general design points about aiming for variety of height, growth habit etc, apply particularly to permanent plants. Make a mess of a seasonal planting scheme, and you'll only have to put up with it for a few months before it's due to be replanted anyway; but changing what was intended to be a permanent display requires a conscious effort–an effort that you may not feel like making once planting is complete.

Fig. 26. A permanent window box planted for year-round interest and colour. From *left to right*: variegated ivy trained up canes or trellis, *Armeria maritima*, trailing aubrieta, *Dianthus deltoides*, winter heather (*Erica carnea* var.*)*, *Euonymus fortunei* 'Silver Queen', and trailing *Polygonum vacciniifolium*.

EVERGREENS

Since evergreen foliage plants form the 'backbone' of the permanent window display, let's look at these first.

Ivy

The ivies, *Hedera* species and varieties, really are the most useful; tough, easy and fast growing; suitable for use both as climbers and trailers, either in sun or shade;

and available in a wide range of leaf shape and colour. Being self-attaching, ivies grown as climbers may be planted to cling to the wall beside and around the window. However, most can get very large in time, and it's easier to keep them trimmed and under control if they're growing up canes or a section of trellis (tied in to the support).

You should find a good selection of different types amongst the house-plants on sale in local stores and markets. These can be grown outside, but they should only be planted in late spring or early summer when there's no danger of frost, to give them a chance to get used to outdoor life. The ivies sold as house-plants are the same as the ones sold for the garden; it's just that those kept under cover will have grown soft and therefore need time to adapt and toughen up. Better still, buy ivies that have been grown outdoors specifically for garden use.

Before looking at different types of ivies for foliage interest, this is a good place to refer you back once again to my suggestions in the planning and design chapter about mixing climbers and trailers. Planting two different ivies with contrasting leaves to either twine up one another as climbers or to intertwine as they trail out of the box really can look very good.

In the average window box, small-leaved ivies are most in keeping with the scale of the planting scheme. *Hedera helix* (common ivy) is excellent, offering many varieties with neat foliage; notably 'Adam' (green, edged with white). 'Chicago' (green) and 'Chicago Variegata' (green and cream). 'Bird's Foot' (handsome deeply divided leaves), and 'Silver Queen' (green and silver).

H. helix 'Goldheart' is one of the best yellow-variegated ones, each leaf having a bold central gold zone. Some change colour in winter, like 'Shamrock' and 'Deltoidea' which both become tinged with copper or bronze during the cold months. 'Buttercup' is notable for its bright yellow new leaves, turning pale green as they age. And there are also some dwarf varieties which make tiny bushes, like the cream-mottled 'Little Diamond'.

For variety, however, and especially in spacious window boxes, large-leaved ivies can make an attractive change. The largest of all are the forms of *Hedera canariensis* (Canary Island ivy) and *H. colchica* (Persian ivy); both are available as plain-leaved and variegated plants. 'Hibernica' is a good large-leaved form of the common ivy.

Conifers

Dwarf conifers are superb for adding height to a permanent planting scheme, offering a variety of shape and foliage tints rivalled by few other evergreens. Be sure to choose truly dwarf types, otherwise they'll quickly outgrow the window box. Even some of the slow-growing ones can get quite large after a few years and may have to be removed to the garden, to be replaced with younger specimens.

One of the loveliest is *Juniperus communis* 'Compressa', a tiny spire-shaped juniper which will never outgrow the smallest of window boxes. It puts on no more than 1 cm ($\frac{1}{2}$ in) of growth a year and looks marvellous with low-growing plants and trailers, like the neater rock plants (of which, more later).

Slow-growing forms of *Chamaecyparis lawsoniana* (Lawson's cypress) make similar spire-shaped trees but are much faster growing: the varieties 'Ellwoodii' and 'Ellwood's Gold' will be all right in a decent-sized window box for a few years but will eventually become too large and need to be replaced.

The same comments apply to the prostrate mat-forming conifers. One of these would look good trailing down from a corner of the window garden.

Another of my favourites is the conical Christmas tree-shaped *Picea glauca* 'Albertiana Conica'. This is quite slow-growing, a bright fresh green in colour. Of the more rounded and bushy types, look out for the following: the yellow-tinted *Chamaecyparis lawsoniana* 'Minima Aurea'; the bright blue-grey *Juniperus squamata* 'Blue Star'; *Thuya orientalis* 'Aurea Nana' (green, tipped with yellow); *Abies balsamea* 'Hudsonia' (dark green), and *Cryptomeria japonica* 'Vilmoriniana', a tight bun of tiny foliage which turns bronze in winter (a real little beauty).

Raised planting troughs brighten a city street: if only more businesses and stores would take the trouble to enliven our dusty towns with flowers and greenery.

Shrubs

Dwarf box trees are also good; clipped to shape, they make an interesting alternative to dwarf conifers and will never grow too large. Try the dwarf hedging box, *Buxus sempervirens* 'Suffruticosa' or the even neater *B. microphylla*.

As for dwarf evergreen shrubs for foliage colour, the small variegated forms of *Euonymus fortunei* are good; particularly the very neat 'Silver Queen', its green leaves edged with bright cream white. 'Emerald and Gold' is still more colourful, tinted pale green, gold and pink. They benefit from spring trimming, to encourage production of new shoots, these showing better colour than old growth.

Heathers

Heathers are marvellous in window boxes, especially the neat-growing winter-flowering types, and their foliage looks good all year round. However, most valuable as far as foliage is concerned are those with golden leaves, like the *Erica carnea* varieties 'Aurea' and 'Foxhollow' (winter and spring flowers); *E.* × *darleyensis* 'Jack Brummage' (winter-flowering); the *Calluna vulgaris* varieties 'Golden Carpet' and 'Gold Haze' (summer-flowering); and *Erica cinerea* 'Golden Drop' (usually non-flowering, but a fantastic foliage plant).

There are also varieties with silvery grey foliage; *Calluna vulgaris* 'Silver Rose' and 'Silver Queen', for example. But the range of leaf tints is so wide that you could create an attractive planting scheme using heathers alone; there are all shades of dark greens, pale greens and rich bronze-greens.

The heathers look perfect with dwarf conifers, and you could do a lot worse than stock a window box purely with these two kinds of plant, for a variety of foliage tints all year, plus summer, winter and spring flowers from the different types of heathers.

Remember that the summer-flowering heathers generally need lime-free soil. If you're planting these, be sure to use a lime-free growing compost of the type used for potting rhododendrons and azaleas. The winter-flowering *Erica carnea* and *E.* × *darleyensis* varieties aren't fussy, and any growing compost will do.

Rock plants

Various other small plants, mainly rock plants, provide evergreen foliage of varying hues. Best of all are the succulent sedums (stonecrops) and sempervivums (houseleeks). These are also useful for their summer flowers, but the main attractions are the grey, red, purple and pink tinted leaves. The *Sedum spathulifolium* varieties are some of the best, like the purple-leaved and golden-flowered 'Purpureum', or the grey rosettes and yellow summer flowers of 'Capablanca'. *Sempervivum arachnoideum* 'Laggeri' is one of the most striking houseleeks, its rosettes covered cobweb-fashion with silvery hairs; and there are numerous others with brightly-coloured fleshy cactus-like rosettes. All are best in a sunny window garden, planted to trail over the front of the box.

Grasses

Dwarf evergreen ornamental grasses can play a part in the year-round window garden as well. I've already mentioned the golden-striped *Carex morrowii* 'Evergold' as something to bulk out the seasonal winter display; but it's just as much at home in a permanent planting scheme. *Festuca glauca* is a bright silvery blue grass which makes small evergreen tufts and looks perfect with heathers; *F. scoparia* is similar, but a beautiful bottle-green.

Ferns

There are one or two hardy evergreen ferns which would be ideal for a window garden in a shady situation; notably, *Polypodium vulgare* (common polypody), especially the dwarf forms; the tiny *Asplenium trichomanes* (maidenhair spleenwort), and the various forms of *Phyllitis scolopendrium* (hart's tongue fern) some of which have wonderful crimped edges to the evergreen fronds.

Now for a selection of neat flowering plants and dwarf shrubs: these are arranged according to flowering times, to simplify the choice of plants for colour in different seasons. Virtually all are evergreens with attractive foliage.

SPRING

We're spoiled for choice here, since there are so many neat spring-flowering rock plants that can be used in the window garden, including some excellent trailing plants.

Most popular and colourful are the aubrietas (commonly known, and often mis-spelled, as aubretias). These are spreading, mat-forming plants, easy to grow, ideal for tumbling over the front of a window box, and a solid mass of long-lasting brilliant colour. Mixed seedlings are frequently offered, and you can raise your own from seed; but these are usually disappointing compared with the clear colours of the named red, pink, mauve, blue and purple varieties. Trim them back hard after flowering, to keep them neat and bushy.

Another superb and easily-grown trailer is *Alyssum saxatile*; bright yellow flowers throughout spring, over grey-green foliage. Good varieties include the double-flowered 'Flore Pleno' (a very compact plant) and the silvery leaved, pale primrose yellow flowered 'Citrinum' (also sold as 'Silver Queen'). Cut them back after flowering.

White rock cress, *Arabis caucasica* (also sold as *A. albida*) is another strong grower that's best trimmed hard after flowering; there are white flowers from late winter to early summer.

The stronger-growing rock garden phlox are also ideal, making trailing mats that bloom from late spring to early summer in a range of colours from rose-red, through pink, mauve and lilac to pure white. The strongest growers are the varieties of *Phlox subulata*, like 'Red Wings' (crimson), 'Alexander's Surprise' (deep pink), 'Oakington Blue Eyes' (lilac-blue) and 'White Delight'. Neater and suitable for small window boxes are the pink, mauve and white forms of *P. douglasii*.

Other low-growing plants for spring include the bushy white-flowered *Iberis sempervirens* (perennial candytuft), a tough thing that always does well even in heavily polluted city air; the best variety is the compact-growing 'Little Gem'; *Armeria caespitosa* (dwarf thrift) with pink flowers, and *Primula auricula* varieties (show auriculas).

Small spring-flowering evergreen shrubs suitable for window gardens include the tiniest dwarf rhododendrons and dwarf evergreen azaleas. It's well worth trying these, although they may eventually grow too large for smaller window boxes and, like the conifers, need to be replaced after a few years. They cope well with city air pollution but are best where they're not too exposed to strong winds.

You could also try the tiny, slow-growing evergreen *Berberis stenophylla* 'Corallina Compacta' for its handsome dark green foliage and orange spring flowers; or that very classy dwarf alpine shrub *Daphne retusa*, for its sweetly scented flowers, white tinged with rosy violet.

Dwarf spring bulbs may be used to add extra colour to the spring display; simply push a few bulbs of crocus, snowdrop, *Scilla*, *Chionodoxa*, dwarf *Narcissus*, *Iris reticulata*, or whatever, into the growing compost between the plants, or around the edges of the box, in autumn. Carefully scoop them out and dry them off for the summer when the leaves start to die down, taking care not to disturb the plant roots too much.

SUMMER

Dianthus (perennial garden pinks and carnations) are a good choice for summer. Their tight hummocks of grey-green leaves look attractive all year round, especially when contrasted with darker foliage. Modern garden pinks tend to flower over a longer period than the older hybrids, often all summer long; and many are deliciously fragrant. Try both single and double flowered varieties. Some of the stronger rock garden species are also useful, and I'd recommend *Dianthus deltoides* (maiden pink) as a plant to spread and trail over the front of the window box; deep green foliage and small red or deep pink flowers endlessly throughout summer.

Rock garden campanulas are wonderful as trailing plants, cascading their bright blue flowers out of the box. The strongest-growing ones, like *Campanula porscharskyana* and *C. portenschlagiana* will take over the window garden and swamp everything else. Neater ones like *C. garganica*, 'W. H. Paine', and small forms of *C. carpatica* like 'Turbinata' are fine.

Rock garden achilleas are good both for their yellow flowers and their finely-cut grey leaves; try *Achillea tomentosa* and any others that you can find. Some of the alpine saxifrages also have handsome silvery grey foliage, particularly the 'encrusted' types with their lovely leaf rosettes and delicate summer flower plumes.

Armeria maritima (sea thrift) is a nice low, bushy plant with spiky foliage, larger than the dwarf thrift of spring, and in flower for a couple of months. 'Vindictive' is a good rose-pink variety, and for a change there's the white-flowered 'Alba'; both go well with dianthus.

For aromatic evergreen foliage and summer flowers, try the varieties of the common thyme, *Thymus drucei* (previously *T. serpyllum*). There are various named forms, mostly pink or red in flower.

Veronica prostrata (rockery speedwell) in its many named varieties is another favourite strong-growing rock plant that's at home trailing over the edge of a window box; it flowers in early summer, generally blue, but there are pink and white forms as well. This is a vigorous spreader and may need regular trimming back after flowering. The same goes for the popular *Helianthemum* (rock rose). It's an excellent trailing spreader with single yellow, pink, red or white rose-like flowers over a long period; and it's a fast grower which will soon fill out the display, but trim it hard after flowering.

In a lime-free growing compost you could try the stunning sky-blue flowered *Lithospermum diffusum*, a low spreading shrubby plant with true gentian-blue flowers. The varieties usually grown are 'Grace Ward' and 'Heavenly Blue'.

Perfect companions for the blue *Lithospermum* are the golden-flowered dwarf shrubby hypericums. The species *Hypericum olympicum*, *H. polyphyllum* and *H. reptans* all produce their large yellow blooms from mid-summer to autumn. Also good for a splash of yellow is the low-growing *Oenothera missouriensis* (evening primrose). This, too blooms right through to autumn, with huge canary-yellow flowers. And don't forget the summer-flowering heathers; most bloom for months, continuing into autumn.

AUTUMN

Since there are few small perennials which flower in autumn, the crocus mentioned earlier under seasonal plants for autumn can be used for extra colour at this time of year (*Crocus speciosus*, *C. kotschyanus* and *C. medius*). Use them as suggested for spring bulbs amongst perennials; pop them in between the permanent plants in late summer, and lift them when they start to die down in late spring or early summer.

Of the neat-growing plants that do bloom at this time, the gentians are noteworthy. *Gentiana septemfida* is an easy one to grow, flowering from late summer into autumn, its blue trumpets carried at the ends of long trailing stems. Rather less easy are the Himalayan autumn gentians. These are some of the loveliest of all, but they need lime-free growing compost and plenty of summer moisture, and they're seldom long-lived. However, the brilliant sky-blue *G. sino-ornata* is the most reliable and well worth trying in a window garden that isn't too hot and sunny (a good companion for ferns, ivies and such-like in a shady window box).

By way of contrast, the low-spreading shrubby *Polygonum vacciniifolium* couldn't be easier to grow, and it will quickly spill over the edge of a window box in a curtain of glossy evergreen leaves. Spikes of rose-red flowers appear from late summer well into the autumn.

Wide windows, as here, may take two boxes side by side. Note the conifers: dwarf varieties are fine in a window garden for a few years, although most will eventually grow too large and need to be replaced.

Plenty of permanent evergreen foliage interest in this window box: slow-growing conifers and variegated ivies, with one or two temporary bedding plants popped in for summer colour.

A dwarf hardy fuchsia like 'Tom Thumb' or 'Lady Thumb' would also provide late colour well into autumn (as well as flowering freely during late summer), but these small fuchsias are only evergreen in very mild, fairly frost-free regions. In areas subject to severe winter cold they may be killed when grown in a box (although they're reasonably hardy if grown in the garden, the roots will be more exposed to frosts in a box).

One of the neater ground-hugging evergreen cotoneasters might be tried in a large window box, for bright red autumn berries, but would probably need regular clipping back. *Cotoneaster congestus,* the slowest and neatest grower, would be the best bet. Alternatively, in lime-free growing compost, *Vaccinium oxycoccos* (the cranberry) and *V. vitis-idaea* (cowberry or mountain cranberry) could be tried for their attractive red fruits and evergreen foliage.

WINTER

Here again, the permanent display can be given a boost by popping in a few winter-flowering dwarf bulbs in autumn; those types mentioned under seasonal plants for winter are suitable.

Apart from these, we have to rely heavily on attractive evergreen foliage (and especially variegated leaves) plus the bright flowers of the winter heathers, the *Erica carnea* and *E. × darleyensis* varieties. Luckily, these winter heathers bloom over an exceptionally long period, often from late autumn or early winter right through to spring; so you don't need many for a good show, and even one will provide colour for months.

Fig. 27. A 'rock garden' window box. Use only one of the very slowest-growing dwarf conifers, such as *Juniperus communis* 'Compressa' shown here. Other plants depicted *(left to right)*: *Phlox* 'Douglasii', *Armeria caespitosa, Saxifraga burserana, Gentiana verna, Saxifraga cochlearis* and *Dianthus alpinus.*

My favourite–apart from the golden-leaved ones already mentioned–is *E. carnea* 'Vivellii', a slow-growing variety with dark bronze and green foliage, and ruby-red flowers. 'Springwood Pink' and 'Springwood White' are excellent, and the pink-flowered 'Darley Dale' and 'Arthur Johnson' are particularly long-flowering, often providing colour from late autumn to winter's end.

THE ROCK GARDEN WINDOW BOX

From these plants lists, it's obvious that rock plants are ideal for window gardens, being low-growing and usually fairly compact. Indeed, it's quite possible to create a complete miniature rock garden, using a dwarf conifer or two and a selection of the neatest rock plants (Fig. 27).

In this case, you needn't be restricted to just the strong-growing rock plants. Most of those suggested so far have been tough, easy things which should thrive even when neglected, but should you make a

hobby of rock plants, and are prepared to give them what they need – most importantly, very well-drained gritty growing compost – then you can check out the specialist growers' catalogues and try some of the smaller species and varieties.

A very important point to remember, however, is that the smaller rock plants hate being constantly dripped on during winter. If rain tends to drip heavily onto the window box, tuck your smallest rock plants towards the back, close to the window and away from the drips, or, better still, if you possibly can, choose a window ledge sheltered from prevailing winds and heavy rains.

Of these smaller rock plants, I'd strongly recommend the 'kabschia' saxifrages, the *Saxifraga burserana* forms for example. All make tight little mats or buns of silvery or grey-green foliage studded with almost stemless ruby-red, pink, white or yellow flowers during late winter and early spring. *S. oppositifolia* is similar, but a lovely trailing plant with purple-red or deep pink flowers.

The dainty alpine primulas, too, would look good brightening up a rock garden window box in spring. The lilac-blue forms of *Primula marginata* are superb with their silvery, toothed leaves, and there are some charming little forms of *P. auricula*, the wild parent of the florist's auricula.

Should you concentrate on lots of neat rock plants instead of a few large ones, you could also try the stunning sky-blue spring gentian, *Gentiana verna*, some of the more refined rock garden pinks, like *Dianthus alpinus*, and the dwarf summer-flowering geraniums. Add a rock and one of the tiniest dwarf conifers (e.g. *Juniperus communis* 'Compressa') to complete the picture, plus a top-dressing of grit or fine gravel, and there's your rock garden.

PLANTS FOR PERMANENT DISPLAYS

Evergreen foliage plants

Asplenium trichomanes; evergreen fern, 8–15 cm (3–6 in).

Carex morrowii 'Evergold'; golden-leaved evergreen grass, 30 cm (1 ft).

Conifers; all slow-growing dwarf varieties are suitable; see 'Permanent planting schemes' chapter for suggestions.

Euonymus fortunei; silver, gold and pink variegated forms, 20–30 cm (8–12 in).

Heathers; golden and silvery foliage varieties of *Erica carnea*, *E × darleyensis* and *Calluna vulgaris*, 15–30 cm (6–12 in).

Festuca; evergreen grasses; *F. glauca* (silver-blue) and *F. scoparia* (green), 15–20 cm (6–8 in).

Hedera (ivies); as climbers and trailers, green-leaved or silver and golden variegated.

Phyllitis scolopendrium; evergreen fern, 20–30 cm (8–12 in).

Polypodium vulgare; evergreen fern, 30 cm (1 ft).

Sedum (stonecrop); many varieties with colourful leaf tints, 5–8 cm (2–3 in).

Sempervivum (houseleek); most have colourful leaf rosettes, 5–8 cm (2–3 in).

Spring flowers

TOUGH ROCK PLANTS AND DWARF SHRUBS

Alyssum saxatile; trailer, grey-green leaves and yellow flowers, 15–20 cm (6–8 in).

Arabis caucasica (*A. albida*, rock cress); trailer, white, 15 cm (6 in).

Armeria caespitosa (alpine thrift); cushion plant, pink flowers, 10 cm (4 in).

Aubrieta (aubretias); trailer; red, pink, mauve, blue, 10–20 cm (4–8 in).

Azalea; dwarf evergreen varieties are suitable; must have lime-free compost.

Berberis stenophylla 'Corallina Compacta'; dwarf evergreen shrub, orange flowers, eventually 45 cm (18 in) but slow growing.

Daphne retusa; dwarf evergreen shrub, fragrant mauve-white flowers, eventually 60 cm (2 ft) but very slow.

Iberis sempervirens (candytuft); bushy, white flowers, 15–20 cm (6–8 in).

Phlox (alpine phlox); trailer; red, pink, mauve, lilac and white varieties of *P. subulata* and *P. douglasii*, 10–20 cm (4–8 in).

Rhododendron; the tiniest dwarf species and varieties are suitable; lime-free compost essential.

Summer flowers

TOUGH ROCK PLANTS

Achillea; trailers, mostly yellow flowers and silver-grey leaves, 13 cm (5 in).

Armeria maritima (sea thrift); cushion plant, red, pink or white flowers, 15 cm (6 in).

Calluna vulgaris; summer-flowering heathers, purple-red, pink and white, 15–30 cm (6–12 in).

Campanula (bell flower); trailers, blue or white flowers, 10–20 cm (4–8 in).

Dianthus (pinks); cushion plants; alpine species and modern border 'pinks', pink or white flowers, 10–25 cm (4–10 in) according to variety.

Helianthemum (rock rose); trailers; yellow, orange, red, pink and white, 15 cm (6 in).

Hypericum; dwarf shrubby alpine species are suitable, yellow flowers, 10–20 cm (4–8 in).

Lithospermum diffusum; shrubby trailer, blue flowers, 15 cm (6 in).

Oenothera missouriensis (evening primrose); trailer, huge yellow flowers, 20 cm (8 in).

Thymus drucei (*T. serpyllum*, thyme); aromatic trailer, pink or red flowers, 5 cm (2 in).

Veronica prostrata (speedwell); trailer, blue, 10 cm (4 in).

Autumn

ROCK PLANTS

Gentiana septemfida; trailer, blue flowers, 13 cm (5 in).

G. sino-ornata; trailer, blue flowers, 13 cm (5 in); lime-free compost essential.

Polygonum vacciniifolium; trailer, pink flowers, 16 cm (6 in).

See also autumn bulbs under 'Seasonal plants'.

Winter

Erica carnea (winter heather); crimson, pink and white (some with golden foliage), 15–25 cm (6–10 in).

E. × *darleyensis* (winter heather); as above.

See also winter-flowering bulbs under 'Seasonal plants'.

Specialist rock garden window box

Dianthus alpinus (alpine pink); rose-red summer flowers, 8 cm (3 in).

Gentiana verna (spring gentian); sky-blue flowers, 8 cm (3 in).

Juniperus communis 'Compressa'; one of the tiniest and loveliest dwarf conifers, spire-shaped 60 cm (2 ft) maximum after many years.

Primula auricula; yellow spring flowers, 10–15 cm (4–6 in).

P. marginata; lilac-blue, spring, 10 cm (4 in).

Saxifraga; cushion-forming 'kabschia' types (e.g. *S. burserana*), spring; and rosette-forming 'encrusted' types, summer; 8 cm (3 in).

Fruit, vegetables and herb suggestions

Note: no sizes are given for herbs, since these will be kept small and bushy by nipping off shoots for kitchen use:

Strawberries (especially alpine varieties); dwarf bush tomatoes, lettuce, radish and spring onions; basil, bay (eventually makes large shrub, but suitable for a while), chervil, chives, garlic, marjoram, mint, parsley, rosemary, sage, thyme.

An exotically-planted urn lends a Mediterranean atmosphere to a town centre frontage where there's only limited space available for a window box display.

15

FRUIT, VEGETABLES AND HERBS

This short chapter will probably be of most interest to those who live in apartments. Where there's no garden to grow fresh fruit and vegetables, and not even a balcony or yard where tubs and pots may be stood, the window box can provide at least one or two vitamin-rich home-grown delicacies for the kitchen.

Office workers might also like to consider planting a box at work with some colourful dwarf tomatoes or some herbs, to liven up those lunch-time sandwiches and add a little extra interest to the working day. A box filled with a selection of culinary herbs outside any kitchen window would be a handy thing from the point of view of a busy cook; simply reach out, snip, and you've a handful of chives or a fresh sprig of parsley to garnish that dish.

Apart from herbs, the best food plants for window gardens include compact-growing things like dwarf bush tomatoes, strawberries (especially the tiny alpine strawberries), and fast-growing small salad vegetables like radish, spring onions and lettuce.

A whole window box may be devoted to these culinary plants, outside the kitchen window for example; either a selection of herbs, a few mixed salad vegetables, a few strawberries, or even a mix of all three in a large box.

Alternatively, if you're in an apartment with only one or two window gardens, then some of these could actually be grown amongst the flowering plants. None of them are ugly, the herbs, dwarf tomatoes and strawberries in particular being quite attractive. If you don't want them to be too obvious from the street, keep them towards the back of the box; in fact, a row of bush tomatoes with their bright red fruits would make a rather fine backing to a flowering display.

Remember, though, that if they're squeezed into a box with lots of flowering plants, or if they're grown crowded together in a box of their own, then they'll need very regular watering; probably every day in hot weather, and sometimes twice a day. And they'll also need feeding from time to time with liquid fertilizer, especially the fast-growing salad crops.

VEGETABLES

Dwarf bush tomatoes are particularly suited to window-box culture, the fruits ripening well in the warmth reflected from the walls and bathed in reflected sunlight from the window.

There are some excellent very dwarf varieties around now, producing small bite-size tomatoes that are often tastier than larger fruits. You can grow them in pots and slip them into the window box amongst flowering pot plants, but they're better actually planted in a box filled with growing compost. All are easily raised from seed sown on a windowsill indoors in late winter or early spring, and planted out in late spring or early summer when there's no danger of frosts or cold nights to stunt the growth. These tiny tomatoes should need no support under normal conditions, but on a very windy ledge they might be safer tied in to short sticks. Remember to keep them well watered, never allowing them to dry out completely, and feed regularly with liquid fertilizer (special tomato fertilizer is best, but any liquid feed will do).

Radish, lettuce and spring onions may be sown in

the box any time from spring to early summer for summer cropping; the earlier the sowing, the earlier you'll get your salad. All should be kept well watered and fed with liquid fertilizer once a week.

The thinly upright-growing cos lettuce varieties like 'Little Gem' and 'Paris White' are the best space-savers for a window box; or try one of the dwarf butterhead varieties like 'Tom Thumb' which are fast-maturing and produce neat tennis-ball size heads. Better still, grow a loose-leaf variety such as 'Salad Bowl' which produces a mass of curly leaves that can be picked a few at a time without pulling the whole plant; 'Red Salad Bowl' is a novel reddish-brown leaved variety of the same sort that makes an interesting addition to salads.

FRUIT

Of fruits, the only one really suitable for window boxes is the strawberry; and plants grown with their runners trailing over the edge of the box (and cropping on these trailing runners) can look very attractive.

Pot-grown runners may be bought and planted in autumn, to fruit the following summer, but in areas subject to severe winter weather, it's safer to put in young plants in spring, although these won't crop properly until the following year. In regions with extremely low winter temperatures, strawberries are not such a good choice.

Better even than the ordinary garden strawberry are the 'Alpine' varieties like 'Alexandria'. 'Baron Solemacher' and the golden-fruited 'Yellow Alpine'. These produce small but delicious fruits (perfect for garnishing fruit cocktail and ice cream) which are carried above the plants on elegantly arching wiry stems. They crop all summer long, so there are always a few tasty fruits to pick, and birds don't seem to like them as much as larger varieties, which is an added bonus. The

Fig. 28. A window box Herb garden. Left to right: young bay tree, rosemary *(foreground)*, parsley, chives, thyme, *(foreground)* and mint.

plants make tidy clumps without runners, and they can be left in the box and cropped year after year. Water and feed frequently in the growing season.

HERBS

Evergreen herbs are very good in a window box, looking attractive and providing garnishes and ingredients for the kitchen all year round (Fig. 28). One of the most popular is thyme, a low-growing twiggy bush with dark evergreen leaves and pretty mauve-pink summer flowers. Common thyme (*Thymus vulgaris*) is the strongest-flavoured. Lemon thyme (*T. x citriodorus*) is milder with a citrus flavour that makes it good for adding to sweet dishes. There are handsome golden-leaved forms of both, excellent for variety of leaf colour and equally useful in the kitchen.

Rosemary is also evergreen and an attractive little shrubby plant with needle-shaped leaves and blue flowers. Regular picking or clipping of the upper shoots will keep it low and tidy, but it will still grow to over 30 cm (1 ft) so place it to one side of the window box.

Chervil is another tallish evergreen best to one side of the window box, but it can easily be kept to under 30 cm (1 ft) by nipping off the upper leaves regularly. The foliage is very attractive, a fresh green, deeply cut and fern-like.

Parsley will grow throughout the year, but it's best to cut it down in early autumn, to make it produce fresh new leaves for winter, as the old growth becomes tough late in the year; once again, very decorative foliage.

The sweet bay (so good in stews and casseroles) is normally grown as a shrub or small tree, often in a tub sheltered against a sunny wall, but it's fairly slow growing, and a young bush may be grown in a deep window box for some time before it gets too big; regular picking of the leaves and pruning of the shoots will help to keep it small. In severe winters it may be damaged by frost but will often grow away again from the base in spring.

Other herbs to try include chives, marjoram, sage, savory, tarragon, basil and mint. Those that are not evergreen can of course be dried or frozen for winter use. Don't forget about garlic; simply buy a head of garlic from the market, split it up, plant the cloves in early spring and lift fresh juicy bulbs in summer.

These herbs may be planted in a window box filled with growing compost, or they may be grown in pots sitting inside a box, perhaps amongst flowering pot plants. Having them in pots does make it easy to lift them in through the window for picking; and pots of non-evergreen herbs may then be brought inside the window in autumn, to keep them growing into winter for a longer supply of fresh leaves. However, it's not much more trouble to lean out and snip leaves from a herb garden actually growing in a box, and with plenty of evergreens, it'll look good all year.

The exception is mint, which is so strong growing and fast-spreading by underground stems that it will quickly take over the window garden. This should always be grown in a pot. If the rest of herbs are permanent plantings in a box full of compost, then the mint pot may be plunged amongst them, but it should be lifted regularly to remove any underground runners that escape from the pot.

Most herbs may be quickly raised from seed, but it's generally simpler to buy ready-grown plants. Some are annuals (like basil) which must be raised afresh from seed each year (or new plants bought in spring); and some like parsley) are short-lived plants which must also be replaced frequently (although not necessarily every year); but many, including the evergreen shrubby ones, keep going year after year.

A well-stocked hanging basket, but note how the white petunias disappear against the whitewashed wall at the top. Try to choose colours to contrast with the background: this situation cries out for more splashes of bright red.

16

HANGING BASKETS

It's impossible to discuss window boxes without also mentioning hanging baskets. These look superb one each side of a door, as they're so often used, but they're equally attractive as window decorations. To my eye, hanging baskets complete the picture, draping the window in a cascade of flowers and foliage to complement and balance the box display below, but the placing of them depends greatly on the shape and size of the window.

A narrow window looks best with a single basket fixed above it, and a window which is both narrow and tall simply cries out for this treatment (Fig. 29). The eye is caught by the brimming display in the window-ledge box, and then drawn upwards in a pleasing way to the basket above; the whole forming a classical pyramidal arrangement. Be sure to fix the basket so that it hangs down in front of the top part of the window, so that it may be admired from within as well as from without.

Wider windows call out for a hanging basket on each side, the trailing plants spilling down to almost meet the tall plants and climbers reaching up from the ends of the box below. Indeed, if it can be contrived so that the climbers and tall plants at each end of the window box do actually reach up to mingle with the cascading leaves and flowers of the hanging basket, this 'framing' effect can be truly lovely.

Very large windows might call for a combination of these, with both hanging baskets to each side and one or more baskets above; but take care not to over-do it, or the effect will end up looking cluttered. Better to keep any arrangement of hanging baskets and window boxes fairly simple.

Fig. 29. Fixing a hanging basket over the window, above your box garden, will complete the picture. Where the window is small, site the basket to one side to avoid blocking the light and the view, but make sure you can reach the basket easily for watering purposes etc.

Brackets for hanging baskets may be quickly and easily fitted by any handyman with an electric drill, but do remember that the baskets, once hung, must be within easy reach for watering and other maintenance tasks. Baskets by ground-floor windows pose no real problems, but those fixed around upper-storey windows should be easily reached from within the window without any necessity for dangerous leaning out over the ledge. Planting and other maintenance tasks will be discussed later, with window boxes, in a separate chapter. For now, let's look at which plants may be grown in hanging baskets and what effects may be obtained with these.

THE PLANTS

Hanging baskets are only really suitable for summer displays in most regions. Holding only a small volume of growing compost, they're too small for most perennial plants, and they freeze solid and dry out fast in cold winter weather, which does not suit winter and spring flowering bulbs. In mild, fairly frost-free regions, of course, they can provide colour from annuals and tender plants almost the whole year round; but for most of us they are unfortunately a summer phenomenon.

Many of the annuals and tender plants mentioned under temporary plants for summer colour in window boxes are of course suitable for hanging baskets. Very tall plants are obviously not ideal, and the major part of the planting scheme will involve trailing plants.

However, the same rules apply about obtaining a balanced mix of types, and at least one tallish plant should ideally be included, in the centre of the basket, to add height to the display, with trailers planted around it. In a wire basket with open sides, trailers may also be planted to grow out between the wires (see 'Planting and maintenance' chapter).

Pelargoniums and fuchsias are perfect as central 'height' plants in a basket. Hanging baskets tend to be more exposed to wind and rain than window boxes, so any tall plants need to be sturdy; these two suggestions are ideal, whereas tall annuals tend to flop over.

Of trailing plants, the following are all excellent. For foliage: small-leaved ivy varieties, the silvery-leaved *Helichrysum petiolatum* and *Senecio maritimus*, *Saxifraga stolonifera* (mother of thousands) and the stripy-

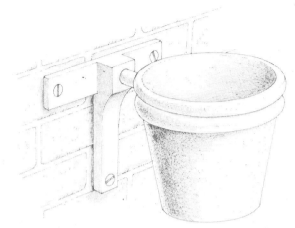

Fig. 30. Brackets to hold pots, fixed to the wall alongside a window, are yet another alternative for brightening up the house; almost as good as hanging baskets.

leaved *Zebrina pendula* (wandering Jew). Flowering plants include trailing begonias (*Begonia ×tuberhybrida* 'Pendula' varieties), trailing fuchsias (e.g. 'Cascade', 'Swingtime' and 'Marinka'), the ivy-leaved *Pelargonium peltatum* varieties, *Lobelia erinus* 'Pendula' varieties (e.g. 'Blue Cascade' and 'Red Cascade'), petunias (e.g. the pink 'Blush Cascade' and the red 'Ruby Cascade'), *Lysimachia nummularia* (creeping Jenny), *impatiens* (busy Lizzie) and *Tropaeolum majus* (nasturtium). For hanging baskets in shade, the following are the best choices: *Lysimachia nummularia* (and its golden-leaved form 'Aurea'), the ivies, *Saxifraga stolonifera*, *Zebrina pendula*, lobelias, nasturtiums, trailing fuchsias and begonias.

Finally, if hanging baskets seem like too much trouble, how about fixing wall-mounted pot holders (Fig. 30)? These are almost as attractive, spilling over with colourful trailing plants. If possible, try to get ones that will hold a largish pot with more than one plant; say a trailer plus a bushy plant; and small wall-mounted 'planters' (small plastic troughs or semicircular containers) fixed with brackets, one each side of the window, provide yet another interesting alternative.

Sweet peas trained on canes clothe this house wall with summer colour; but even so, the effect is greatly enhanced by the addition of a well-stocked hanging basket.

17

PLANTING AND MAINTENANCE

As in any form of gardening, the more care you take over planting, watering, feeding and so forth, the better the end result will be. The most carefully thought-out planting schemes are so easily spoiled by careless planting and indifferent maintenance; which, in the end means wasted time and effort. Annuals in particular need good quality growing compost plus regular watering and feeding if they're to grow fast, come into flower early and make a superb display.

GROWING COMPOSTS

Never use unsterilized garden soil in containers; the chances are that it will contain soil pests, weed seeds and plant disease spores which can cause havoc in the confines of a pot or window box. The average garden soil is, in any case, often far from perfect as a growing medium. It may be too heavy and sticky or very sandy and dry, or short on essential plant foods and trace elements necessary for healthy growth.

You can make up your own growing compost by sterilizing garden soil, adding peat and fertilizers, but that's a long and tiresome process. Better to buy bags of commercially-produced composts which are guaranteed pest and disease free, with a correct balance of ingredients to ensure strong growth.

Soilless peat-based potting compost is best for fast-growing temporary plants like annuals, tender perennials, spring bedding plants and bulbs; the plants can root into it quickly, and it's light and easy to work in when it comes to regular seasonal planting, lifting and replanting.

There's no need to replace the compost every time you replant for a new season; it'll do for the whole year with just a little topping up as necessary when you replant. Once it has been used to grow your summer, autumn, winter and spring displays, it will be exhausted and in poor condition; so use the old compost as a soil improving material in the garden, and start again with fresh potting compost.

Soil-based potting compost is better for permanent plants (including perennial herbs). It stays in good condition for much longer and retains plant foods better, so your permanent planting display can be left undisturbed for quite a few years.

Should you wish to grow the smaller, more 'special' alpines in a 'rock garden box' as described earlier, then these should be given a particularly well-drained, gritty soil. Mixing three measures of soil-based potting compost with one measure of horticultural grit or fine gravel (measured by bulk) is ideal. Don't forget to top-dress with a layer of grit or gravel, tucking this under the leaves of the tiny rock plants to help keep their necks dry and prevent rain splashing soil onto the delicate flowers.

DRAINAGE

It's essential that any window box should have holes in the base for drainage of excess water, to prevent the growing compost becoming waterlogged and going sour. Roots simply cannot grow in waterlogged soil, and where drainage is poor or even non-existent, the plants are liable to die very quickly, especially if waterlogging occurs during winter. This applies particularly to boxes filled with compost, but also to boxes intended to hold pots or removable liners; water collecting around the pots or liners will make the compost in them equally wet and sour.

Make sure that the drainage holes are reasonably large and that there are enough of them–four or five in a medium-sized box; more in a very large container. To ensure that they won't become blocked by the growing compost, place a small pile of broken flower-pot pieces, broken bricks or small stones over each hole. The box may then be filled with growing compost, taking care not to disturb the drainage material. Better still, to ensure perfect drainage, cover the holes as suggested, then also cover the base of the box with a 2-cm (1-in) layer of gravel or grit, the compost going in on top of this drainage layer; this is particularly advisable for permanent plantings, to ensure good long-term drainage.

If you're planning to grow the tiniest rock plants in a specialized rock garden window box, use a gritty compost mixture as mentioned earlier, but also put an extra-deep layer of drainage grit or gravel in the base; preferably 4 to 5 cm (1½ to 2 in).

PLANTING

Your plants should not be crammed into the box so close together that there's no room for root growth. Make sure that there's some compost between the rootballs for them to grow out into, but don't space them out too much; you want their top-growth to mingle together in a luxuriant mass of flowers and foliage.

Always water the plants (in their pots or trays) before planting them, to be sure that their rootballs are moist; never plant anything with dry roots. Water thoroughly after planting; a really good soaking until water seeps out of the drainage holes. Don't over-fill the box with compost. The surface of the compost should be about 2.5 cm (1 in) below the rim of the container, to catch and hold water.

When mixing bulbs with bedding plants (for a winter or spring display) always put the plants in first, then pop the bulbs in around them; do it the other way around, and you may damage the bulbs with the trowel when you put the plants in later. Use your hands for planting, of course, and this problem doesn't arise.

Remember that the larger the bulb, the deeper it should be. Dwarf bulbs need only have their tips about 2.5 cm (1 in) below the surface, but larger daffodils and tulips should have more like 5 to 8 cm (2 to 3 in) of compost over their tips, preferably more. Much depends on the depth of the box, though; don't put large bulbs so deep that their bases sit almost at the bottom of the container.

If you're using climbers that need support from canes or trellis, put the support in first, and then the plant, to avoid spearing and damaging roots. Tie the climbers in to the supports gently with soft twine, not too tightly so that their stems may grow and expand.

On a general point, don't forget the design suggestions made in my first chapter. Do go for a variety of plant types, with tall focal plants or climbers to the sides of the box, grading down to smaller, bushier things in the centre, and trailers towards the front. Don't start planting straight away, either. Stand back and imagine the effect you're aiming for, double-checking that everything is going in its right place. If the plants are pot-grown, try placing them on the surface of the compost, arranging and re-arranging them until you're happy with the layout.

WATERING

Try not to let the window box dry out completely at any time, and particularly when young plants are growing fast before flowering.

Never wait for plants to start wilting before you bother to water. If they're short of water, they'll stop growing and suffer a setback long before wilting becomes obvious; and they can then take some time to recover, so that flowering may be delayed.

In hot weather you'll probably find that a well-stocked window box in a sunny position may need watering once a day or perhaps even twice a day. Watering in the mornings and evenings is best, and you should always avoid splashing the plants' foliage in sunny summer weather; water droplets on leaves act like magnifying glasses, concentrating the sun's rays and scorching the plants.

However, too much water can be as bad as none at all. Test the compost with your finger to see if it's drying out below; if so, fill the box to the rim with the watering can. Do not water again until the compost once more starts to feel just barely moist. The ideal is to keep it damp but not soaking wet. Watering should be minimal in winter, just enough to stop the growing compost drying out, and it may not be required at all. Small rock plants in particular need hardly any watering at this time of year.

FEEDING

Seasonal plants will need more feeding than a permanent planting display, since things like annuals, tender perennials and bulbs grow fast and quickly exhaust the soil. Peat-based composts used for seasonal plants also tend to lose their plant foods quickly, these being easily washed out by rain and watering. Peat composts will feed the plants adequately for a few weeks after first being planted, but after that, you should water with liquid fertilizer every two or three weeks during summer. Feed winter and spring seasonal plants including bulbs) less frequently, say once immediately after planting and once or twice in the spring.

The best liquid fertilizers to use are those with a high-potash content, which encourages flowering rather than excessive foliage growth (tomato fertilizer is suitable, being very high in potash). Liquid feeds which also contain trace elements are particularly good, preventing deficiencies of these essential minerals.

Permanent plantings require less heavy feeding. For one thing, the soil-based composts in which they're usually grown hold plant nutrients longer; secondly you don't want the plants to grow too vigorously or they may quickly become too large for the box; and thirdly, most of the smaller flowering perennials generally bloom more freely when not over-fed. One dose of a high-potash liquid fertilizer in the spring should do (with a second dose in summer only if the plants look like they really need a boost).

If the growing compost is dry, give your plants some water before feeding with liquid fertilizer; applied to dry compost, it may harm the roots, and never make the mixture stronger than recommended on the bottle.

HANGING BASKETS

Wire baskets should be lined with moss (available from garden stores) and filled with a peat-based potting compost. One or two trailing plants may be inserted in the sides, to grow out through the wire and moss. Place these in position as you line and fill the basket. Finally, plant the top with more trailers and some taller and bushier things (Fig. 31). Bring the moss right to the brim of the basket, but the compost level should be below this, to allow for watering. After planting, give the basket a good soaking and keep it out of the sun for a couple of days, if possible, to let the plants settle in before hanging.

Baskets do dry out fast and may need watering once or even twice a day in hot weather. The most effective way to water is to take the basket down and dunk it in a bowl of water until the compost is soaked through. In very hot weather, it's best to do this at least once or twice a week, in addition to a daily sprinkling with the watering can. Feed with liquid fertilizer every two or three weeks.

If you're unable to carry out such frequent watering in summer, put a lining of polythene inside the moss to help conserve the moisture. But be sure to punch some holes in the base of the polythene to allow for drainage of excess water; and make slits in the sides to allow you to plant trailers. Placing a saucer on the moss lining in the base, before filling with compost, also helps to

Hanging basket plants trail downwards and mingle attractively with border plants below: note the choice of red flowers to contrast with the whitewashed wall; while paler blooms stand out well in the shade, against the green of the conifer.

Classic hanging basket plantings: tall fuchsias and pelargoniums in the centre, circled with bushier plants, and trailing lobelias planted through the sides of each basket.

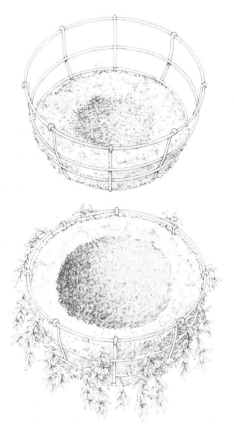

Fig. 31. *(a)–(c)* Making up a hanging basket. First place a pad of sphagnum moss in the bottom of the basket, then place a handful or two of compost on the moss and push two or three trailing plants through the wires. Repeat the process with another series of plants; bushy plants can be placed in the top.

prevent water from draining away too quickly, and to hold a small reserve of moisture for the roots.

Solid plastic hanging plant containers require less frequent watering (although they'll still dry out quite fast) but then you can't plant trailers in the sides of these; and I do like the attractive moss-lined effect of the traditional open basket.

GENERAL CARE

One of the most important periodic tasks is to nip off dead flower heads, to prevent energy being wasted on seed production and to encourage prolonged flowering instead.

Often, trimming a plant with shears or scissors after it finishes flowering will induce it to produce a second flush of colour. This is worth trying with all plants that make strong, straggly growth, although not all will respond. Trimming is to be recommended in any case for the strongest-growing perennials like aubrietas, arabis, *Alyssum saxatile,* campanulas, helianthemums and *Iberis sempervirens* (candytuft). Cutting back the spent flowering shoots keeps them neat as well as ensuring good flowering the following year, and quite possibly some extra flowers the same year. Try this with annuals, too.

Weeding is the only other regular task. In the crowded conditions of a window box or hanging basket, added competition for root space, water and food is the last thing your plants need, so get any weeds out as soon as you spot them, and before they become large enough to provide serious root competition.

18

PROBLEMS WITH YOUR PLANTS

Give your window garden plants good quality growing compost, water them regularly (not too much, not too little), feed as suggested earlier, and you should have few real problems. Healthy, well-grown plants will be better able to survive unseen disasters like insect or disease attack, scorching hot weather, frosts and other gardening plagues. Poorly grown plants, on the other hand, will often give up the fight at the first sign of any trouble.

To fully describe and discuss all the diseases, pests and cultural disorders that can strike plants down would fill a book in itself. Let's look briefly, however, at some of the most common troubles that might crop up.

GROWING PROBLEMS

Stunted growth, wilting, brown-scorched leaves and dying shoots may be due to various causes, but look first to the growing conditions. These symptoms are classic signs of drought, but they can also be due to waterlogged soil causing the roots to rot. Always check the growing compost first to see whether it's either too dry or too wet (both conditions are equally serious).

Plants which have suffered drought damage in hot weather will revive more quickly if they're given some shade and shelter from the wind in addition to watering. Pop plant pots over them, or pin shading material (netting or even sheets of newspaper) over the entire window box for a day or two after watering.

Frost damage, when severe, shows on tender plants and young annuals as a blackening and shrivelling of soft shoots and leaves. Mild frost damage may appear only as a yellowing of the leaves, and the plants will recover. Even hardy plants used in permanent displays may be damaged by severe frosts, this usually showing as a browning of the leaves. Where frost damage is bad, cut out all affected shoots to prevent rot setting in, and hope that new growth will appear. Annuals and tender plants killed to soil level will seldom recover and should be replaced.

If sharp frosts are forecast after you've planted tender things, protect them by pinning sheets of newspaper over the box as insulation. Always check that any annuals and bedding plants you buy in have been 'hardened off'; that is, they've been grown under cold conditions outside or in cold frames for a while, to acclimatize them to outdoor life and toughen them up.

PESTS

Birds may sometimes damage window box plants, pulling out seedlings, pecking leaves and tearing at flowers (especially in spring). If this happens, tie some strands of black sewing cotton between small sticks, criss-crossing the window box. Only two or three strands towards the front will be needed and shouldn't look too unsightly. This will keep the birds off without harming them, and it can be removed after a week or so when the birds have given up and gone elsewhere.

Aphids are the commonest and most serious insect pests, crippling plants by sucking sap from young leaves and shoot-tips, and also sometimes infecting plants with serious virus diseases. Watch out for infestations on new growth, particularly in late spring and early summer, and spray immediately with malathion or (better still) a long-lasting systemic insecticide.

Slugs and snails may find their way up walls into window gardens, particularly in wet seasons. If they become a problem, scatter some slug-killer pellets into the box, underneath the foliage of the plants where these creatures hide.

Other insect pests are too numerous to list, but symptoms such as pale yellow-mottled leaves, notches eaten out of leaves, white 'tunnels' burrowed through leaves and twisted, malformed foliage often indicate insect activity. If serious symptoms appear, the best thing to do is to spray with a systemic insecticide recommended for dealing with a wide range of different pests (your local gardening store will advise on available brands).

DISEASES

Grey mould (botrytis) is one of the commonest diseases affecting the kinds of seasonal plants and bulbs used in window boxes, particularly where these are grown in crowded conditions, and most frequently in damp weather. It shows as a furry grey growth on soft shoots and leaves, which eventually rot and collapse. On many plants, and especially on bulbs, this starts low down, at or near soil level. It can be halted by spraying with a fungicide containing benomyl.

Other typical signs of plant disease include mouldy, sooty grey or powdery white coatings on leaves and stems; sudden wilting despite the compost being neither too dry nor too wet; and brown spotting of leaves. The simplest thing, if symptoms like these appear, is to spray with a systemic fungicide that deals with a wide range of diseases (once again, local stores will advise on brands).

Finally, any plant which has suffered a setback from poor growing conditions, weather damage, insect or disease attack, may be given a quick boost towards recovery by foliar feeding. This 'shot in the arm' treatment is great for any plant that isn't doing well, the foliar fertilizer being sprayed onto the leaves and absorbed straight into the plant tissues.

Do not spray insecticides, fungicides or foliar fertilizers onto plants in hot sun, otherwise scorch damage may occur. In hot weather, it is better to wait for lower temperatures in the evening.

HERBS

INTRODUCTION

Herbs, of course, are ideally suited to small gardens and many may be grown in containers. Culinary herbs, especially, are enjoying great popularity today, as over the last 20 years or so our eating habits have changed in favour of more highly flavoured foods, especially from other nationalities and cultures.

Also, the movement towards natural, unprocessed foods, simply cooked, has brought with it an increased use of herbs to provide flavour and interest in the place of rich sauces, salt and artificial flavourings.

Herbs are the most satisfying plants to grow. It's not just their many uses, their attractive foliage and flowers, or even the tantalizing scents that are given off at the slightest touch that make them so rewarding. As much as any of this, it's the fascination of their long history, the knowledge that you are continuing a tradition of growing plants that have been cultivated for centuries, that turns herb growing from an interest into a life-long addiction.

This section opens with a chapter on designing herb gardens, from the intricate precision of an Elizabethan knot garden to a free-flowering wilderness of scented plants. The chapter also considers growing herbs in paving, walls and raised beds, in containers, and even creating herb lawns and hedges.

A comprehensive table lists herbs for various condi-tions and purposes, and those with particularly attractive foliage.

Chapter 20 is very much a practical chapter, describ-ing preparation of the planting site, planting techniques, general cultivation, planting in containers, and pests and diseases (of which there are few which attack herbs).

Once you have your herbs established, you will probably want to increase your stock by propagating from them and there are various ways in which you can do this, such as sowing seeds, dividing plants and tak-ing cuttings, as outlined in this chapter.

Chapter 21 deals with the all-important subject of using herbs in the kitchen and other parts of the home. It explains how to preserve herbs by drying, freezing and other methods. Then follow numerous culinary recipes, some traditional, some new. There is also advice on making *pot pourri*, both dry and moist, which preserves the scent of summer flowers all the year round. Herb pillows and baths are also included, as is advice on making herbal teas.

Chapter 22 is an alphabetical selection of popular herbs, from angelica to thyme. Here full descriptions of the plants are given. This is followed by cultural information. Detailed advice on uses is then given.

19

DESIGN

From the intricate precision of an Elizabethan knot garden to a free-flowering wilderness of scented plants —a herb garden can be anything you like to make it. Before planting any herbs, it does pay to sit down with a pencil and paper and make some rough plans to avoid annoying mistakes later on.

OVERALL PLANNING

The first question is always — where? Most gardens have only limited space and the herb border must fit in with everything else. As a general rule, the nearer the house it can be the better. Here the scents can be more frequently appreciated, and there's not too far to go to pick the few sprigs that will make all the difference to a meal.

A sheltered position is always best. Most herbs are natives of warm climates and will grow more readily in a protected position; also, fragrances linger on warm, still air far longer than they do in a breezy, open spot. At the same time, plenty of air and sunshine are necessary for the majority of species, so shelter should not mean heavy shade. Which is the best spot for sitting out in summer? For that's probably the ideal position for your herb garden.

Once you've decided on the position, see how much space you can allow yourself. A large, formal herb garden can give a great deal of pleasure, but bear in mind it will need careful planning, be quite expensive to plant up, and it will take a lot of maintenance to keep it looking its best. However, few things are more irritating than being constrained by a tiny border

which it is impossible to extend sensibly, and collecting herbs generally becomes quite addictive!

Because shelter is so important, it's an excellent idea to enclose a herb garden with walls or hedges. You may be lucky enough to have an existing walled garden to convert to herbs — otherwise building walls from scratch is prohibitively expensive. Hedging can be arranged, though: it should be evergreen, preferably dark leaved to act as a foil for light coloured herbs, and not too greedy—privet, for example, will drain the soil of plant foods for a considerable distance, so that anything planted near it has a struggle to survive. Bear in mind that a formal garden means neat, well-trimmed hedges, with all the extra work that entails.

Fencing should not be despised, for although it does not look very attractive to start with, it can be much improved by climbing plants. It is relatively cheap and easy to erect, and could make all the difference to a garden in an exposed situation. Walls, fences and hedges all cast shade as well as shelter—another point to remember before putting them up.

Those gardens fortunate enough to be reasonably warm and sheltered do not need to be enclosed, and herbs can be planted out in the open.

Once you have decided on the position and size, you can get down to the detailed planning. Let's start with a large, formal herb garden.

FORMAL HERB GARDEN

The design of the formal garden is very important. The overall shape should be regular, divided into a

Gravel paths give all-weather access to the plants. Wooden surrounds to the beds ensure they remain well-defined: they also help to keep invasive herbs in their place.

Lavender *(left)* is an excellent plant with which to edge a path. The strongly fragrant flowerheads have been used for centuries to scent linen.

number of equal sections to form a repetitive pattern. There should be a focal point; usually in the centre, though not necessarily.

The epitome of a formal herb garden is the knot garden, which is purely decorative. Bushy herbs in contrasting colours are planted to form low hedges which run through and over each other in complex patterns like ropes forming a knot. Knot gardens need to be viewed from above for the best effect: if you have a suitable garden—and an orderly mind!—they can be most effective and impressive, and are not as difficult to lay out as they look.

Knot Garden

The design shown in Fig. 32 is fairly simple. When planning a knot garden it really is essential to draw it to scale on paper first.

Plant the marked lines with suitable herbs such as santolina, wall germander, hyssop and lavender. Buy small but bushy plants and set them about 8–15 cm (3–6 in) apart, depending on size. At the planning stage, decide which 'rope' runs over or under at each intersection: generally each one goes under and over alternately to give an entwined effect. If you just impose the circle on top of the loops, on top of the diamond, this is not a true 'knot'.

Clip the newly planted 'ropes' back quite hard to encourage even, bushy growth, and trim the plants very regularly in the growing season. The spaces between the 'ropes' can be filled with pea gravel, shingle, flint chippings, forest bark or similar materials, using either one for the whole garden or, more effectively, several contrasting colours and textures to emphasize the patterns.

The knot garden is a masterpiece of precision, but it is not meant for cropping. A formal herb garden can, however, be both beautiful and useful.

The shape must be regular for the best effect, but can be anything within those lines: square, rectangular, diamond, circular, semi-circular, oval or triangular. The focal point is marked by something like a sundial or a white-painted, old fashioned beehive (with or

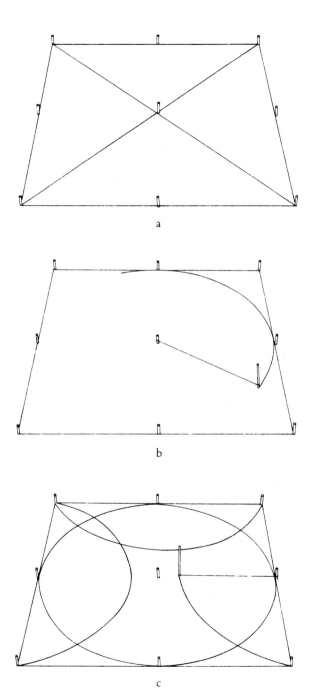

a

b

c

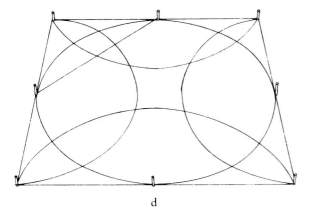

d

without occupants!), a small pool or fountain, a small evergreen tree or clipped shrub, an ornament or even just a large, striking herb like angelica.

Where the focal point falls is quite important, and depends on the shape of the garden, the direction from which it is approached, and many other factors. The dead centre of the herb garden is usually a safe bet, but if you can, try out some easily moved object in several different places, viewing it from all angles to see where it looks most comfortable. The natural focal point — the point to which the eye is most easily led — is not always where you might expect it to be. The rest of the herb garden design should radiate from that focal point.

Use paths to form the basis of the design. (They have a practical value, too, for you should be able to reach every herb from paved ground.) Two intersecting paths dividing a square garden into four equal parts is a pleasing, simple and well-tried pattern (Fig. 33). Where

Fig. 32. Knot garden *(a)* Mark the mid point of each side of the square. Stretch strings diagonally across to find the centre and mark it with a peg.

(b) Draw the circle with a stick and string tied to the centre peg.

(c) Move the mid point pegs slightly outside the square and use the stick and string, tied to these, to mark the semi-circles.

(d) Move the mid point pegs back to the edges and mark the diamond by running a stick along string stretched tautly between them.

(e) Use herbs in contrasting colours to plant up the 'ribbons'.

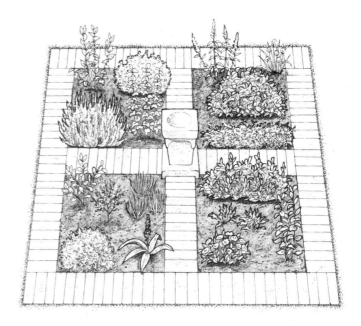

Fig. 33. A square herb garden with intersecting paths is a popular pattern. Add interest with a central focal point.

193

Fig. 34. Another simple design—a chequerboard of alternate paving slabs and herb plants.

they intersect, you can position a seat, sundial, small pool or what you will. Plant fairly low-growing herbs near the centre of the garden with the taller ones towards the back.

There are many more complicated designs you could work out for any particular shape, but remember not to make it too fiddly. Bold shapes and fairly simple patterns are usually the most effective.

For many people the herb 'garden' is, in fact, just a bed. This too can be of a formal design: one that is both practical and pleasing is a chequerboard of plants and paving slabs (Fig. 34). Don't try to cram too many herbs into each planting space—one reasonable-sized bush or perhaps two smaller subjects is usually plenty.

INFORMAL HERB GARDEN

Most herb beds are informal, whether by accident or design. In fact, these are even more difficult to make effective than formal plans. Many herbs have an annoying habit of not knowing their proper limits. The books might say 90 cm (3 ft) high by 50 cm (1½ ft) spread—but try telling that to the plant! In your soil it

may refuse to grow more than half that height while deciding to sprawl to double the spread. Or another compact, low growing variety might romp away to twice its normal dimensions, obscuring the more reticent, supposedly larger-growing plant behind it. In a small area where every inch counts, these mistakes show up badly, and there will be a continual juggling and shifting of positions until you find just how things grow in your particular site.

But an informal garden can be a beautiful, blowsy muddle where finding a choice plant almost hidden by another only adds to the charm, and the sheer exuberance of plants jostling for space more than makes up for their untidiness. There is a fine line between magnificence and messiness, though, and you will need to take care that your herbs don't escape your control. Fortunately many of them have no objection to being brought back into line by some drastic work with the secateurs before things go too far.

It's an unfortunate fact that truly beautiful informality can only be achieved by sheer good luck—unless you happen to be one of those people who have an instinct for plant associations and manage to hit the jackpot every time without knowing how they do it. For most of us, the informal garden needs a little basic planning to make it work. The following points about plants are just as relevant to plantings within the formal garden.

BASIC REQUIREMENTS FOR THE HERB GARDEN

The first essential is to know your soil and have at least a rough idea of the size each plant is likely to reach (though as I've said, this is not always easy). It might seem obvious but it's still worth saying—put the taller plants at the back and the lowest ones at the front. If your bed is viewed from all sides (an island bed) then the tallest herbs must go in the centre.

Many herb gardens look very bleak in winter. To

An informal border filled with strong-growing plants; tall tansy and rosemary at the back, brightly variegated ginger mint in the centre and purple sage and savory in the foreground.

give some visual winter interest (and provide fresh herbs for the kitchen in all months) make sure you have several evergreens, and use them to form the backbone of your planting scheme.

Then jot down the main season of interest of the herbs you particularly want to grow. Some appear very early in the spring (others so late that every year you're sure they've died). Some have brightly marked young foliage that fades as it matures: some reach their best in late summer when they are fully grown. There are flowers at various times from early summer through to autumn (though if you are growing herbs for culinary use you will probably cut these off, so don't rely on them for decoration). Then there are foliage colours—dark green, bronze, silver, steely blue, brilliant yellow—and textures; from finely divided to big and bold, soft and hazy to sharp and spiky.

Now you have to plan your planting so that all the different aspects complement, not clash. As to what's complementary and what's clashing—well, that's up to you! Basically you want to ensure the interest is spread right through the herb garden, not grouped together at any one season. You may wish to grade the colours, starting at one end with cool greys and blues, and working down through greens to warmer golds and reds, or you may prefer to have the different colours dotted about and evenly distributed.

TYPES OF PLANTS

Tall, bold, architectural plants are shown to their best advantage when they are accompanied by soft, fluffy foliage to form a complete contrast. In general, fine feathery foliage is best when used as a foil for the more robust-leaved plants.

So far I have only talked about the visual impact of herbs, but there are all sorts of other ways you could plan them to form a satisfying design. Group them according to their use—medicinal, culinary, household and so on—for an interesting and educational garden, or by scent, from citrus to spicy, sweet to sharp and

pungent. A collection of herbs particularly attractive to bees will also attract butterflies and moths.

Although herbs are very often set apart and grown in their own plot, there's no reason at all why they shouldn't take their place amongst the border plants and shrubs. Many of them already do—rosemary, rue and lavender, for instance, are just as widely (if not more widely) grown as decorative plants as they are for any other purpose.

Make sure you know just where all the different herbs are and you can continue to gather them for use in the home, though you will have to be careful to pick shoots judiciously to leave a well-shaped bush.

Many herbs make particularly good edgings to beds, curled parsley, chives or dwarf lavender amongst them.

In small gardens, finding room for all the plants you want to grow is always a problem. Here, they must fit in as best they can, and every inch of space must be used.

HERBS IN PAVING AND IN WALLS

Because they can often grow in very dry, poor soils, herbs are naturals for planting in gaps in paving. Here there is the bonus of fragrance as they are brushed past or occasionally trodden on. Low, spreading plants are the most suitable. If you are laying a patio or path, leave slightly wider gaps every so often to accommodate plants: where different sizes of slabs are being used, leave one of the smaller ones out here and there. In existing paving you can often chisel out a small corner or squeeze plants in the gaps already there.

Walls offer similar planting sites (Fig. 35), particularly dry stone walls where it's easy to prod plants into cracks and cavities. The tops of walls can be planted, too, if sufficient soil is held there. As walls often provide exceptionally dry growing conditions, mix into the soil one of the water-retaining polymers now available in granular form.

Fig. 35. Herb planting in a wall *(a)* When planting herbs in walls, carefully shape the rootball to fit the cavity.

(b) Put a little good loam in the hole and pack the roots in snugly.

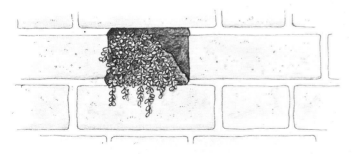

(c) Several herbs are suitable for wall planting, but trailing thymes are particularly good.

Plants for walls and paving are best raised at home if possible. Cuttings should be rooted in very small containers and planted out while still young to ensure the root system fits oddly shaped crevices without too much damage.

RAISED BEDS

Raised beds are a convenient way of growing herbs, too. They can be constructed on a totally paved garden where they will give much better growing conditions than containers. They are useful where soil conditions are not the best for herbs — heavy, sticky clays for example — and provide the free-draining conditions many herbs love. Invasive herbs can be grown without fear of them spreading all over the garden, and weeding, picking and trimming become much simpler.

Raised beds are ideal for disabled gardeners (including the elderly) who have trouble bending or who garden from a wheelchair; blind gardeners will also appreciate the advantages of having scented and textured plants within easy reach and nearer nose level!

Make a raised bed as large as is practical, building it of materials sympathetic to the rest of the garden and the house. Choose the height to suit the purpose: 30 cm (1 ft) might be sufficient depth for most herbs, but if the raised beds are meant for wheelchair users obviously they must be much higher. Place rubble in the base if necessary to ensure good drainage before filling the bed with good quality, light loam (Fig. 36).

Raised beds dry out fairly quickly so they could need frequent watering in hot, sunny weather; try to position them within reach of a hose to make this easier.

HERB LAWNS

Many gardens—even small ones—give up quite a lot of their space to a lawn. Why not be different and try a herb lawn?

Contrasting foliage colours between santolina *(centre)* and winter savory make this very simple bed effective at Hatfield House.

Angelica archangelica: a statuesque herb whose leaves and stems are both used as flavouring.

Fig. 36. Raised bed (a) Laying the first course of bricks.

(b) Filling the bed with compost.

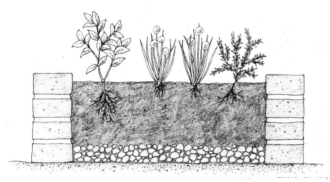

(c) Sectional view of planted bed.

I should say straight away that herbs won't give a close, even sward like turf. At certain times of the year they look distinctly patchy—and weeds can be a terrible problem. (You can't use the normal selective lawn weedkillers on herbs.) Added to which, they won't take the normal wear and tear, rough and tumble that grass does, and getting them planted and established takes not a little time (and money). But, against all that, a well-grown herb carpet can be such a beautiful and fragrant thing it's worth every bit of trouble, and more, that goes into it.

The best known 'lawn' herb must be chamomile, with its rich, fruity apple scent: it has been used for generations. The variety 'Treneague' does not flower and this makes it especially suitable; however, seed of this variety is not, of course, available, and establishing a lawn from plants is more expensive and labour intensive. The various creeping thymes are quite spectacular when in flower and will attract so many bees that walking on the plants is quite impossible! For a damp, shady corner, try one of the mints: pennyroyal or the tiny, creeping Corsican mint.

Keep herb lawns small. Prepare the soil for them very thoroughly, removing all weed roots: sow seed thickly or set plants about 10 cm (4 in) apart. Keep the new lawn well watered and weed it regularly, removing every weed you see. Once the plants have made good growth and knitted together they will help suppress weeds, but in the early stages it's up to you.

Once established, clip the lawns over with shears or use a hover mower to lightly top them: this helps to keep them close and compact. Occasional walking will do no harm, but a permanent pathway in a herb lawn will soon kill the plants in that area.

HERB HEDGES

Those herbs that do not mind being clipped make excellent formal hedges, while one or two make good, flowering, informal hedges and screens. As with all hedges, the soil should be thoroughly prepared before planting, being deeply dug, with a reservoir of plant food provided by the incorporation of well-rotted garden compost or animal manure, plus a long-lasting fertilizer such as bonemeal.

Buy young, well-shaped plants for a hedge. Most should be pruned back by about half after planting to ensure a bushy habit with plenty of new growth at the base of the hedge. As the plants grow, tip the sideshoots back lightly to keep them compact. Allow the plants to reach just above the required final height of the hedge, then cut the tops back to just below this height for a good finish. Trim according to the plant you are using: formal hedges require clipping two or three times in the growing season; informal hedges usually just once, after flowering.

Herbs suitable for close clipping can also be grown as single specimens, trimmed to a pleasing shape — something simple, like a pyramid or sphere, or more adventurous, like corkscrews or fantastic birds or animals.

While herbs like rosemary will make average size hedges, many can be grown as dwarf hedges to edge borders or form knot gardens. These miniature hedges need even more careful clipping to keep them bushy and compact: don't underestimate the amount of work involved in surrounding your herb garden or vegetable plot with a dwarf herb hedge!

HERBS IN CONTAINERS

If you have a really tiny garden, or even no garden at all, you may have to grow all your herbs in containers. More skill is needed to keep a container-grown plant happy and healthy, but many herbs adapt to this method of cultivation very well.

While they can be grown, if necessary, indoors, all herbs will do better outside even if it's only on a windowsill or balcony. Here they will receive better light and fresh air to keep them strong and sturdy.

Large containers for patios include half barrels, urns, large earthenware pots, troughs, sinks and tubs. Always use the largest container possible — it makes cultivation much easier. Any pot is liable to both waterlogging and drying out, so make sure there is a source of water close at hand.

Terracotta has a pleasant, rustic, warm look that goes well with herbs, but many of the beautifully decorated pots available today are liable to be damaged by frost. Unglazed terracotta absorbs water, a sharp frost freezes and expands the water and shatters the pot. In cold areas, choose frost-resistant pots, or keep them in a sheltered position. They can also be protected by lagging them with sacking, straw or loft insulation material.

Strawberry pots — urns with planting holes in the sides — offer great scope for trailers such as thyme. Separate containers for invasive herbs like mint will keep them under control, but mixed collections of other herbs can be planted in sinks, troughs and barrels. Don't cram too many in together, and choose the most valuable types, whether for scent, flavour, colour or general appearance. Steer clear of the very large, strong growers.

Since there is only a relatively small volume of soil in a container, plant foods will be used up fairly quickly. For this reason you might like to stick to annual or easily raised herbs that could be replaced, using fresh compost, every year — especially in small containers.

Just because you are restricted to growing herbs in pots doesn't mean you should forget design entirely. A mixed planting in a large tub must be chosen carefully, bearing in mind many of the same principles as for designing a large herb garden. Even a windowbox needs planning! A selection of herbs each in 10 cm (4 in) pots, can be arranged pleasingly and artistically in a window. The variegated or coloured-leaved varieties grow in pots just as well as their plain-leaved relatives — in fact many of them are slower growing and therefore more suitable.

The following tables indicate preferred locations, and soils for herbs, the types of foliage, what herbs are suitable for hedges, lawns, walls, paving and bees, and those growing under or over certain heights.

The soft colour of purple sage contrasts well with variegated ginger mint. In the background is a steel–blue rue and the pale pink flowers of chives.

This small, formal garden benefits from the shelter of tall beech hedges. Fragrant lilies add height to the low-growing herbs.

Table 1
Preferred locations and soils

HERBS FOR FULL SUN

Basil	Juniper
Bay	Lavender
Bergamot	Rosemary
Caraway	Sage
Coriander	Savory
Cotton lavender	Thyme
Hyssop	

HERBS FOR DAPPLED SHADE

Angelica	Lovage
Borage	Mint
Chervil	Parsley
Chives	Pennyroyal
Fennel	Sorrel
Lemon balm	Sweet cicely

*poisonous

HERBS FOR HEAVY SHADE

Comfrey	Valerian
Lily of the valley*	Violet
Lungwort	Woodruff
Tansy	

HERBS PREFERRING MOIST SOIL

Angelica	Elecampane
Bergamot	Lovage
Chervil	Mint
Chives	Sweet cicely
Comfrey	Valerian

HERBS WHICH REQUIRE WELL-DRAINED SOIL

Bay	Lavender
Caraway	Marjoram
Coriander	Myrtle
Cumin	Rosemary
Hyssop	Savory
Juniper	Thyme

Table 2
Types of foliage

HERBS WITH BLUE/SILVER FOLIAGE

Artemisia	Pinks
Cotton lavender	Rosemary
Curry plant	Rue
Eucalyptus	Sage
Lavender	

HERBS WITH VARIEGATED FOLIAGE

Geraniums, scented	Rue, variegated
Lemon balm, variegated	Sage, variegated
Marjoram, gold tipped	Thymes (several)
Mints (several)	

HERBS WITH DARK FOLIAGE

Basil, Dark Opal	Myrtle
Bay	Purple sage
Bronze fennel	

HERBS WITH FEATHERY OR LACY FOLIAGE

Anise	Dill
Caraway	Fennel
Chamomile	Parsley
Chervil	Southernwood
Coriander	Sweet cicely
Cumin	Wormwood
	Yarrow

*poisonous

HERBS WITH BOLD FOLIAGE

Angelica	Ladies' mantle
Burdock	Lovage
Comfrey	Lungwort
Costmary	Mullein
Dandelion	Nasturtium
Foxglove*	Rue
Hop	Sorrel
Horseradish	Thornapple*

Table 3
Herbs for hedges, lawns, walls, paving and bees

HERBS FOR HEDGES

Low:	Southernwood
Box	Wall germander
Cotton lavender	*Medium height:*
Hyssop	Rosa rugosa (informal)
Lavender	Rosemary (formal)

HERBS FOR BEES

Bergamot	Marjoram
Catmint	Rosemary
Eucalyptus	Sage
Hyssop	Thyme
Lavender	

HERBS FOR LAWNS

Chamomile	Thyme
Corsican mint	Yarrow
Pennyroyal	

HERBS FOR WALLS

Hyssop	Sempervivum
Lavender Dwarf Munstead	Thyme
Rosemary (prostrate vars)	Wall germander
Savory	

HERBS FOR PAVING

Chamomile	Pink
Creeping mint	Thyme

Table 4
Herbs growing under 50cm (1½ft) or over 2m (6ft)

HERBS GROWING UNDER 50cm (1½ft)

Basil	Marjoram
Chamomile	Parsley
Chives	Pennyroyal
Corsican mint	Pink
Cotton lavender	Lungwort
Lavender Dwarf Munstead	Thyme

HERBS GROWING 2m (6ft) OR MORE

Angelica	Fennel
Bay	Lemon verbena
Chicory	Lovage
Elecampane	Rose
Eucalyptus	Rosemary

A close-up of the herbs shown in the previous photograph: *(upper step)* lavender and melilot (fresh and dried); *(lower step, rear)* dried woodruff, dried thyme; *(lower step, middle)* pomanders, rosemary, costmary; *(lower step, foreground)* feverfew, eau-de cologne mint, southernwood *Artemisia abrotanum*, and a home-made pot pourri.

20

GROWING AND PROPAGATING

SELECTION, PURCHASING AND SITE LOCATION

The common, culinary herbs are fairly easy to buy these days, though some of the more unusual varieties might give you a little more trouble. A good garden centre is the best place to start. Here you should find a reasonable selection of plants, usually in 5 cm (2 in) pots, which will establish quite readily virtually all year round when planted out in the garden.

Selecting herbs is no different from choosing any other container-grown plant. You want a sturdy, bushy, healthy specimen of good shape; reject plants which are badly pot-bound, with diseased or pest-infested foliage, or which look drawn and 'soft' and have obviously been grown in protected conditions (unless you are prepared to harden them off carefully yourself before planting).

Check also (as far as you can) that the plants are correctly labelled, for misnaming of herbs is unfortunately common. If you are not familiar with any particular varieties you will have to buy them on trust, but check them out afterwards. It's always embarrassing to give another gardener a cutting of some especially choice herb only to have them tell you you've been nurturing some totally different plant for months!

Exchanging specimens with other herb enthusiasts is another good way of getting plants, especially some of the rarer ones. To start with, though, you will probably have to buy them from a specialist nursery.

There are increasing numbers of these all over the country, but if you cannot find one within travelling distance you will have to use the mail order service many of them offer. Plants are usually despatched in spring, but you will need to order as early as possible to be sure of receiving all the plants you want, particularly choice varieties. Postage is, unfortunately, expensive, but because plants are small, costs can be kept down to a reasonable level.

The site for the vast majority of herbs should be warm, sheltered and in full sun. It should also be convenient to the house, as culinary herbs need to be picked just before cooking if they are to retain all their flavour.

Exposed sites can be improved by protecting them with walls or hedges (see Chapter 19 for more details). One or two herbs grow better in light shade, so if your herb border can include a shady area, so much the better.

SOILS AND DRAINAGE

As a general rule, herbs are not fussy plants and they will grow in most soils and situations. A deep, moist, rich soil will promote plenty of lush foliage growth on most types, but the flavour will be inferior to those grown in poorer, dry soils. Many Mediterranean herbs in their native habitat grow in arid, dusty, stony soils so they are quite capable of coping with these conditions in the garden.

However, very poor, dry soils will not produce very attractive plants, and the plants will certainly not be able to cope with continual harvesting. So a balance must be drawn between good growth and good flavour.

Freely drained soils are essential for some herbs which quickly rot away in damp conditions. However, such soils should also be reasonably moisture-retentive to keep growth steady. This combination is not impossible, as it might first sound. It relies mainly on good soil structure, to allow drainage of excess water, and some organic matter (such as garden compost) to act as a sponge and hold some moisture in reserve.

Herbs require rather better drainage than many other garden plants. Free draining soils are composed of relatively large soil particles and are sandy or gritty. Heavy, clay soils, consisting of tiny particles which stick together and do not allow water to run freely between them, are the least suitable for herbs. The addition of plenty of organic matter will greatly improve their texture and drainage: working in sharp sand will also make them more suitable for herb growing. If you have a very light, sandy soil, add a small amount of organic matter to improve water retention and help stop plant foods being rapidly leached out of the soil.

Heavy applications of fertilizer are certainly unnecessary, but if you have poor soil, add a light dressing of bonemeal while preparing the bed, and incorporate this well. Bonemeal releases its nutrients gradually over an extended period, so will give the plants a steady supply of food without causing rapid lush growth.

In difficult growing conditions, due to bad weather or something similar, herbs might begin to suffer. In these cases a foliar feed sprayed over the plants will give them a quick boost and see them over the critical period. Regular fertilizing is not normally necessary.

PLANTING

Container-grown herbs can be planted at any time of the year except when the soil is frozen. However, it is

not a good idea to plant them out in a very hot, dry period—wait until a cool, fairly showery spell if possible. This way they will establish much more quickly. Bare root plants — those lifted direct from the open ground — are planted in early spring.

Dig a planting hole large enough to accommodate the plant's roots freely. If you haven't been able to improve the soil in the whole bed, work some peat and sand or similar material into the bottom of the planting hole. It is vital to plant at the right depth—the crown must not be buried.

Firm the newly planted herbs well to ensure that the roots are in good contact with the soil, and if conditions are dry, water them in thoroughly.

For quick effect, plant closely using two or three plants of each species so that the herbs soon fill out and make the bed look established. Some perennials will then have to be removed after a few years as they grow and need more space, so bear this in mind when planting. It is cheaper to space the plants more widely to start with; you will have to wait longer for the bed to fill out, of course, and there will be more room for weeds between the plants, too.

WEEDING

As weeds compete with the herbs for light, space, moisture and nutrients, they should be removed as soon as possible, particularly while young herb plants are getting established. Hoeing is quick and efficient in dry weather, using a hoe with a very sharp blade to slice seedling weeds off at ground level (being very careful to avoid damaging the herbs, of course!). When the soil is damp, hand weeding is the answer—after all, as Kipling said 'half a proper gardener's time is spent upon his knees'! Hand weeding amongst herbs has, at least, the compensation of the various fragrances released as you brush against different plants, and gives you the opportunity to form a really close relationship with your herb border.

I suspect that most gardeners would rather not use weedkillers (or insecticides) among their herbs, but if you have no such objections, a paraquat/diquat mixture could be used (carefully) to kill off seedling weeds. This will kill the green parts of any plant that it touches. Perhaps the most useful weedkiller is glyphosate, as this will deal with the problem weeds, like bindweed, that are very difficult to control by any other method. This is carried throughout any plant to which it is applied, so it kills roots as well as topgrowth. Again, great care must be taken to keep this chemical off the herbs. Once you have eradicated difficult weeds like this, it should not be necessary to use chemical herbicides again unless the border is allowed to become very overgrown.

Weeds can also be kept at bay by using mulches. Make sure the soil is reasonably damp first, then apply a fairly thick covering of peat, pulverized bark or similar material. This will retain soil moisture as well as suppress weed growth. Well-rotted garden compost can also be used, though because this is not sterilized, as proprietary mulching materials are, there is more chance of it containing weed seeds and weeds will appear in it more quickly.

In reasonable soil, most herbs should not require much watering except while they are getting established: the moisture-loving types such as angelica may, of course, need more frequent watering in dry spells. The best time to water is in the evening, when the sun is off the plants.

PLANTING IN CONTAINERS

If you have only very limited garden space, or you want fresh herbs through the winter, you will want to grow some plants in pots. They are never quite as happy as they are when in the open ground, but with a little skill you can keep them growing well.

In a large outdoor tub (Fig. 37) which will not need moving about you could use garden loam or a loam-based compost; if you do need to move it, use a lighter, peat-based compost. Herbs will grow quite well in either, though many gardeners swear by one or the other. I have always found peat-based composts give the best results, but if you prefer the loam-based, John Innes type, the herbs won't mind!

Make sure any container, large or small, has adequate drainage, with holes in the base and crocks over the holes: it's much easier to add water than to try to take it away. Drying out will, however, be a problem in dry weather and the smaller the container, the more difficult it will be to get the moisture level right. Be prepared for daily watering.

If you have no garden space at all, herbs can be grown in the house. If at all possible, keep them outside, on a balcony or even a windowledge. Otherwise, keep the pots in the lightest position available. They will all lean towards the light source, so every few days you should turn them round to keep them straight. Lack of light will lead to pale, drawn, sickly looking plants, and this will be a particular problem in winter, when light levels are low. Special horticultural electric light bulbs are available to supplement natural daylight: they are far more effective than ordinary or fluorescent lights because they transmit the correct part of the spectrum for plant growth. They are fairly expensive, but very worthwhile if you are trying to grow plants in a rather dim house (not everybody has nice, bright, sunny windowsills!).

If you want a variety of herbs indoors, 9 cm (3½ in) pots are probably the most practical size, though you should be prepared to replace plants as they outgrow these rather small containers. Use peat-based or loam-based compost, and give regular liquid feeds (any pot plant fertilizer will do). Keep the compost just moist at all times, and remember that overwatering kills more plants than underwatering.

Bringing potted herbs indoors is one way to keep fresh supplies available through the winter. Good pot subjects are parsley, basil, thyme, savory, marjoram and possibly (for a short time) rosemary and sage. If you have the facilities, raise seedlings in late summer for potting on and growing indoors in winter. This is more satisfactory than digging existing plants up and trying to pot them.

Some of the laundry herbs at Eyhorne Manor. Clockwise from bottom left: lavender, melilot (dried), melilot (fresh), rosemary, costmary, mint, mixed dried herbs *(in trug)*, southernwood and (centre) feverfew.

Fig. 37. Tub planting *(a)* Pour in gravel 2.5 cm (1 in) deep.

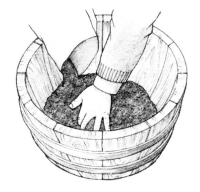

(b) Pour in compost until tub is two-thirds full.

(c) Set the plant in the tub.

(d) Fill the remaining space with soil.

(e) Water the plant in well.

PESTS AND DISEASES

Fortunately herbs are not generally troubled by many pests and diseases. The point to remember is that strong, well grown plants are more resistant to pest and disease attack (though they are not necessarily less likely to be attacked in the first place). Because herbs are used in small quantities, a few insect pests can fairly quickly be washed or brushed off after picking.

Aphids (greenfly and blackfly) are likely to appear on any plant making soft lush growth, generally clustering near the growing tips. Because of their remarkably efficient method of reproduction, huge numbers can build up very rapidly. Watch out for them particularly on herbs which are growing in the house or greenhouse. Often the easiest method of control is to pinch out and crush the infested tips of plants. Another remedy is to spray with water to which you have added a small amount of detergent.

Lovage can be disfigured by celery leaf miner, a grub which tunnels within the leaves, leaving a thin ribbon of dead tissue. Pick off and crush affected leaflets. Parsley is often attacked by carrot fly. This small fly lays eggs in the soil near the roots of carrots, parsnips and parsley: the grubs which hatch out live in the roots, eating tunnels out of them. Because this reduces the efficiency of the plants' system for obtaining food and water from the soil, they soon begin to show symptoms of distress, though a minor attack will not produce very serious results. The older leaves begin to yellow and flag, and become tinged with red; plant growth slows or stops. Carrot fly attack is much worse in some years than others. It can be halted by using a soil insecticide (see precautions below). Raising two batches of parsley seedlings a year ensures you will have some replacement plants coming along. To some extent carrot fly can be carried over from one season to the next in the soil, so choose a fresh site or grow in containers of sterilized potting compost after an outbreak.

The most troublesome disease that's likely to attack your herbs is mint rust. This can attack all varieties of mint and is characterized by rusty orange, powdery spots on the undersides of the leaves. It has a very severe effect on plants and there is no cure. One way round the trouble is to lift some of the creeping underground stems in autumn, wash off the soil and immerse them in hot water, 44°C (110°F), for about ten minutes. This should kill the disease, but take care not to damage the rhizomes by allowing the temperature to go any higher. Rinse in cold water before replanting in a fresh bed of clean soil.

A different type of rust sometimes affects chives, especially in mild areas. If plants are badly affected it is best to destroy them and raise new stock from seed.

When using any chemical on edible plants, whether it is a fungicide or insecticide, you must take certain precautions. First read the instructions on the bottle or pack fully, making sure the particular chemical is suitable for use on edible crops, and if so, how long you must wait between application and harvesting. Wherever possible, choose a chemical that has a short interval between spraying and picking—some require only a day, while others could be up to a fortnight. Also, read the small print, where you could well find a list of specific plants that could be damaged by the chemical concerned.

PROPAGATION

Once you have your herbs established, you will probably want to increase your stock by propagating from them and there are various ways in which you can do this.

Seed

You can save seed from your own plants or buy packets of seed of the most common herbs from most garden centres. Seed always seems to be a cheap way of obtaining plants but this is not necessarily true. A packet of seed costs roughly the same as one small, pot-grown plant. If you use a seed tray and compost, you must add this to the cost: remember, too that it will take several weeks before seedlings reach the same size as a bought plant. A packet of seed will of course give you a large number of plants, but if you want only one or two of each type of herb that's not much of an advantage.

Raising plants from seed is always satisfying, though, and many herbs grow very easily by this method. Many of the variegated or coloured foliage varieties will not come true from seed and must be propagated by other methods, so your choice of these is limited.

Early plants can be obtained by sowing in a frost free greenhouse in early spring. Fill a tray with sowing compost, firm and level it with a presser, then sprinkle seed carefully and evenly over the surface (Fig. 38). Cover lightly with a further layer of compost or fine silver sand. Water with a fine rose on the can and cover the tray with a piece of glass and a sheet of newspaper.

When the seedlings begin to appear, remove the newspaper; when the first one touches the glass, remove the glass. Water just sufficiently to keep the compost moist, always using a fine rose. As soon as the seedlings are large enough to be handled, prick them out into another tray with more space between them, or into individual pots. Handle them at all times by their seed leaves — never by their stems.

When they have made sturdy little plants, they can be planted outdoors. For bushiness, pinch out the growing tip when the seedling is 10 cm (4 in) high.

Some herbs can also be sown outside, direct where they are to grow—in fact some must be sown like this as they dislike being transplanted. Rake the soil level and break it down into small, even crumbs (Fig. 39). Draw out one or two shallow drills with a cane in the patch where you want your herbs to grow, then sprinkle seed along these drills. Cover with soil, patting it firm, and label the patch. Water with a fine rose. The herb seedlings will be distinguishable from the weeds because they are growing in neat rows. Once they are large enough, thin them out in stages to the correct number.

Division

In spring, when plants that died down the previous autumn are starting to re-emerge, many of the clump forming types (such as chives) can be divided. Dig up the entire plant with a garden fork and pull it to pieces carefully with your hands, making sure every piece has some strong, healthy shoots and good fibrous roots (**Fig.39a**). Replant the section straight away. Many plants are improved by regular division, making stronger growth than if they had been left alone.

Cuttings

Softwood, semi-ripe or hardwood cuttings can be taken according to the variety of plant. Soft tip

Fig.38. Seed sowing in tray *(a)* Firming the compost in the corners of the tray.

(b) Sowing seeds evenly over the surface.

(c) Covering the seeds with a layer of compost.

213

Fig. 39·a Division of border plant (a) Lift the whole plant with a garden fork.

Fig. 39. Using a rake, carefully pull the soil back over the newly sown seeds.

(b) Separate into smaller pieces by gently pulling apart.

cuttings are successful with most herbs; semi-ripe and hardwood are suitable for shrubby varieties. Another method is root cuttings — used for horseradish.

Softwood cuttings are taken in spring and early summer. Choose healthy young shoots, and trim them to between about 5 and 10 cm (2–4 in). Cut the stems cleanly just below a leaf joint using a very sharp knife or a razor blade and remove the lower leaves. If you like, you can dip the base of the stem into rooting powder and tap off the excess to leave a light dusting, though this isn't essential. Insert the cuttings in a mixture of peat and sand or a sowing and cuttings compost and water them in well. Softwood cuttings must be kept in a humid atmosphere. Spray them with water in a hand mister, and cover the tray or pot with a clear plastic propagator top or even an inflated plastic bag. Gentle warmth will encourage rapid rooting: softwood cuttings root quickly anyway, sometimes within a few days.

Semi-ripe cuttings are taken later in the summer, when the stems have started to ripen at the base but are

(c) Replant the new portions straight away.

Tansy *(Tanacetum vulgare)* has attractive finely cut foliage and yellow button flowers, but is very invasive.

still flexible. Take sideshoots of the current season's growth: if they are 15 cm (6 in) long or less, tear them away from the main stem with a small heel of older wood (Fig. 40). Longer sideshoots should be trimmed below a leaf joint with a sharp knife, making them 8–15 cm (3–6 in) long. Remove all the lower leaves and dip the base in rooting powder before inserting in a pot of sandy cuttings compost. Water in with a fine rose.

Semi-ripe cuttings are tougher than softwood and don't need so much mollycoddling. The best place for them is a garden frame out of direct sun. Keep the compost moist, but there's no need to provide the very humid conditions required by softwood cuttings. Rooting is not very fast: usually the cuttings are left in the frame (or a very sheltered spot in the garden) until growth starts the following spring.

Hardwood cuttings are a less usual way of propagating herbs but this method can be used for some shrubby types such as bay, rosemary and myrtle. The cuttings are taken in autumn, when the leaves have fallen on deciduous plants, and when plants are completely dormant. Take a well-ripened shoot of the current season's growth up to 30 cm (12 in) long, depending on the plant. Remove lower leaves of evergreens. Insert the cuttings to about half their length in light, weed-free soil in the open garden — one end of the vegetable plot is a favourite place — and firm them in with your foot. They can be left there for about 12 months. They root slowly but are trouble free.

Horseradish is the only herb that is commonly increased from root cuttings. If the large, fleshy root is dug up it can be cut into a number of sections with a knife, and each one will form a new plant.

Layering

This is almost like taking cuttings but without separating the cutting from the parent plant. Take a branch and bend it down to the soil; peg or hold it in contact with the soil with a stone. The underside of the branch can be nicked lightly to encourage rooting. Once roots have formed, the new plant can be separated from the parent, dug up and replanted.

'Mounding' is a similar method, where a spreading herb such as thyme is partially covered with soil in the centre. This holds down the branches all round, so that eventually large numbers of new plants can be separated.

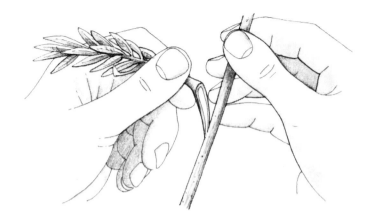

Fig. 40. Semi-ripe cuttings *(a)* Tearing off shoot with heel.

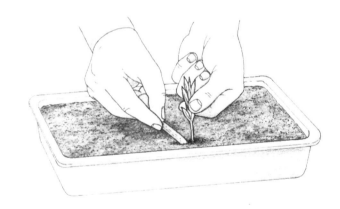

(d) Inserting cutting in tray.

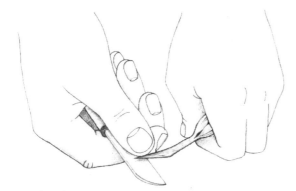

(b) Trimming shoot.

(c) Dipping shoot into rooting powder.

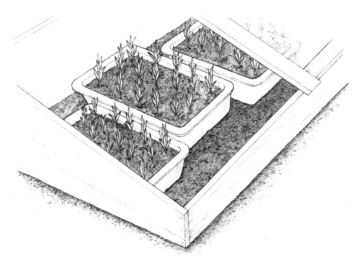

(e) Tray in cold frame.

(f) Rooted cutting.

Herbs can be mixed with border plants. The ornamental grey-leaved *Stachys lanata* blends well with cream and green variegated apple mint in the left foreground.

21

USING HERBS

You can start harvesting your herbs as soon as the plants are reasonably well established and have made enough growth not to mind the odd sprig being tweaked off. It is perfectly acceptable to pinch out the growing tips of quite small plants as this encourages them to become compact and bushy; however, it should only be the very tips of the shoots on young herbs—not half the plant!

It is the foliage that is most often used for culinary purposes. Just when you pick it and how it is used depends on the plant, but generally you should pick fairly young growth (though not the very newest shoots) which is fresh, unblemished and pest and disease free. Use it as soon as possible after harvesting—preferably within minutes as the flavour will then be at its best.

For most dishes where the herbs are to be eaten, they should be finely chopped as this ensures an even distribution of the flavour: in some dishes the whole, uncut herbs are infused into the dish and removed before serving. Even here it is a good idea to crush them lightly before adding them to the food, just to ensure the full release of their flavour.

Herbs are always best used fresh, but if you are to carry on using them in reasonable quantities through the winter, you will have to have a supply that has been preserved in some way. Because there is always some loss of flavour during the preservation process, you should gather the herbs when they are at their peak. This is generally just before flowering begins: choose a dry, sunny day and if possible pick them in the morning as soon as the dew has dried off the leaves. This is when the flavour should be at its strongest.

DRYING

Drying is the time-honoured—though not always the best—method of preserving herbs (Fig. 41). There are two schools of thought about the actual process. One is that flavour loss is kept to a minimum if the herbs are dried slowly in a reasonably cool atmosphere; the other that the drying should be completed as quickly as possible, using gentle heat. The problem with slow drying is that the herbs can get sticky and dusty (especially if they are hanging in the kitchen, which is the favourite place). A reliable method is to use a *very* cool

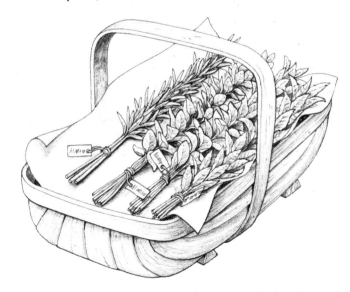

Fig. 41. Tie herbs for drying in small bunches.

oven—only just on—with the door open. Spread the herbs on cooling racks or greaseproof paper and turn them once or twice until they are quite dry and can be crumbled between the fingers.

HERBS SUITABLE FOR DRYING

Anise (seed)	Lovage
Bay	Marigold
Caraway (seed)	Marjoram
Coriander (seed)	Parsley
Cumin (seed)	Rosemary
Dill (seed)	Sage
Fennel (seed)	Savory
Hyssop	Tarragon
Juniper berries	Thyme

If you prefer to use the slow method, hang small bunches of herbs in a dry, airy place out of direct sun. Don't make the bunches large, or the centre of the bunch will remain damp and start to go mouldy. In very warm, dry weather, they will take only a few days to dry.

The flavour is preserved best if the dried herbs are left whole and crumbled just before using, but they take up more storage space like this. Once they are completely dry, they should be packed into small, tightly stoppered jars, crumbling them lightly if necessary. Keep the jars in a cool, dry cupboard, in the dark. It is better to use several small jars than one large one, because every time you take the jar out of the cupboard and remove the lid, a little more of the precious flavour and aroma escapes.

Seeds which are to be used in cooking also need to be stored dry, but these are allowed to ripen, very nearly, on the plant so that they are already dry when harvested. Because seeds have a habit of sowing themselves as soon as they are ripe, you must keep a careful eye on the plants as they approach maturity. Pick them when the first seed capsule has split open, cutting the whole stem. Be very careful when picking the stems, as a sudden movement can shower seeds everywhere! Hang the stems in bunches, upside down, with the heads securely enclosed in a paper bag: as the seed capsules gradually split open, the seeds will be shed into the bag.

Seeds should also be stored in sealed jars. Don't crush them until you are ready to use them, as the flavour is preserved much more successfully in the entire seed.

FREEZING

In most households, freezing has taken over from drying as the most popular and convenient method of food preservation, and it's ideal for herbs—especially those with delicate foliage and flavour, which do not dry successfully anyway.

Herbs should be gathered when they are in their prime and frozen as quickly as possible. They can be left whole, in sprigs, and frozen in small plastic bags. When you are ready to use them, rub the bag between your palms and the frozen herbs will be 'chopped' for use. They are no good for use as a garnish once they have been frozen as they emerge looking very bedraggled.

One of the most convenient ways of freezing herbs is as ice cubes. Chop either single herbs or mixtures finely (Fig. 42), pack them into ice cube trays, cover

Fig. 42. Chop herbs finely with a sharp knife.

with water, and freeze. Turn the frozen cubes out into polythene bags to save freezer space: a shot of soda water in each bag should stop the cubes sticking together. Just add one or two cubes to whatever dish you are cooking.

Herb butters can also be frozen; freezing them ready made is far more successful then trying to incorporate thawed herbs into butter.

HERBS BEST PRESERVED BY FREEZING

Basil	Dill	Parsley
Chervil	Fennel	Tarragon
Chives	Lemon balm	

HERB SALTS

Salt is a natural preservative and herb salts are very convenient to use. Again, you can use single herbs or make up a favourite mixture. Make sure any moisture has dried off the herbs you are using, then chop them well. Mix the chopped herbs with a good quality salt such as Maldon sea salt. The proportion of herb to salt varies according to the plant being used, but add as much herb as possible without making the salt too wet. Spread the salt and herb mix out on a baking tray and dry it in gentle heat. Break up any lumps that form before storing in airtight jars. Herb salt should replace ordinary salt on the table and in cooking; it has a very subtle flavour.

Herbs used for sweet dishes—such as sweet cicely, bay and angelica—can be mixed in a similar way with sugar. Caster sugar is best.

HERBS FOR HERB SALT

Basil	Marjoram	Thyme
Bay	Savory	

HERB SUGARS

Anise	Lemon balm	Scented geraniums
Bay	Mint	Sweet cicely

HERB VINEGARS

Use a mild-flavoured vinegar such as white wine, distilled or cider vinegar; the stronger flavoured dark malt will overpower the flavour of the herbs. Pack a jar or bottle with lightly crushed herbs and heat the vinegar (do not let it boil). Pour the hot vinegar over the herbs and seal the jar (don't use a metal cap). Shake occasionally and keep in a warm place for two to three weeks. Strain into a clean bottle and add a tall sprig of the herb you have used — this looks appealing and identifies the vinegar without the need for labelling. Use in mustards, mayonnaise and salad dressings; add sparingly to casseroles.

HERBS FOR VINEGAR

Basil	Lovage
Coriander	Mint
Dill	Rosemary
Fennel	Tarragon

HERB OILS

Good quality oil absorbs the flavour of certain herbs well. Pack a jar or bottle with lightly crushed herbs as for the vinegar and pour gently warmed oil over them. Cap loosely and leave in a warm place (a sunny windowsill is ideal), shaking or stirring frequently, and pressing the herbs. After two or three weeks strain the oil into a fresh jar of herbs and repeat the process. Herb oils can also be used in salad dressings, to rub on meat before grilling or barbecueing, in marinades, and to dress cooked vegetables lightly before serving.

HERBS FOR OILS

Basil	Savory
Fennel	Tarragon
Marjoram	Thyme
Rosemary	

221

Salvia officinalis 'Tricolor', another variegated sage. This variety has green leaves marked with cream, or purplish leaves marked with pink. The small purple flowers are popular with bees.

Sage is one of the most decorative herbs, particularly in its variegated forms. This is golden variegated sage, *Salvia officinalis* 'Icterina'.

HERB MIXTURES

There are no hard and fast rules about which herb goes with which food, and you should experiment to see what appeals to you most. However, you might find it handy to have some ready-made-up mixtures of dried herbs available to speed up food preparation when you are in a hurry. These mixtures could also form a base to which you can add other herbs and spices as available.

FOR PORK

2 parts sage
1 part rosemary
1 part chives
1 part thyme
or
2 parts juniper berries
1 part thyme
1 part lovage
1 part savory

FOR LAMB

2 parts rosemary
1 part marjoram
1 part lemon balm
or
2 parts ginger mint
1 part fennel seed
1 part cumin seed

FOR GAME

2 parts juniper berries
1 part thyme
1 part marjoram
or
2 parts caraway seed
2 parts sage
1 part lovage

FOR BEEF

1 part thyme
1 part marjoram
1 part sage

FOR FISH

1 part dill
1 part lemon thyme
Bay leaf
or
2 parts lemon balm
1 part coriander
1 part anise
1 part sweet cicely

FOR POULTRY

2 parts tarragon
1 part savory
1 part parsley
1 part lemon thyme
or
2 parts sage
2 parts parsley
1 part chives

USEFUL SPICES TO ADD TO HERB MIXTURES

Allspice
Cinnamon
Fresh ginger root
Mace
Mustard (black and white)
Nutmeg
Peppercorns (white, black and green)

Suitable for all meat and vegetable dishes.

CHEESE AND EGG DISHES

Cheese and egg dishes are usually delicately flavoured and herbs are often best used singly rather than in mixtures which could overpower the dish.

HERBS FOR CHEESE DISHES

Chives
Caraway
Chervil

Lemon thyme
Lovage

HERBS FOR EGG DISHES

Chervil
Chives

Parsley
Tarragon

HERB RECIPES

Virtually any recipe can be adapted to include herbs. The following are a few ideas, some traditional, some new, that you could try. Don't be afraid to adjust the amount and variety of herbs to suit yourself. There are no hard and fast rules in herb cookery!

Two classic mixtures to start with:

Bouquet garni

Tie together a bay leaf, 2 stems of parsley, 2 sprigs of

thyme, 2 sprigs of marjoram. (If dried herbs are used, tie them in a muslin bag.) Add to casseroles, soups etc at the start of cooking and remove before serving. Rosemary, sage, savory or other herbs can be added or substituted as appropriate.

Fines herbes

Finely chop and mix equal quantities of parsley and chervil with half the amount of tarragon and chives. Add to dishes (especially egg dishes) just before serving. Always use fresh herbs.

Herb butter

Useful for serving in pats on vegetables or meat. Try spreading a split French loaf with herb butter, wrapping in foil and warming in the oven to make herb bread — a nice change from garlic bread.

Large bunch mixed dried or (preferably) fresh herbs —
parsley, thyme, savory, marjoram, basil etc.
50g (2oz) softened butter
1 teaspoon lemon juice

Chop herbs very finely and work them and the lemon juice into the butter with a broad-bladed knife. Shape into a long block or roll, wrap in greaseproof paper and refrigerate or freeze until ready to use.

Herb stuffings

A stuffing or forcemeat is a traditional way of adding flavour to roast meat or fish.

SAGE AND ORANGE STUFFING
rind and flesh of half an orange
75g (3oz) wholemeal breadcrumbs
1 finely chopped onion
2 tablespoon chopped sage
salt and pepper
1 small egg
1 tablespoon vermouth (optional)

Grate the rind and chop the flesh of the orange and mix with the breadcrumbs, onion, sage and seasonings. Beat the egg with the vermouth if using, and add to the breadcrumb mixture. Use to stuff joints of pork or duck.

THYME AND SAVORY STUFFING
50g (2oz) wholemeal breadcrumbs
juice and grated peel of small lemon
1 tablespoon lemon thyme leaves
1 tablespoon savory leaves
1 tablespoon chopped chives
½ finely chopped onion
pinch of ground ginger

Mix all ingredients with sufficient water to bind. Shape into balls with damp hands, dot with margarine and bake in a moderate oven for 15–20 minutes.

Herb dumplings

250g (8oz) self raising flour
pinch of salt
125g (4oz) suet
2 tablespoons chopped fresh mixed herbs (or half the
amount of dried mixed herbs)
water to mix

Sift flour and salt and add suet and herbs. Mix to a soft dough with water and with floured hands form into small dumplings. Add to soups or stews about 20 minutes before the end of cooking time.

Barbecues

The warm, spicy flavours of herbs are ideal for barbecues. Try laying a few branches of rosemary on the coals to give off aromatic smoke while the food is cooking.

MARINADE FOR MEAT
150ml (¼pt) red wine
1 tablespoon vegetable oil
1 shallot or small onion
1 tablespoon wine vinegar
bay leaf
3 sprigs thyme
2 sprigs sage
3 allspice berries
½ teaspoon chopped root ginger

Warm all ingredients together and allow to cool before using.

BASTING OIL
1 clove garlic
3 sprigs oregano
3 sprigs basil
2 sprigs rosemary
4 tablespoons vegetable oil (preferably herb flavoured oil)

Crush the garlic and lightly bruise the herbs. Put all ingredients into a saucepan and warm together for 10 minutes. Allow to cool. Use to brush on meat or fish before and during barbecueing.

Pasta

The bland taste of plainly cooked pasta is the ideal foil for herb flavoured sauces.

PESTO
large bunch fresh basil—about 75g (3oz)
pinch of salt
50g (2oz) pine kernels
2 garlic cloves
50g (2oz) grated Parmesan
4–5 tablespoons olive oil

Pound basil, salt, pine kernels and garlic cloves in a pestle and mortar. Add Parmesan, then gradually add the oil until it is well blended. A blender or food processor can be used to amalgamate all the ingredients instead. Store in a refrigerator: stir through freshly cooked pasta.

TOMATO SAUCE
1 rasher streaky bacon or 25g (1oz) vegetable margarine
1 garlic clove
1 small onion
500g (1lb) ripe tomatoes
½ teaspoon brown sugar
salt and pepper
1 tablespoon chopped fresh oregano
1 tablespoon chopped fresh basil

Chop bacon and cook over a low heat to extract the fat, or melt margarine. Add crushed garlic clove and finely chopped onion; cook until soft but not brown. Roughly chop the tomatoes (skinned if you prefer) and cook until thoroughly softened. For a smooth sauce, blend and sieve. Season, add the sugar and stir in the herbs.

Salads

Finely chopped herbs of all sorts can be sprinkled over salads or mixed with dressings. Make oil and vinegar dressings with herb vinegar, or try this attractive mayonnaise.

GREEN MAYONNAISE
6 stems of watercress
6 stems of parsley
12 large sorrel leaves
300ml (½pt) mayonnaise

Pour boiling water over the herbs and leave them for 5 minutes. Drain thoroughly, add to mayonnaise and blend in a liquidizer.

Herb jellies

Mint jelly is the best known, and infinitely superior to mint sauce. Sage or rosemary can also be used.

2.5kg (5½lb) cooking apples or crab apples
large bunch of fresh mint
1.3l (2¼pt) water
1.3l (2¼pt) vinegar
sugar
8 tablespoons finely chopped mint leaves

Even a small garden has room for a herb border. Strategically placed stone slabs make all the plants accessible but are unobtrusive.

Chop the apples and put in a large pan with the bunch of whole mint. Cover with the water and simmer until the apples are soft, then add the vinegar and boil for a further 10 minutes. Strain through a jelly bag. Measure the amount of juice and add 450g (1lb) sugar to every 500ml (1pt) juice. Boil until setting point is reached. Remove from the heat and allow to cool for about 10 minutes before stirring in the chopped mint. Pour into warm jars and seal.

Apple fool

This can also be made with gooseberries or rhubarb.

250g (½lb) apples
1 tablespoon chopped sweet cicely
honey
small carton double cream or plain yogurt
1 egg white

Peel and chop the apples and cook them with sweet cicely until pulped. Add honey to taste (be careful not to add too much). Fold in the whisked cream or yogurt and the stiffly beaten egg white. Chill. Decorate with candied angelica.

POT POURRI

The scent of summer flowers can be preserved all year round by making *pot pourri*. There are two methods, moist and dry. Moist *pot pourri* has a better, longer lasting fragrance, while dry *pot pourri* has a more attractive appearance.

The basis of most *pot pourri* is rose petals. Old-fashioned roses are best, but any highly scented variety will do. Collect the petals when the flowers are at their peak. Add whatever other scented flowers and leaves are available, together with some spices, and a fixative to preserve the scent—gum benzoin and orris root are the most readily available.

For dry *pot pourri*, spread the petals and leaves on newspaper or a drying frame in an airy room to dry slowly until they are crisp before mixing them. For moist *pot pourri*, leave them to dry for only one or two days, until they are limp.

Varying the proportions of the different flowers, foliage and spices will give very different fragrances.

Dry pot pourri

Store dried petals and leaves separately in airtight containers until you have enough, then tip them into a large mixing bowl. To each 2 litres (½ gallon) add 1 teaspoon each of finely ground cinnamon, allspice and cloves, and one bay leaf torn into pieces. Mix thoroughly, then add 8g (¼oz) gum benzoin and 30g (1oz) orris root powder. Store in a tightly closed jar, shaking daily, for about two months, then tip into containers. The two months' storage is necessary to allow the full fragrance to develop.

Moist pot pourri

Dry petals and leaves for one or two days until they are limp and leathery. Pack into an earthenware jar or similar container to make a layer about 10cm (4in) deep, then cover with rock or sea salt to about 5mm (¼in). Add further layers as materials are available, stirring the contents of the pot first. Weight the *pot pourri* down after adding each new batch if possible. At the end of the season, break up the mixture and add dried orange peel, cloves, cinnamon, mace, bay leaves, orris root powder and a small amount of brandy to moisten. Put it back in the jar, pressing well down, weight it and leave it to mature for several months.

Pot pourri should be kept in closed jars, with the lids taken off as required to scent the room: this way their aroma lasts much longer. In open bowls they will have a shorter life, but can be stirred occasionally and revitalized with essential oils if necessary.

Suitable ingredients for pot pourri

FLOWERS

Roses, carnations, lavender, pinks, jasmine, stocks, wallflowers, honeysuckle, lily of the valley, philadelphus, thyme, bergamot, mignonette, myrtle, violets, heliotrope, choisya, peonies.

LEAVES

Thyme, lemon verbena, scented geraniums, mint, rosemary, bay, sweetbriar, lavender, southernwood, sweet cicely, lemon balm, bergamot, myrtle, choisya, sage, costmary, eucalyptus, marjoram, chamomile.

SPICES

Allspice, cinnamon, mace, coriander, cloves, nutmeg, aniseed.

This is not a complete list — virtually any scented flower or leaf can be added to a pot pourri.

SACHETS

Make up small muslin sachets and fill with dried herbs such as lavender or dry *pot pourri* mix to store among linen or to hang in the wardrobe. Use a mixture of insect-repellent herbs to keep moths away —mint, rue, cotton lavender, rosemary, tansy, southernwood and wormwood.

Remember that the fragrance does not last for ever —you should make up new sachets every year.

HERB PILLOWS

Use a double thickness of cotton to make a pillow slip, to prevent dust from the herbs from escaping from the pillow. Dried hops are traditionally used to ensure sound sleep, otherwise fill the pillow slips with any pleasantly scented, dried mixture.

HERB BATHS

To scent a bath, make a muslin bag containing your chosen herbs plus a tablespoon of oatmeal. Hang this from the hot tap so that the water runs through it. Alternatively, pour boiling water over a handful of bruised herbs in a large jug, leave it to brew, then strain into the bathwater. Good bath herbs are rosemary, mint, lemon verbena, chamomile, peppermint.

SIMPLE SKIN CREAM

500 g (1 lb) pure clarified lard or petroleum jelly
Elderflowers, stripped from their stems

Melt the lard or petroleum jelly and pack in as many elderflowers, pressed well down, as can be covered. Keep on a very low heat (do not boil) for an hour. Strain into jars. Use as a soothing and protecting hand and face cream.

MEDICINAL HERBS

Many herbs have strong medicinal properties, but self-medication is not recommended. Apart from the dangers of overdosing or even poisoning, there is a risk of herbal treatments masking the symptoms of a more serious disease. Illnesses and recurrent problems should always be taken to your doctor.

Herbal teas (in moderate amounts) are pleasant and refreshing to drink and can help to alleviate the symptoms of simple illnesses like colds or stomach upsets. Pour boiling water on to dried or lightly crushed fresh herbs and leave to infuse for about 10 minutes. Strain. Add lemon juice and honey to taste.

Rosemary, peppermint, lemon verbena, elderflowers, sage, lavender, chamomile and rose hips make good teas.

SMALL GARDENS: HERBS

TO ALLEVIATE COLDS AND COUGHS:

Chamomile	Mallow
Fennel	Rosemary
Garlic	Sage
Horehound	Thyme
Hyssop	

TO AID THE DIGESTION:

Anise	Dill
Caraway	Fennel
Chamomile	Marjoram
Coriander	Peppermint

MILD DIURETICS:

Parsley	Savory
Sage	Tarragon

POISONOUS HERBS:

Belladonna	Henbane
Bryony	Lily of the valley
Foxglove	Monkshood
Hemlock	Thornapple

The papery pink flowers of chives *(Allium schoenoprasum)* are particularly attractive and are very freely produced.

22

A-Z SELECTION OF POPULAR HERBS

ANGELICA
Angelica archangelica (Umbelliferae)
Biennial or short-lived perennial
Angelica is a majestic herb, commonly growing from 2–2.5 m (6–8 ft) tall. When grown from seed, in the first year a small rosette of leaves is all that appears. In the second or perhaps third year, the thick, hollow flower stems shoot up, carrying great cartwheels of tiny, sweet-smelling, pale green flowers in early summer. Leaves in the second year are larger, with broad petioles, and are divided into leaflets.

Wild angelica is a plant of woodland and river banks, and the cultivated variety retains the preference for rich, moist soil and a lightly shaded position. The life of the plant is prolonged if the flowerheads are cut off before seed is set: self-sown seedlings appear in large numbers if the seed is allowed to fall naturally.
Uses: Stems, leaf stems, root, seed and leaves are all used, though the candied stems are the most familiar. All parts are pleasantly aromatic, particularly the seeds, which are used to flavour drinks including gin and vermouth. The leaves and roots can be added to stewed fruit to reduce its acidity.

ANISE
Pimpinella anisum (Umbelliferae)
Annual
A sweet, aromatic herb with a very distinctive flavour, anise is a native of Mediterranean regions. The plant grows from 45–60 cm (1½–2 ft) with rounded, lobed basal leaves having serrated edges, and feathery, finely cut upper leaves on the flower stems. Flowers are small and cream, held in typical umbels appearing in July and August. They are followed by pale brown, ribbed seeds which are widely used as a flavouring.

Anise likes a warm climate and seeds do not ripen well in northern regions. In cold areas, sow the seeds in fibre pots in a greenhouse in early spring, planting the complete pot outside in a sunny position after the risk of frost is over. Otherwise sow direct in a sunny spot after frosts have finished; mark the position as anise is slow to germinate.
Uses: Ripe seeds are used as flavouring for sweet dishes and in curry mixtures; they have medicinal value as an aid to digestion, and they help soothe coughs. Their most important commercial use is in *pastis* such as Pernod, and liqueurs. The foliage can be added to fish dishes or used in salads.

BALM
Melissa officinalis (Labiatae)
Perennial
Another Mediterranean native, but one that grows well in both northern and southern climates. Lemon balm, or bee balm, is a bushy herb reaching around 60 cm (2 ft). It has bright green, rounded leaves which are wrinkled and rough: a variegated variety, splashed with yellow, is known as golden balm. White, nettle-like flowers appear in midsummer and are very attractive to bees.

Plants can be raised from seed, cuttings, or by division. They will grow in most soils, though a reasonably moist position is preferred.
Uses: Leaves have a strong, pleasant citrus scent, and

can be used in any dishes where a lemon flavour is appropriate. They make a refreshing herbal tea which helps relieve headaches. Balm is best used fresh for culinary purposes, but dried leaves can be added to *pot pourri* or stored with linen both to scent it and to repel insects. Harvest the stems just before flowering; the aroma is very volatile and is soon lost.

BASIL
Ocimum basilicum (Labiatae)
Annual

Sometimes called king of herbs, basil grows to around 45 cm (1½ ft), forming a bushy plant with smooth, light green, tender leaves and spikes of small white flowers. 'Dark Opal' is a particularly attractive variety with deep purple foliage. Basil likes a warm climate, and in cool areas seed should be raised in a greenhouse in early spring, plants being set out after frosts are over.

Grow basil in a sunny spot on free draining soil: sow more seeds outside in summer to ensure a succession of young plants. Pinch out flowering shoots to promote leafy growth.

Uses: The foliage is very pungent, with a warm, sweet, spicy scent similar to cloves. It is traditionally used with tomatoes, but can be added to many savoury dishes.

As basil has a powerful flavour it should be used with discretion; the fresh foliage is far superior to dried. Basil aids the digestion and stimulates the appetite: sniffing the crushed foliage helps to clear the head. A few basil leaves added to a *pot pourri* give it a pleasant, spicy fragrance.

BAY
Laurus nobilis (Lauraceae)
Perennial

This rather tender evergreen tree has lanceolate, shiny, deep green leaves. It can grow to around 9 m (30 ft) in warm climates, but is very amenable to clipping and is often grown trained as a standard or pyramid. Fluffy white flowers in early summer are followed by black berries.

Plant bay in a sheltered position on light, well-drained soil. In cold areas, grow plants in tubs so that they can be taken indoors in cold spells. Propagate from soft or semi-ripe cuttings in summer. Watch out for scale insects on the undersides of the leaves—these eventually lead to disfiguring sooty mould growth.

Uses: The mature leaves are dried and used whole in soups, stews, sauces and rice pudding; they also form part of a *bouquet garni*. Tear the edges of the leaves before use. They have a powerful flavour and dry well. Remove them from the dish before serving. In Greek and Roman times, a 'laurel wreath' (of bay) was an award of honour.

BERGAMOT
Monarda didyma (Labiatae)
Perennial

A decorative plant from North America, bergamot stands about 90 cm (3 ft) high with long, toothed, mid-green leaves. Flowers appear in midsummer in shaggy, scarlet whorls; there is also a pink-flowered variety. Bergamot prefers a rich, fairly moist soil with some organic matter such as garden compost added. It can be grown from seed, but is more usually propagated by division in spring.

Uses: The leaves have a strong, rich, citrus fragrance and can be used to make tea. This was a common drink of the Oswego Indians and has given bergamot its alternative name of Oswego tea. The foliage is an excellent addition to a *pot pourri*. Leaves can be dried throughout the summer; they are at their most fragrant if picked just before flowering.

Bergamot is a favourite plant of bees, who visit the lipped flowers whenever they are open. The bergamot oil of perfumery is derived not from this plant, but from the Italian bergamot orange which has a very similar fragrance.

BORAGE
Borago officinalis (Boraginaceae)
Annual

This fast growing plant quickly reaches around 90 cm (3 ft) high, with a very hairy stem and rough, wrinkled, bristly leaves. The flowers are star-like, pink in

Tanacetum vulgare 'Crispen': this form of tansy has particularly good, bright green foliage.

Melissa officinalis aureus: golden variegated balm. This easily grown plant adds a splash of bright colour to the herb garden. The leaves have a distinct lemon scent and flavour.

bud, becoming brilliant blue on opening, with prominent black anthers. The flowers characteristically hang their heads.

Borage is a hardy annual and very easy to grow on virtually any soil. It seeds itself with great enthusiasm, but the tough-looking seedlings, with their large seed leaves, are easy to spot and rogue out if they are not wanted.

Uses: The foliage has a refreshing cucumber flavour and is often used in summer drinks, especially fruit cups. It can also be used in salads, but pick only the young leaves, before they become too hairy. The bright blue flowers have a similar mild flavour and can be added to salads or used to decorate cold dishes; they can be floated on drinks or frozen into ice cubes. Borage has an age-old reputation as a promoter of cheerfulness and courage.

CARAWAY
Carum carvi (Umbelliferae)
Biennial

Caraway has pale green, feathery, divided leaves: in its second year it produces heads of pinkish white flowers which are followed by dark brown, ridged seeds. If the flower stems are removed the plants can be kept growing for another year but they self-seed readily if allowed too, ensuring a perennial supply.

Seeds can be sown in spring or autumn in any moderately rich soil in a sunny position. Self-sown seedlings should be thinned out as soon as they can be identified. Plants grow to around 60 cm (2 ft).

Uses: The seeds are the most strongly flavoured part of the plant, with a warm, spicy, characteristic taste and aroma. Familiar as the flavouring for 'seed cake', they are also widely used in bread and biscuits, and with cabbage in the German *sauerkraut*.

The foliage and stems can also be used, having a flavour similar to, but milder than, the seeds. They are especially suitable for fish and cheese dishes, and are good in salads, too. Caraway seeds aid digestion, so they are often eaten with rich foods. They are used commercially as a flavouring for *kummel* and other liqueurs.

CHAMOMILE
Anthemis nobilis (Compositae)
Perennial

This low-growing, creeping plant goes under several other Latin names, the commonest being *Chamaemelum nobile*. It has finely divided, apple-scented, ferny leaves and daisy-like white and yellow flowers which stand about 30 cm (1 ft) tall.

Chamomile is frequently grown as a lawn substitute, sometimes in the mistaken belief that it is labour saving. Small chamomile lawns can be effective and pleasantly aromatic, but need painstaking hand weeding while they are getting established. They will stand less wear than grass. The variety 'Treneague' is best for lawns — it is neater because it does not flower.

Chamomile likes a well-drained position in full sun. Ordinary varieties can be raised from seed but 'Treneague' must be propagated by division of the runners.

Uses: Chamomile has no real culinary use, but the fresh or dried flowerheads can be made into a tea which is taken for stomach upsets, headaches or colds. It can also be applied externally to soothe minor wounds, and forms a pleasant rinse for light-coloured hair. Commercially it is used in some cosmetic preparations.

CHERVIL
Anthriscus cerefolium (Umbelliferae)
Annual

Chervil is a dainty, fragile-looking plant, with pale green, lacy leaves and small umbels of delicate white flowers. It grows to between 60 and 90 cm (2–3 ft) on lightly shaded, moisture-retentive soil.

Chervil should be sown several times in a season, starting in late spring and continuing until midsummer for a succession of leafy plants. Sow where it is to grow, as the plants resent root disturbance. If seedheads are allowed to form the plant will sow itself readily, but to promote maximum foliage growth the flowering stems can be removed.

Uses: The soft foliage has a fresh, delicate flavour of aniseed. It disperses very quickly, so the herb should be used as soon as possible after harvesting and must be added to cooked dishes just before serving. It is particularly good with fish and eggs, and in salads.

Chervil also makes a pretty garnish for delicately flavoured dishes, in place of the more robust tasting parsley.

CHIVES
Allium schoenoprasum (Liliaceae)
Perennial
Chives are the smallest and prettiest member of the onion family, growing to about 22–30 cm (9–12 in) tall. The grass-like leaves are cylindrical, tapering and hollow, forming large clumps with small bulbs just below the surface of the soil. In summer, round, pink, papery flowers are produced. While these are very decorative, they should be removed to stimulate maximum foliage growth. The answer is to grow two clumps, allowing one to flower and keeping the other for culinary use.

Chives are easily grown from seed, and once established the clumps should be divided every two or three years in spring. If yellow, withered leaves appear, water the plants with a liquid feed. Chives like a fairly moisture-retentive soil.
Uses: Chives have a delicate onion flavour and can be used in any dish where this is appropriate. Their mild flavour is particularly suitable in salads, with eggs and cheese, and as a garnish for soup. Chop finely, and add to dishes shortly before the end of cooking.

CORIANDER
Coriandrum sativum (Umbelliferae)
Annual
The divided, mid-green leaves—broad at the base and finer towards the top of the plant—and small, pinkish white flowers are typical of the umbellifer family. The flowers are followed by clusters of round, brown, strong-smelling seeds.

Seeds of this 60 cm (2 ft) hardy annual can be sown in autumn or early spring in free-draining soil in a sunny position. Sow where the plants are to grow, as they do not like root disturbance.
Uses: The foliage and unripe seeds have a very strong, penetrating scent which some people find unpleasant: it is warm and spicy but difficult to describe accurately. When ripe, the seeds lose some of these unpleasant undertones, and these, together with the fresh leaves, are widely used in Indian cookery. They are suitable for any strongly spiced savoury dish, particularly curries.

Coriander is thought to have a beneficial effect on the digestion.

COSTMARY
Balsamita major (Compositae)
Perennial
This plant has long, pale green leaves with toothed edges, and small yellow flowers. It grows to about 90 cm (3 ft) but tends to sprawl unless supported. Its general weed-like appearance is reinforced by the fact that it is very invasive. The roots should be restricted to prevent costmary taking over the whole herb bed.

It can be raised from seed, but once established is easily increased by division in autumn or spring. Well-drained soil is preferred.
Uses: Costmary is also known as alecost and bible leaf: alecost because it was once used to flavour beer (like hops) and bible leaf because the pressed leaves were used as scented bible bookmarks. They have a sweet, spicy fragrance rather like balsam and can also be stored amongst linen and in *pot pourri*. It has insect repellent properties.

Costmary is not much used as a culinary herb but can be added in very small amounts to strongly flavoured dishes.

CURRY PLANT
Helichrysum angustifolium (Compositae)
Perennial
A small, evergreen shrub growing to about 60 cm (2 ft) with narrow, needle-like silvery leaves: a good decora-

tive plant grown for its bright effect. Flowers are yellow, button-like and not particularly decorative. They are produced from midsummer. Plant in full sun in light, free-draining soil. The curry plant can be propagated from tip cuttings during the summer months.

Uses: The foliage of this plant gives off a warm curry scent not just when the foliage is touched, but when it is in hot sunshine. It is a pleasant fragrance which carries for some distance. The flavour is not as strong as the scent, but a few sprigs can be added to delicately flavoured foods to give them a mild, spicy aroma. Dried leaves can also be added in very small quantities to a *pot pourri*, and they can be used to ward off insects.

DILL
Anethum graveolens (Umbelliferae)
Annual

Dill makes a striking plant of about 90 cm (3 ft) high, with finely cut, feathery leaves. The flat heads of yellow flowers are followed by brown, ridged, aromatic seeds.

Sow dill in moist soil in spring, where the plants are to grow: they prefer a sunny position. A second sowing in early summer will provide a further supply of foliage while the first sowing is allowed to set seed. Do not allow the soil to dry out.

Uses: The delicate anise flavour of the leaves goes well with fish and vegetables. Add dill leaves to a dish shortly before serving as prolonged cooking destroys the flavour. The seeds are more strongly aromatic, warm and spicy; they can be added to pickles, bread and cakes as well as being used in fish dishes. Dill water is made by infusing the crushed seed and is often given to babies to soothe them and aid digestion.

FENNEL
Foeniculum vulgare (Umbelliferae)
Perennial

A plant which looks similar to dill, fennel is taller—up to 2 m (6 ft) — with even more feathery, thread-like foliage. The yellow flowers are borne in broad umbels from midsummer and set curved, aromatic seeds. Bronze fennel is a variety with dark, purple-bronze foliage, good for decorative borders; Florence fennel has swollen leaf bases which, in fennel's native Mediterranean countries, form a large, crisp 'bulb'. (In northern climates it takes a very warm summer to produce anything resembling this bulb!)

Sow fennel in spring in an open, sunny position in moisture-retentive soil.

Uses: Both foliage and seeds are used, the seeds having the stronger aroma. Their anise flavour is similar to that of dill, and fennel should be used in much the same way. The seeds aid digestion, and fennel is traditionally thought to cure a wide number of assorted ailments as well as protecting against witchcraft.

GARLIC
Allium sativum (Liliaceae)
Perennial

One of the most famous herbs, this member of the onion family forms a compound bulb containing several 'cloves', each of which produce tall, slender leaves growing between 30 and 45 cm (12–18 in). Small round heads of pinkish flowers may appear in a warm midsummer.

Garlic does best in the warmth of Mediterranean summers but grows reasonably well in northern climates. Buy a bulb from the greengrocer or supermarket and break it into separate cloves: plant these in well-drained soil in a warm, sunny position in late summer to overwinter. In heavier soils, plant in early spring. Harvest when the leaves begin to die down in summer.

Uses: The leaves are strongly aromatic and may be used in cooking to give a less pungent flavour than the bulb. It is the bulb that is mainly used, however, in almost any savoury dish. Use it very sparingly, for the flavour is penetrating and lingering. Garlic has been credited with dozens of health-giving attributes and is thought to be a good general tonic and guard against infection when eaten regularly.

The feathery foliage and yellow flowerheads of fennel *(Foeniculum vulgare)* make this a valuable garden plant.

GERANIUM
Pelargonium species *(Geraniaceae)*
Perennials

The name geranium is, strictly, inaccurate, for these are the tender pelargoniums which need to be over-wintered in a house or greenhouse in cold climates. There are many different species and varieties with strongly scented foliage. They must be overwintered in a frost-free place and started into growth in spring: the best plants are produced from cuttings taken from the new young shoots. In summer they can go outside in pots or tubs. Flowers are small, white or pink and usually fairly insignificant.

Uses: The scents include lemon, balsam, southern-wood, peppermint, rose, apple, eucalyptus and clove: some are amazingly powerful. On most varieties, the foliage needs to be lightly rubbed before the fragrance is released. Apart from their uses in *pot pourri* and scented sachets, leaves can be used to flavour cakes and drinks.

HORSERADISH
Armoracia rusticana (Cruciferae)
Perennial

The leaves of horseradish look rather like dock leaves; they are large and coarse. Sometimes in midsummer white or pale pink flowers are produced in loose panicles: they are the typical four-petalled cruciferous flowers.

The roots of horseradish are large and very invasive; this is a plant that becomes a determined weed if it is not kept under control. Plant the roots in old bottomless buckets sunk in the soil, or in trenches lined with slate (traditionally) or heavy duty polythene. Rich, moisture-retentive soil produces the best roots.

Uses: Young leaves are sharp, hot and spicy, but they are rarely used. It is the thick, white root, peeled and grated, that gives us one of our most powerful seasonings. A traditional accompaniment to roast beef and smoked mackerel, horseradish can also be used to zip up many other meats, fish and salads. It is related to mustard and has the same hot, biting tang: it is far worse than onions for making the eyes water! Mix the grated root with a little vinegar and thick cream to make horseradish sauce.

HYSSOP
Hyssopus officinalis (Labiatae)
Perennial

A bushy plant with small, narrow leaves and blue, pink or white hooded flowers, hyssop grows to around 90 cm (3 ft) high. It likes a warm, sunny position in free-draining soil.

Seed can be sown in spring, or tip cuttings of young shoots can be taken in early summer. Established bushes may be clipped back in spring to prevent them from becoming leggy and untidy. Hyssop stands clipping well and can be grown as a low hedge.

Uses: Leaves are strongly aromatic, slightly bitter and somewhat minty. The flavour is strong, so hyssop should be used sparingly. It is good in sausages or with any form of pork, and is a useful herb for stuffings, particularly to accompany rich meats.

Tea made from the foliage is useful for coughs, colds and asthma; it is also a digestive. The foliage can be dried for use in winter (though the plant is semi-evergreen in reasonably warm situations).

JUNIPER
Juniperus communis (Cupressaceae)
Perennial

A shrubby conifer with whorls of spiky leaves: they are blue-green above and shining silver beneath. The tree grows up to 2 m (6 ft) or so in sheltered positions but can be low and spreading on the windswept downland that is its natural habitat. Many decorative garden forms have been bred.

Juniper is an accommodating plant and will grow in most situations, though it prefers sun and free draining soil.

Female plants bear berries which ripen very gradually, over two or three years. They turn from green to black, overlaid by a bluish bloom.

Uses: The berries have a strong, sharp, clean aroma: they are used commercially to flavour gin. Pick them when they are fully ripe and dry them before storing. Crush them lightly before use. They are particularly appropriate with game, but are also useful for winter soups and casseroles. Use them sparingly as the flavour can be overpowering.

LAVENDER
Lavandula species *(Labiatae)*
Perennial

The common lavender, *Lavandula angustifolia*, is a low-growing bush with narrow, pointed, silver leaves and spikes of purple-blue, highly scented flowers. It loves hot sun and is happiest in very free-draining soil.

Allowed to grow freely, it will reach about 90 cm (3 ft), but the stems will be gnarled and twisted, bare at the base and rather unlovely. To keep growth compact and bushy, trim the shrubs back fairly hard after flowering. *Lavandula spica*, *L. vera* and *L. officinalis* are synonymous with *L. angustifolia*. Good varieties include 'Hidcote', neat and compact, and 'Twickel Purple', with deep blue flowers. French lavender, *L. stoechas*, is a more compact grower: its flowers have large bracts and a quite distinctive appearance.
Uses: Lavender is *the* herb for scenting linen: it is also very widely used commercially as a fragrance for cosmetics. The flowers are at their most aromatic as the first buds on a spike begin to open; pick them on a sunny morning and hang them up in an airy room to dry. Use them in *pot pourri*, sachets and for scenting bath water (the name itself originates from the Latin *lavare*, meaning to wash).

LEMON VERBENA
Lippia citriodora (Verbenaceae)
Perennial

This graceful shrub, which used to go under the name of *Aloysia citriodora*, grows to around 2 m (6 ft) with long, tapering light green leaves. In late summer it bears clusters of pinkish flowers. It is rather tender, and though it may well grow outdoors in milder regions, there is always a risk of it being killed by prolonged or particularly sharp frost.

Take cuttings of healthy young shoots in early summer and overwinter these in a frost-free place as an insurance against winter losses. Grow the plant on light, very well drained soil and give winter protection: in cold areas keep it in a pot and move it under cover for the winter.
Uses: The leaves have a sharp, pleasant, citrus scent which will enliven a *pot pourri* or make an aromatic infusion. They can be added, finely chopped, to a variety of sweet or savoury dishes: as the flavour is quite strong, only small amounts need to be used.

LOVAGE
Levisticum officinale (Umbelliferae)
Perennial

This tall, stout herb is similar to angelica, with divided leaves and flowering stems up to 2 m (6 ft), carrying large, greenish yellow umbels of flowers. It will grow in sun or light shade, and likes a moist, rich soil.

The foliage dies down in winter, but strong young shoots grow again in mid spring. The foliage is sometimes attacked by leaf miner: affected leaflets should be picked off and destroyed. For maximum foliage, flower stems can be snapped off as soon as they appear, but the large plants can normally provide ample supplies in any case, and can be allowed to flower and seed.
Uses: Foliage and seeds have a strong celery or yeasty aroma and flavour and can be added to many savoury dishes. Use in small quantities as lovage can be overpowering: it is too strong for very delicately flavoured foods. Seeds are useful in winter when the topgrowth has died down.

MARIGOLD
Calendula officinalis (Compositae)
Annual

These very popular bedding plants are often called pot

marigolds—not because they are grown in pots, but because they are used in cooking. There are many decorative varieties available. The leaves are quite large and coarse, pale green, and growing to about 30 cm (1 ft). Flowers, in shades of orange, are daisy-like with many petals. They are produced in great profusion above the leaves all summer.

Marigolds are very easily grown. Sow the seed where it is to flower in March or April and thin the seedlings as they develop. Make a further sowing in late August to provide plants which will overwinter and flower early the following year — though they generally sow themselves very freely in any case.

Uses: The petals add a golden colour and subtle flavour to savoury dishes. They can be sprinkled on salads or added to cooked dishes such as risotto, casseroles and soups, as well as puddings and cakes. Cooked petals look a bit bedraggled: you can infuse them in boiling water and strain the infusion into the dish instead of adding the petals direct if you prefer.

MARJORAM
Origanum species *(Labiatae)*
Perennial
There are several different marjorams, all of which have a warm, sweet flavour. The most commonly grown is sweet marjoram, *O. marjorana*, a tender perennial which is usually treated as an annual. It grows to about 25 cm (10 in) tall with small, mid-green, slightly hairy leaves and purple-pink flowers. *O. vulgare*, wild marjoram or oregano, is hardy and makes a spreading plant about 60 cm (2 ft) tall. It has a good, strong flavour; a golden leaved form is available. Pot marjoram *(O. onites)* is also hardy, slightly more compact, with a mild flavour.

Marjorams of all types grow well in a sunny position in light soil. Trim them back in midsummer if they become leggy.
Uses: Marjoram is particularly good with tomatoes, but is suitable for any savoury dish or salad, especially delicately flavoured meats. Sweet marjoram is a pleasant addition to scented sachets.

MINT
Mentha species *(Labiatae)*
Perennial
Surely one of the best known herbs, 'mint' may be one of many species, with widely differing foliage and fragrance. Nearly all the mints are very invasive, spreading by creeping underground stems. They are easy—almost too easy!—to grow, and need to be kept firmly under control.

Plant in moist soil in sun or light shade. Restrain the roots by planting within a bottomless bucket sunk up to its rim in the soil, or in a hole with the sides lined with heavy duty polythene, or use some similar trick to prevent mint taking over the entire garden. It has a disconcerting habit of racing along underground and popping up cheerfully several yards away where you don't notice it until it has thoroughly established itself.

The major disease is rust, which can be quite devastating. Look for rusty orange spots under the leaves; as soon as any are seen, cut off affected stems and burn them.

Good varieties include spearmint *(Mentha viridis)* with pointed, light green leaves; apple mint *(M. rotundifolia)* rounded, hairy leaves with a fruity scent; peppermint *(M. piperata)* deep, reddish green foliage, well-known aroma; ginger mint *(M. gentilis)* spicy mint scent and golden variegated leaves; and eau de Cologne mint *(M. citrata)* which smells just as you might expect. Pennyroyal *(M. pulegium)* and Corsican mint *(M. requienii)* are prostrate, small leaved species good for ground cover.
Uses: Mint is a good culinary herb, a traditional accompaniment to lamb. It has many other uses, though: try it in salads; with young, early summer vegetables (not just peas and new potatoes!); with any simply cooked meat. It can also be added to sweet dishes. Include the fruit-scented mints in *pot pourri* and sachets; hang it in the kitchen as a fly repellent, and use a bunch of eau de Cologne mint to scent bath water.

Armoracia rusticana variegata: variegated horseradish. The pungent roots of this herb are very invasive if they are not contained in some way.

MYRTLE
Myrtus communis (Myrtaceae)
Perennial
A sprig of myrtle was once traditionally included in every bride s bouquet. It is a rounded, evergreen, slightly tender shrub which will reach 3 m (10 ft) high in sheltered conditions. The dark green, glossy leaves are small and spiky: in summer creamy white flowers with bunches of prominent white stamens burst open. In warm years, bluish black berries follow.

Myrtle needs a sheltered place in warm gardens; in cold areas it makes a good conservatory plant. It can be propagated by semi-ripe or hardwood cuttings. Give plants outdoors some winter protection.
Uses: Foliage, flowers and stems of myrtle are all strongly and pleasantly aromatic. The leaves and flowers should be added to *pot pourri* and sachets.

Myrtle is not commonly used in cooking, but its spicy scent is appropriate to game and pork. The berries are also edible.

PARSLEY
Petroselinum crispum (Umbelliferae)
Biennial
Surely this is a herb that everyone knows! The frilly edged, tightly curled leaves are deep green and grow to about 25 cm (10 in): the compact plants make good edging. In the second year, tall flower stems with heads of white flowers are produced.

Parsley has an unwarranted reputation of being difficult to grow. Seed is slow to germinate in cold conditions, but given a little warmth seedlings can appear in days rather than the six to eight weeks usually expected. Make one sowing in spring and another in late summer: allow some plants to flower and seed and you should get a perennial supply of parsley from self-sown seedlings. If the early sowing is made in a warm greenhouse, it will germinate much more rapidly; it can then be planted out later (unless you are superstitious!).

There is a plain-leaved form of parsley sometimes known as Italian parsley, which has a good flavour and grows well in poor conditions.
Uses: Parsley is most familiar as an uneaten garnish—a terrible waste! Leaves and leaf stalks have a strong, appetising flavour and can be finely chopped and added to many savoury dishes. Parsley is thought to prevent the smell of garlic lingering on the breath.

ROSE
Rosa species *(Rosaceae)*
Perennial
It is the old fashioned roses that are most valuable as herbs, and there are many varieties to choose from. Most have only one, fairly short flowering season, but they make up for that with the quality of their blooms — usually large and blowsy, very strongly scented. Most are pink or white: some turn attractive shades of lavender, maroon and slate-grey as they age. Varieties of *Rosa gallica* are particularly useful. The hybrid sweetbriars, such as 'Lady of Penzance', have the bonus of aromatic foliage.

Roses like a well-drained, moderately fertile soil in an open, sunny position. The old fashioned type need only light pruning, removing dead or weak wood.
Uses: Rose petals are the basic ingredient of most *pot pourri*. They should be gathered just as the flower is fully expanded: if left until they start to fade, some of the fragrance will have gone. The foliage of sweetbriars can also be added to a *pot pourri*.

Rose petals can also be eaten. They have a light, delicate, scented flavour and are useful for decorating fruit desserts and cakes.

Rose hips are an excellent source of vitamin C and are often made into syrup.

ROSEMARY
Rosmarinus officinalis (Labiatae)
Perennial
Rosemary is an attractive, evergreen shrub with long, slender, mid-green leaves, silver on their undersides. In

summer it carries pale blue, hooded flowers. It will grow to around 2 m (6 ft) in a sheltered position — it likes warmth.

Plant rosemary in free draining but moderately rich soil. Bushes can be clipped, and rosemary makes a good hedge in warm gardens. Propagate from semi-ripe cuttings in summer.

Uses: Rosemary is a traditional flavouring for pork and lamb, but can be used with any meat. The dried foliage is sharp and spiky so should be crumbled before use.

The aromatic leaves can be included in *pot pourri*, and an infusion makes an excellent hair rinse, leaving the hair lightly scented and shining. Rosemary can be used to scent many cosmetics.

RUE
Ruta graveolens (Rutaceae)
Perennial

'Jackman's Blue' is the variety you are most likely to come across—it is an intense silvery blue and makes an excellent 30 cm (1 ft) tall, decorative plant. The compound leaves are very attractive and in summer bright yellow flowers appear. Some gardeners think these detract from the steely blue foliage and remove them.

Rue likes a well drained soil and a reasonably sheltered position. It is usually evergreen, though a hard winter may knock it back. It is quite easy to propagate from soft or semi-ripe cuttings.

Uses: Rue is rarely used these days, and one sniff at the bruised foliage will tell you why. The aroma is intensely strong and most people think it unpleasant—our tastes have probably changed over the years! It has undertones of coconut, but is very distinctive; the taste is very bitter.

Rue has medicinal properties but can be toxic and must be used only under medical supervision. It can cause allergic reactions if handled by people with sensitive skin. These days it is grown as a decorative plant, though it does have insect-repellent properties.

SAGE
Salvia officinalis (Labiatae)
Perennial

The soft, grey-green foliage of sage, topped by spikes of purple flowers, make it an attractive evergreen shrub of about 30–60 cm (1–2 ft). There are several varieties with coloured foliage: 'Icterina' is variegated with gold; 'Purpurascens' is plum purple and 'Tricolor' is marked with cream and pink.

Free draining but reasonably fertile soil suits sage best. If it is cut back hard in spring it will make a compact bush, otherwise it is inclined to get leggy.

Increase sage from seed or from soft tip or semi-ripe cuttings. Coloured leaved varieties must be propagated vegetatively.

Uses: The strongly aromatic, slightly bitter leaves are excellent with fatty foods such as pork and duck (sage and onion stuffing is a traditional accompaniment). Leaves can be dried and crumbled to a fluffy powder which retains its flavour well.

Sage has been widely used as a medicinal herb, useful for its antiseptic properties. Sage tea help to relieve headaches and colds, and can be used as a hair rinse for dark hair.

SAVORY
Satureja species *(Labiatae)*
Annual and perennial

There are two types of savory, similar in appearance and flavour. Summer savory (*S. hortensis*) is annual and usually thought to have a finer, more subtle flavour than the perennial winter savory (*S. montana*). Both have thin, pointed, mid-green leaves on slender 30–60 cm (1–2 ft) stems with pinkish lilac, hooded flowers towards the tips. Summer savory is rather more delicate in appearance and is frost sensitive, while shrubby winter savory is largely evergreen in a sheltered position.

Both grow well in poor, stony soil, enjoying free draining conditions. Cut winter savory back in spring to keep it compact.

Sow summer savory where it is to grow in spring;

winter savory can be sown in spring or summer, or increased by soft tip cuttings in early summer.

Uses: The savories are fine-flavoured herbs which deserve to be much more widely used. Traditionally, they are associated with beans of all types, but their warm, spicy, peppery flavour is also good with meat, fish, cheese, eggs and salads. The flowers are attractive to bees.

SORREL
Rumex acetosa (Polygonaceae)
Perennial

This relative of dock has arrow-shaped, fleshy, light green leaves growing in lush clumps. Flowering stems grow to about 1.5 m (5 ft) with panicles of reddish brown flowers that set into rusty seeds. The flowers are one of the least attractive among herbs, and flowering sharply reduces or stops leaf production: cut flower stems down as soon as they are seen.

Sorrel is one herb that likes light shade and a moist soil (which will retard flowering).

Sow seed in spring, indoors or where the plants are to grow. Plants are perennial, but are best replaced by new stock every few years.

Uses: This is an unusual herb in that it is not aromatic, but the young leaves have a sharp, salty, vinegary taste which is very refreshing. They make an excellent, clean-tasting early summer salad. Older leaves can be very lightly cooked (like spinach) to accompany rich foods. Blended with mayonnaise, they add a tang and an attractive green colour.

SOUTHERNWOOD
Artemisia abrotanum (Compositae)
Perennial

Southernwood is one of the most decorative herbs, with pale grey-green, thread-like, feathery leaves. It makes a rounded bush about 60–90 cm (2–3 ft) high. Very small yellow flowers sometimes appear in late summer.

Find southernwood a sheltered spot as it can be damaged by severe frosts. Soil should be freely drained but also moisture-retentive. If the plants get leggy, cut them back in spring once the leaf buds are bursting.

Semi-ripe cuttings, taken in summer, are the best method of propagation.

Uses: Apart from its value as an ornamental garden plant (the foliage is also useful for flower arrangements) southernwood is a good insect repellant. Include it in sachets for storing with linen. The very pleasant, warm scent makes it a useful addition to *pot pourri*.

The flavour is bitter and southernwood is not much used as a culinary herb, though very small amounts can be added to fatty dishes or strong-flavoured foods.

SWEET CICELY
Myrrhis odorata (Umbelliferae)
Perennial

Fresh, light green heads of ferny foliage and heads of frothy, tiny white flowers make sweet cicely a beautiful, delicate herb, usually around 75 m (2½ ft) tall. In soil that suits it, it can become quite invasive, making a large, spreading plant and sowing itself very freely.

Grow in a lightly shaded position and in moist soil. Although the plant dies down completely each autumn, fresh young foliage reappears in very early spring. Propagate from seed: established plants generally produce ample self-sown seedlings which can be lifted and transplanted.

Uses: All parts of the plant have a strong anise scent and flavour. The downy foliage can be added sparingly to salads, or cooked with sharp fruits like rhubarb, gooseberries and redcurrants to reduce their acidity and thus the need to add sugar. This makes sweet cicely a particularly useful herb for diabetics.

In winter the ripe seeds (which are carried in attractive, pointed seed cases when the flowers have faded) can be used instead of the foliage. Even the large tap-root can be eaten, when cooked, in salads.

TANSY
Tanacetum vulgare (Compositae)
Perennial

The finely cut fern-like foliage makes tansy quite a

decorative plant, but it is very invasive and must be planted where it can be kept under control. It grows to about 90 cm (3 ft) and has heads of round, button-like, bright yellow flowers.

Tansy will grow in most soils, and a fairly poor, dry position will help to check the spread of its tough, creeping rootstock. It is easily propagated by division, or from seed.

Uses: Tansy is rarely used as a culinary herb now because of its strong, bitter flavour, but it was once widely eaten at Easter in the form of pancakes or puddings. It was considered to be a tonic, cleansing herb which would purify the body after the winter: it does help to kill roundworms. Tansy has good insect repellent properties, and the strongly aromatic leaves can be hung in kitchens and larders to help repel flies, or included in sachets to store with clothes. The foliage also helps keep cats away from flower beds.

TARRAGON
Artemisia dracunculus (Compositae)
Perennial

This famous herb grows to a straggling plant about 75 cm (2½ ft) tall with deep green, narrow, pointed leaves and tiny, inconspicuous green flowers. There are two types of tarragon, the Russian and the French. French tarragon is generally held to have a much superior, more subtle flavour: Russian is stronger growing and coarser. Russian tarragon is easily raised from seed, while French tarragon rarely sets viable seed and must be propagated by soft tip cuttings or division of the rootstock. It is very difficult to distinguish between the two plants.

Tarragon needs a warm, sunny spot on well drained soil.

Uses: Tarragon has a pronounced, warm flavour and only small amounts are needed. It can accompany fish, meat and vegetable dishes and is used in soups and sauces as well as tarragon vinegar. It is particularly good with chicken. Russian tarragon, with its less spicy flavour, needs to be used in rather larger quantities than French tarragon.

THYME
Thymus species *(Labiatae)*
Perennial

Thyme is one of the most important and useful, as well as decorative, herbs. There are several different varieties, all fairly low and spreading, with small, tough leaves on wiry stems.

Thyme is a plant of hot, dry, stony hillsides, and it is in poor soil in a warm spot in the garden that the flavour is best. It is an excellent plant for growing in paving or on a wall.

Some thymes can be raised from seed sown in spring, while named forms must be propagated by semi-ripe cuttings in summer.

Garden thyme, *T. vulgaris*, has narrow, grey-green leaves and a pungent aroma, with pale pink or white flowers. Like all the thymes, these flowers are very attractive to bees. Garden thyme is easily raised from seed. The variety 'Silver Posie' is a small, slower growing form with mid-green leaves edged white.

Citrus overtones make lemon thyme *(T. citriodorus)* another good culinary herb with softer green leaves that make a compact mound. 'Silver Queen' is marked with silver, while 'Aureus' has golden foliage. *T. herba-barona* is an unusual, caraway-scented type forming a low, spreading mat.

Native wild thyme, *T. serpyllum*, is available in several varieties, including 'Annie Hall' with pale pink flowers; 'Albus' with white flowers; 'Coccineus' with crimson flowers and 'Lanuginosus' with woolly grey leaves and lilac flowers. *T. serpyllum* is another creeping, mat-forming thyme.

Thymes can be divided in spring or late summer; semi-ripe cuttings can be taken in late summer, and the low branches can be layered in summer.

The small leaves dry quickly and well, keeping their full flavour; they can also be frozen.

Uses: The warm, spicy flavour of thyme improves many dishes—all meats, vegetables, eggs and cheese. Flowers and foliage (especially of lemon thyme) are suitable for *pot pourri*. It is a strongly antiseptic herb—the essential oil, thymol, is still used medicinally as an antiseptic and a preservative.

APPENDIX: PLANT LISTS

SMALL TREES

Acer griseum (paperbark maple)
Acer palmatum 'Dissectum' (Japanese maple)
Arbutus unedo (strawberry tree)
Betula pendula 'Youngii' (Young's weeping birch)
Cercis siliquastrum (Judas tree)
Cotoneaster 'Hybridus Pendulus'
Crataegus monogyna 'Stricta' (hawthorn)
Crataegus oxyacantha 'Paul's Scarlet'
Ficus carica (fig)
Gleditsia triacanthos 'Sunburst' (honey locust)
Laburnum × *watereri* 'Vossii' (golden rain)
Magnolia × *soulangiana*
Malus floribunda (Japanese crab)
Malus 'John Downie' and other cultivars (crab)
Prunus subhirtella 'Autumnalis' (Autumn cherry)
Pyrus salicifolia 'Pendula' (silver willow-leaved pear)
Salix caprea 'Pendula' (syn. *S.c.* 'Kilmarnock')
    (Kilmarnock willow)
Sorbus 'Joseph Rock'

SMALL SHRUBS

Berberis × *stenophylla* 'Corallina Compacta' (barberry)
Berberis thunbergii, dwarf cultivars (barberry)
Calluna vulgaris cultivars (ling)
Convolvulus cneorum
Cytisus × *beanii* (broom)
Cytisus × *kewensis* (broom)
Daboecia cantabrica cultivars (St. Dabeoc's heath)
Daphne arbuscula
Daphne retusa
Erica herbacea (syn. *E. carnea*) cultivars (heath)
Erica × *darleyensis* cultivars (heath)
Euonymus fortunei cultivars
Genista lydia
Hebe armstrongii (shrubby veronica)
Hebe pinguifolia 'Pagei' (shrubby veronica)
Ilex crenata 'Golden Gem' (dwarf holly)
Lavandula spica 'Hidcote' (lavender)
Rhododendron, any dwarf species/cultivars
Santolina chamaecyparissus 'Nana' (syn. *S.c. corsica*)
    (cotton lavender)

DWARF CONIFERS

Abies balsamea 'Hudsonia' (dwarf balsam fir)
Chamaecyparis lawsoniana 'Ellwoodii' (dwarf Lawson cypress)
Chamaecyparis lawsoniana 'Minima Aurea' (dwarf Lawson cypress)
Chamaecyparis pisifera 'Boulevard' (dwarf sawara cypress)
Chamaecyparis pisifera 'Filifera Aurea' (dwarf sawara cypress)
Cryptomeria japonica 'Vilmoriniana' (dwarf Japanese cedar)
Juniperus chinensis 'Pyramidalis' (juniper)
Juniperus communis 'Compressa' (juniper)
Juniperus squamata 'Blue Star' (juniper)
Picea glauca 'Albertiana Conica' (dwarf white spruce)
Thuja occidentalis 'Rheingold' (dwarf American arbor-vitae)
Thuja orientalis 'Aurea Nana' (dwarf Chinese arbor-vitae)

SHRUBS FOR CONTAINERS

Acer palmatum cultivars (Japanese maples)
Buxus sempervirens (box)
Camellia cultivars
Choisya ternata (Mexican orange blossom)
Daphne odora 'Aureomarginata'
Elaeagnus, any species or cultivars
Erica herbacea (syn. *E. carnea*) cultivars (heath)
Euonymus, any evergreen species/cultivar
Fatsia japonica
Fuchsia, any hardy cultivar

Hebe (shrubby veronica), any species/cultivar
Hedera helix (ivy) cultivars
Hydrangea macrophylla, Hortensia and Lacecap cultivars
Ilex (holly)
Laurus nobilis (sweet bay)
Pieris formosa forrestii
Rhododendron, dwarf species/cultivars
Skimmia reevesiana
Taxus baccata (yew)
Viburnum davidii
Vinca (periwinkle)
Yucca species/cultivars

PERENNIALS FOR CONTAINERS

Acanthus spinosus (bear's breeches)
Agapanthus
Alchemilla mollis (lady's mantle)
Bergenia species/cultivars
Beschorneria yuccoides
Campanula persicifolia (peach-leaved bellflower)
Eryngium (sea holly) species
Euphorbia wulfenii (spurge)
Grasses, ornamental
Helleborus orientalis (Lenten rose)
Hemerocallis (day lily) hybrids
Hosta (plantain lily) species/cultivars
Kniphofia caulescens (red-hot poker)
Lupins, Russell hybrids
Phormium (New Zealand flax)
Rodgersia pinnata 'Superba'
Zantedeschia aethiopica (arum lily)

VEGETABLES FOR CONTAINERS

Asparagus peas
Beans, climbing and dwarf French
Beans, runner
Beetroots
Carrots
Chicory, red
Cucumbers, outdoor
Endive, curled
Herbs, especially small kinds
Onions, spring
Peas, dwarf early
Radishes
Rhubarb chard
Tomatoes

CLIMBERS AND WALL SHRUBS FOR SHADE

Chaenomeles (ornamental quince)
Garrya elliptica
Hedera (ivy)
Hydrangea petiolaris (climbing hydrangea)
Jasminum nudiflorum (winter-flowering jasmine)
Lonicera japonica 'Aureoreticulata' (honeysuckle)
Parthenocissus (Virginia creeper)
Polygonum baldschuanicum (Russian vine)
Pyracantha (firethorn) species/cultivars

PLANTS FOR RAISED SCREE BED
Sunny and well-drained conditions

Androsace
Calceolaria (slipperwort), alpine types
Daphne, dwarf alpine species
Dianthus, alpine pinks
Draba (whitlow grass) species
Gentiana (gentian) species
Hebe (shrubby veronica), miniature species
Leontopodium alpinum (edelweiss)
Lewisia species/cultivars
Phyteuma comosum
Saxifraga species/cultivars
Sedum (stonecrop), alpine species
Teucrium, alpine species
Veronica, dwarf alpine species

PLANTS FOR RAISED PEAT BED

Arctostaphylos uva-ursi
Cassiope lycopodioides and *C. tetragona*
Gaultheria, small species
Lithospermum diffusum
Phyllodoce aleutica
Pieris japonica 'Little Heath' and 'Little Heath Green'
Rhododendron, dwarf species/cultivars
Vaccinium, small-growing species

ANNUALS/BEDDERS FOR SHADE

Begonia semperflorens (wax begonia)
Fuchsia, greenhouse cultivars
Iberis umbellata (candytuft)
Impatiens (busy lizzie), bedding types
Lobelia, summer-bedding types
Matthiola bicornis (night-scented stock)
Myosotis (forget-me-not)
Mimulus (summer-bedding types)
Nicotiana (ornamental tobacco plant)
Pansies, especially winter-flowering

GROUND-COVER PLANTS FOR SHADE

Alchemilla mollis (lady's mantle)
Bergenia species/cultivars
Cotoneaster horizontalis (fishbone cotoneaster)
Geranium (crane's bill) species/cultivars
Hedera (ivy)
Hosta (plantain lily)
Hypericum calycinum (rose of Sharon)
Lamium (dead nettle)
Pulmonaria (lungwort)
Symphytum (comfrey)
Vinca (periwinkle)

BULBS FOR SEMI-SHADE

Anemone blanda (windflower)
Anemone nemorosa (wood anemone)
Camassia (quamash)
Chionodoxa (glory of the snow)
Colchicum species/cultivars
Endymion (bluebells)
Eranthis hyemalis (winter aconite)
Fritillaria (fritillary) species
Galanthus (snowdrop) species/cultivars
Muscari (grape hyacinth) species/cultivars
Narcissus (daffodil) species/cultivars
Scilla (squill) species/cultivars

INDEX

Page numbers in *italic* refer to the illustrations